The ParaView Guide

Updated for ParaView version 4.3

Utkarsh Ayachit

With contributions from:
  Berk Geveci, Cory Quammen, Dave DeMarle,
  Ken Moreland, Andy Bauer, Ben Boeckel,
  Shawn Waldon, Aashish Choudhary,
  George Zagaris, Burlen Loring,
  Thomas Maxwell, John Patchett,
  Boonthanome Nouanesengsy, Bill Sherman,
  Nikhil Shetty, Eric Whiting,
  and the ParaView community

Editors:
  Lisa Avila, Katie Osterdahl, Sandy McKenzie,
  and Steve Jordan

January 20, 2015

http://paraview.org
http://kitware.com

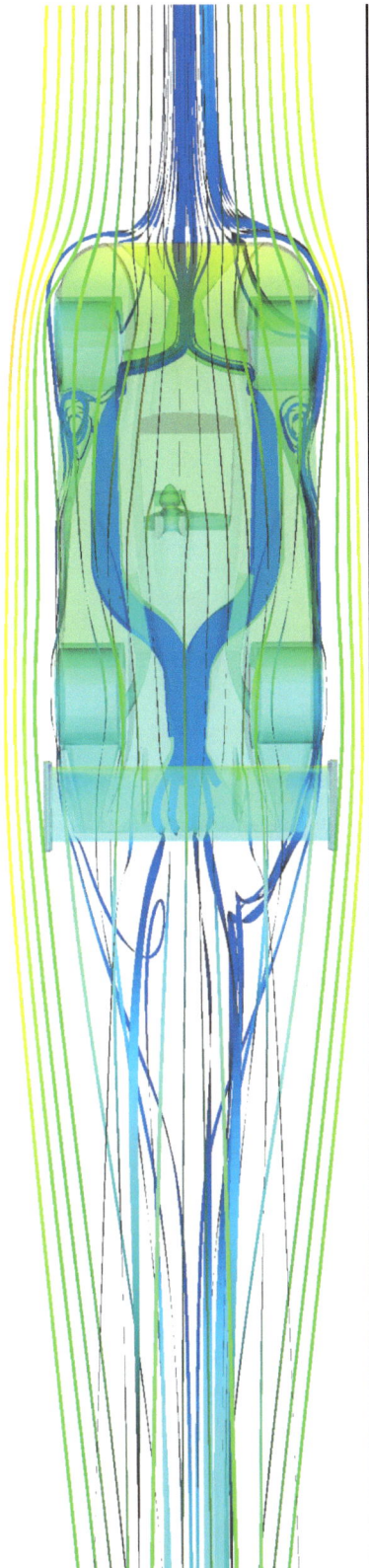

Kitware

Published by Kitware Inc. ©2015

All product names mentioned herein are the trademarks of their respective owners.

Part I and Part II of this document are available under a Creative Commons Attribution 4.0 International license available at http://www.paraview.org/download/.

This project has been funded in whole or in part with Federal funds from the Department of Energy, including from Sandia National Laboratories, Los Alamos National Laboratory, Advanced Simulation and Computing (ASC), and the Army Research Laboratory (ARL).

Printed and produced in the United States of America.
ISBN number 978-1-930934-30-6

CONTRIBUTORS

This book includes contributions from the ParaView community including the ParaView development team and the user community. We would like to thank the following people for their significant contributions to this updated text:

Cory Quammen, **Berk Geveci**, **Ben Boeckel**, **Dave DeMarle**, and **Shawn Waldon** from Kitware for their contributions throughout the text.

Ken Moreland, for large sections of text from his excellent *The ParaView Tutorial*[7] that formed the basis of Chapter 15. **Thomas Maxwell** from National Aeronautics and Space Administration (NASA) , **John Patchett** and **Boonthanome Nouanesengsy** from Los Alamos National Labs (LANL) , **Bill Sherman** from Indiana University, **Nikhil Shetty** from the University of Wyoming, **Aashish Choudhary** from Kitware, and **Eric Whiting** from Idaho National Laboratory, who contributed Chapter 19. **George Zagaris** from Lawrence Livermore National Laboratory who was the primary author of Chapter 20, and **Andy Bauer** from Kitware who was the primary author for Chapter 18. **Burlen Loring** from Lawrence Berkeley National Laboratory authored wiki posts that were made into Chapter 16.

Special thanks to the Kitware communications team including **Katie Osterdahl**, **Sandy McKenzie**, **Lisa Avila**, and **Steve Jordan**. This guide would not have been possible without their patient and persistent efforts.

ABOUT THE COVER

The cover image is a visualization of magnetic reconnection from the VPIC project at Los Alamos National Laboratory. The visualization is generated from a structrued data containing 3.3 billion cells with two vector fields and one scalar field, produced using 256 cores running ParaView on the interactive queue on the Kraken at the National Institute for Computational Sciences (NICS).

The interior cover image is courtesy of Renato N. Elias, Associate Researcher at the CFD Group from NACAD/-COPPE/UFRJ, Rio de Janeiro, Brazil.

The cover design was done by Steve Jordan.

Join the ParaView Commuity at www.paraview.org

CONTENTS

III　Extras　215

IV Appendix   251

Part I

User's Guide

INTRODUCTION TO PARAVIEW

1.1 Introduction

ParaView is an open-source, multi-platform scientific data analysis and visualization tool that enables analysis and visualization of extremely large datasets. ParaView is both a general purpose, end-user application with a distributed architecture that can be seamlessly leveraged by your desktop or other remote parallel computing resources and an extensible framework with a collection of tools and libraries for various applications including scripting (using Python), web visualization (through ParaViewWeb), or in-situ analysis (with Catalyst).

ParaView leverages parallel data processing and rendering to enable interactive visualization for extremely large datasets. It also includes support for large displays including tiled displays and immersive 3D displays with head tracking and wand control capabilities.

ParaView also supports scripting and batch processing using Python. Using included Python modules, you can write scripts that can perform almost all the functionality exposed by the interactive application and much more.

ParaView is open-source (BSD licensed, commercial software friendly). As with any successful open-source project, ParaView is supported by an active user and developer community. Contributions to both the code and this user's manual that help make the tool and the documentation better are always welcome.

🛈 Did you know?

The ParaView project started in 2000 as a collaborative effort between Kitware Inc. and LANL . The initial funding was provided by a three year contract with the US Department of Energy ASCI Views program. The first public release, ParaView 0.6, was announced in October 2002.

Independent of ParaView, Kitware started developing a web-based visualization system in December 2001. This project was funded by Phase I and II SBIRs from the US Arm Research Laboratory (ARL) and eventually became the ParaView Enterprise Edition . PVEE significantly contributed to the development of ParaView's client/server architecture. PVEE was the precursor to ParaViewWeb, a modern web visualization solution based on ParaView.

Since the project began, Kitware has successfully collaborated with Sandia, LANL , the ARL , and various other academic and government institutions to continue development. Today, the project is still going strong!

In September 2005, Kitware, Sandia National Labs and CSimSoft started the development of ParaView 3.0. This was a major effort focused on rewriting the user interface to be more user friendly and on developing a quantitative analysis framework. ParaView 3.0 was released in May 2007.

1.1.1 In this guide

This user's manual is designed as a guide for using the ParaView application. It is geared toward users who have a general understanding of common data visualization techniques. For scripting, a working knowledge of the Python language is assumed. If you are new to Python, there are several tutorials and guides for getting started that are available on the Internet.

> **(i) Did you know?**
>
> *In this guide, we will periodically use these **Did you know?** boxes to provide additional information related to the topic at hand.*

> **Common Errors**
>
> ***Common Errors** blocks are used to highlight some of the common problems or complications you may run into when dealing with the topic of discussion.*

This guide can be split into two volumes. Chapter 1 to Chapter 8 can be considered the user's guide, where various aspects of data analysis and visualization with ParaView are covered. Chapter 9 to Chapter 17 are the user's manual sections, which provide details on various components in the UI and the scripting API.

1.1.2 Getting help

This guide tries to cover most of the commonly used functionality in ParaView. ParaView's flexible, pipeline-based architecture opens up numerous possibilities. If you find yourself looking for some feature not covered in this guide, refer to the Wiki pages (http://paraview.org/Wiki/ParaView) and/or feel free to ask about it on the mailing list (http://paraview.org/paraview/help/mailing.html).

1.1.3 Getting the software

ParaView is open source. The complete source code for all the functionality discussed in this user's guide can be downloaded from the ParaView website http://www.paraview.org. We also provide binaries for the major platforms: Linux, Mac Os X, and Windows. You can get the source files and binaries for the official releases, as well as follow ParaView's active development, by downloading the nightly builds.

Providing details of how to build ParaView using the source files is beyond the scope of this manual. Refer to the ParaView Wiki (http://paraview.org/Wiki/ParaView) for more information.

1.2 Basics of visualization in ParaView

Visualization is the process of converting raw data into images and renderings to gain a better cognitive understanding of the data. ParaView uses VTK, the Visualization Toolkit, to provide the backbone for visualization and data processing.

The VTK model is based on the data-flow paradigm. In this paradigm, data flows through the system being transformed at each step by modules known as algorithms. Algorithms could be common operations such as clipping, slicing, or generating contours from the data, or they could be computing derived quantities, etc. Algorithms have input ports through which they take in data and output ports through which they produce output. You need producers that ingest data into the

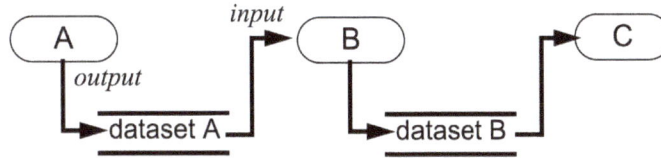

Figure 1.1: Visualization model: Process objects A, B, and C input and/or output one or more data objects. Data objects represent and provide access to data; process objects operate on the data. Objects A, B, and C are source, filter, and mapper objects, respectively.[12]

system. These are simply algorithms that do not have an input port but have one or more output ports. They are called *sources*. Readers that read data from files are examples of such sources. Additionally, there are algorithms that transform the data into graphics primitives so that they can be rendered on a computer screen or saved to disk in another file. These algorithms, which have one or more input ports but do not have output ports, are called *sinks*. Intermediate algorithms with input ports and output ports are called *filters*. Together, sources, filters, and sinks provide a flexible infrastructure wherein you can create complex processing pipelines by simply connecting algorithms to perform arbitrarily complex tasks.

For more information on VTK's programming model, refer to.[12]

This way of looking at the visualization pipeline is at the core of ParaView's work flow: You bring your data into the system by creating a reader – the source. You then apply filters to either extract information (e.g., iso-contours) and render the results in a view or to save the data to disk using writers – the sinks.

ParaView includes readers for a multitude of file formats typically used in the computational science world. To efficiently represent data from various fields with varying characteristics, VTK provides a rich data model that ParaView uses. The data model can be thought of simply as ways of representing data in memory. We will cover the different data types in more detail in Section 3.1. Readers produce a data type suitable for representing the information the files contain. Based on the data type, ParaView allows you to create and apply filters to transform the data. You can also show the data in a view to produce images or renderings. Just as there are several types of filters, each perfoming different operations and types of processing, there are several kinds of views for generating various types of renderings including 3D surface views, 2D bar and line views, parallel coordinate views, etc.

ⓘ Did you know?

The Visualization Toolkit (VTK) is an open-source, freely available software system for 3D computer graphics, modeling, image processing, volume rendering, scientific visualization, and information visualization. VTK also includes ancillary support for 3D interaction widgets, two and three-dimensional annotation, and parallel computing.

At its core, VTK is implemented as a C++ toolkit, requiring users to build applications by combining various objects into an application. The system also supports automated wrapping of the C++ core into Python, Java, and Tcl so that VTK applications may also be written using these interpreted programming languages. VTK is used world-wide in commercial applications, research and development, and as the basis of many advanced visualization applications such as ParaView, VisIt, VisTrails, Slicer, MayaVi, and OsiriX.

1.3 ParaView executables

ParaView comes with several executables that serve different purposes.

`paraview`

This is the main ParaView graphical user interface (GUI). In most cases, when we refer to ParaView, we are indeed talking about this application. It is a Qt-based, cross-platform UI that provides access to the ParaView computing capabilities. Major parts of this user's manual are dedicated to understanding and using this application.

`pvpython`

pvpython is the Python interpreter that runs ParaView's Python scripts. You can think of this as the equivalent of the *paraview* for scripting.

`pvbatch`

Similar to *pvpython*, *pvbatch* is also a Python interpreter that runs Python scripts for ParaView. The one difference is that, while *pvpython* is meant to run interactive scripts, *pvbatch* is designed for batch processing. Additionally, when running on computing resources with MPI capabilities, *pvbatch* can be run in parallel. We will cover this in more detail in Section .

`pvserver`

For remote visualization, this executable represents the server that does all of the data processing and, potentially, the rendering. You can make *paraview* connect to *pvserver* running remotely on an HPC resource. This allows you to build and control visualization and analysis on the HPC resource from your desktop as if you were simply processing it locally on your desktop!

`pvdataserver` **and** `pvrenderserver`

These can be thought of as the *pvserver* split into two separate executables: one for the data processing part, *pvdataserver*, and one for the rendering part, *pvrenderserver*. Splitting these into separate processes makes it possible to perform data processing and rendering on separate sets of nodes with appropriate computing capabilities suitable for the two tasks. Just as with *pvserver*, *paraview* can connect to a *pvdataserver*-*pvrenderserver* pair for remote visualization. Unless otherwise noted, all discussion of remote visualization or client-server visualization in this guide is applicable to both *pvserver* and *pvdataserver*-*pvrenderserver* configurations.

1.4 Getting started with `paraview`

1.4.1 `paraview` graphical user interface

paraview is the graphical front-end to the ParaView application. The UI is designed to allow you to easily create pipelines for data processing with arbitrary complexity. The UI provides panels for you to inspect and modify the pipelines, to change parameters that in turn affect the processing pipelines, to perform various data selection and inspection actions to introspect the data, and to generate renderings. We will cover various aspects of the UI for the better part of this guide.

Let's start by looking at the various components of the UI. If you run *paraview* for the first time, you will see something similar to the Figure 1.2. The UI is comprised of menus, dockable panels, toolbars, and the viewport – the central portion of the application window.

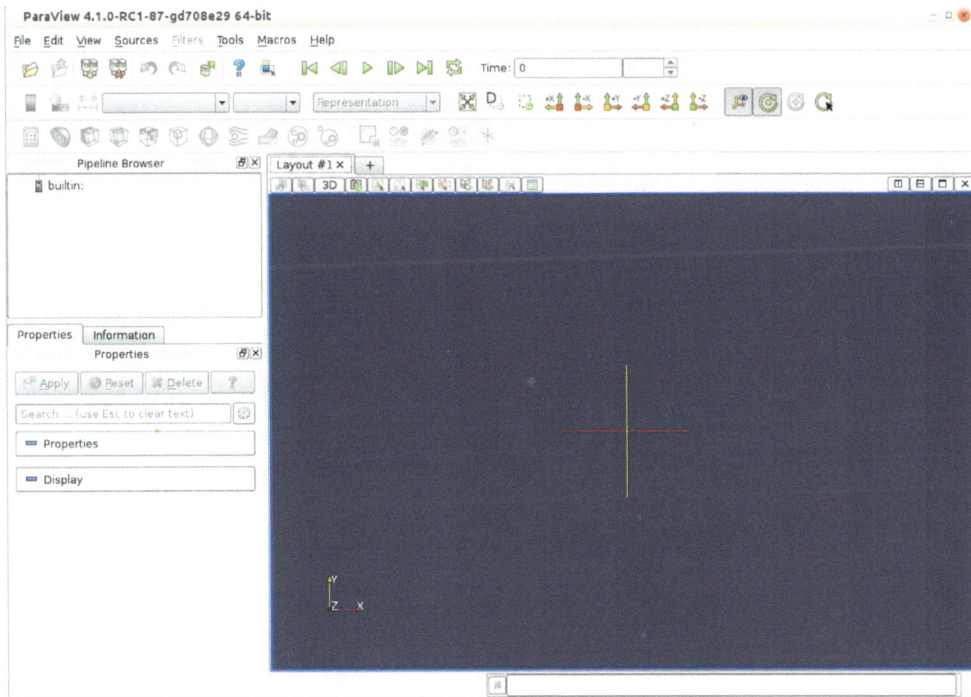

Figure 1.2: *paraview* application window

Menus provide the standard set of options typical with a desktop application including options for opening/saving files (File menu), for undo/redo (Edit menu), for the toggle panel, and for toolbar visibilities (View menu). Additionally, the menus provide ways to create sources that generate test datasets of various types (Sources menu), as well new filters for processing data (Filters menu). The Tools menu provides access to some of the advanced features in *paraview* such as managing plugins and accessing the embedded Python shell.

Panels provide you with the ability to peek into the application's state. For example, you can inspect the visualization pipeline that has been set up (`Pipeline Browser`), as well as the memory that is being used (`Memory Inspector`) and the parameters or properties for a processing module (`Properties` panel). Several of the panels also allow you to change the values that are displayed, e.g., the `Properties` panel not only shows the processing module parameters, but it also allows you to change them. Several of the panels are context sensitive. For example, the `Properties` panel changes to show the parameters from the selected module as you change the active module in the `Pipeline Browser`.

Toolbars are designed to provide quick access to common functionality. Several of the actions in the toolbar are accessible from other locations, including menus or panels. Similar to panels, some of the toolbar buttons are context sensitive and will become enabled or disabled based on the selected module or view.

The viewport or the central portion of the *paraview* window is the area where ParaView renders results generated from the data. The containers in which data can be rendered or shown are called *views*. You can create several different types of views, all of which are laid out in this viewport area. By default, a 3D view is created, which is one of the most commonly used views in ParaView.

1.4.2 Understanding the visualization process

To gain a better understanding of how to use the application interface, let's consider a simple example: creating a data source and applying a filter to it.

Creating a source

The visualization process in ParaView begins by bringing your data into the application. Chapter 2 explains how to read data from various file formats. Besides reading files to bring in data into the application, ParaView also provides a collection of data sources that can produce sample datasets. These are available under the Sources menu. To create a source, simply click on any item in the Source menu.

Did you know?

As you move your cursor over the items in any menu, on most platforms (except Mac OS X), you'll see a brief description of the item in the status bar on the lower-left corner in the application window.

If you click on Sources ⟩ Sphere, for example, you'll create a producer algorithm that generates a spherical surface, as shown in Figure 1.3.

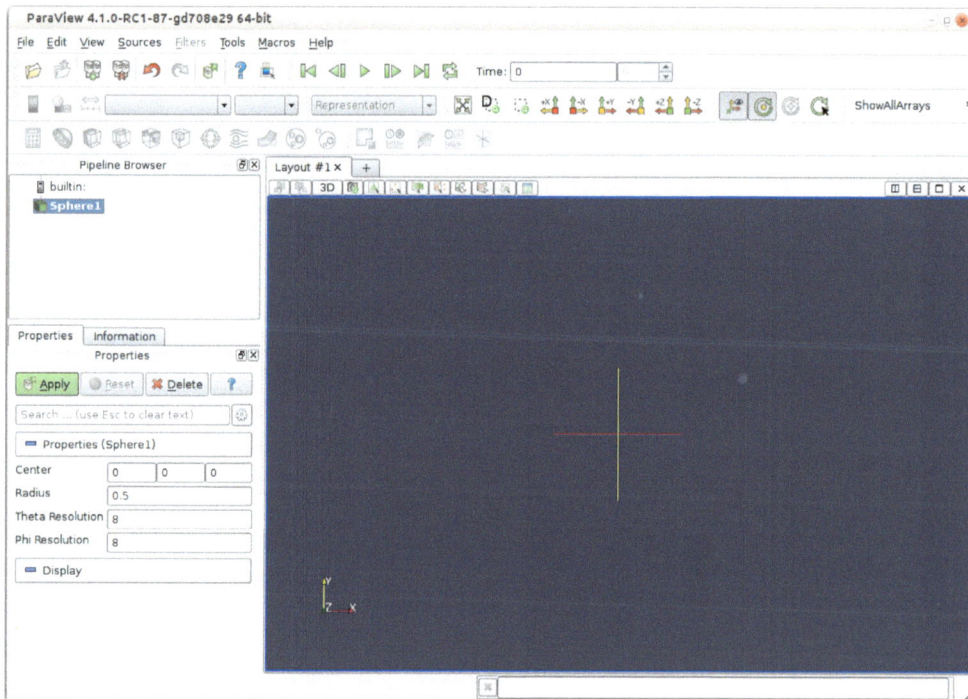

Figure 1.3: Visualization in *paraview*: Step 1

A few of things to note:

1. A pipeline module is added in the `Pipeline Browser` panel with a name derived from the menu item, as is highlighted.

2. The `Properties` panel fills up with text to indicate that it's showing properties for the highlighted item (which, in this case, is `Sphere1`), as well as to display some widgets for parameters such as `Center`, `Radius`, etc.

3. On the `Properties` panel, the `Apply` button becomes enabled and highlighted.

4. The 3D view remains unaffected, as nothing new is shown or rendered in this view as of yet.

Let's take a closer look at what has happened. When we clicked on `Sources` ⟩ `Sphere`, referring to Section 1.2, we created an instance of a source that can produce a spherical surface mesh – that's what is reflected in the `Pipeline Browser`. This instance receives a name, which is used by the `Sphere1` and the `Pipeline Browser`, as well as other components of the UI, to refer to this instance of the source. Pipeline modules such as sources and filters have parameters on them that you can change that affect that module's behavior. We call them *properties*. The `Properties` panel shows these properties and allows you to change them. Since the ingestion of data into the system can be a time-consuming process, *paraview* allows you to change the properties before the module executes or performs the actual processing to ingest the data. Hence, the `Apply` button is highlighted to indicate that you need to accept the properties before the application will proceed. Since no data has entered the system yet, there's nothing to show. Therefore, the 3D view remains unaffected.

Let's assume we are okay with the default values for all of the properties on the `Sphere1`. Next, click on the `Apply` button.

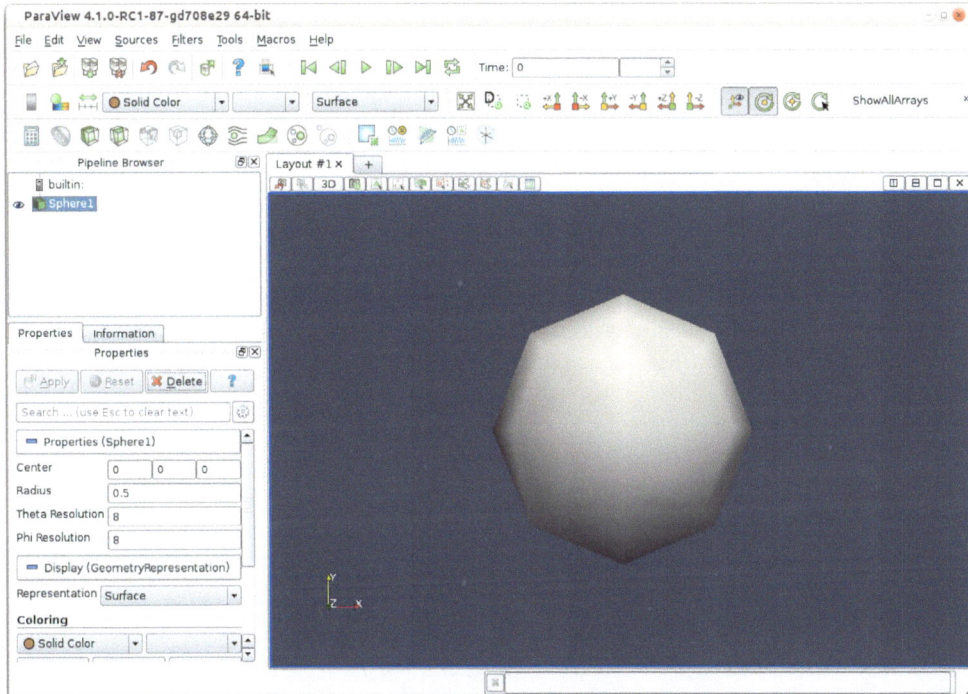

Figure 1.4: Visualization in *paraview*: Step 2

The following will ensue (Figure 1.4):

1. The `Apply` button goes back to its old disabled/un-highlighted state.

2. A spherical surface is rendered in the 3D view.

3. The `Display` section on the `Properties` panel now shows new parameters or properties.

4. Certain toolbars update, and you can see that toolbars with text, such as `Solid Color` and `Surface`, now become enabled.

By clicking `Apply`, we told *paraview* to apply the properties shown on the `Properties` panel. When a new source (or filter) is applied for the first time, *paraview* will automatically show the data that the pipeline module produces in the current view, if possible. In this case, the sphere source produces a surface mesh, which is then shown or displayed in the 3D view.

The properties that allow you to control how the data is displayed in the view are now shown on the `Properties` panel in the `Display` section. Things such as the surface color, rendering type or representation, shading parameters, etc., are shown under this newly updated section. We will look at display properties in more detail in Chapter 4.

Some of the properties that are commonly used are also duplicated in the toolbar. These properties include the data array with which the surface is colored and the representation type. These are the changes in the toolbar that allow you to quickly change some display properties.

Changing properties

If you change any of the properties on the sphere source, such as the properties under the `Properties` section on the `Properties` panel, including the `Radius` for the spherical mesh or its `Center`, the `Apply` button will be highlighted again. Once you are finished with all of the property changes, you can hit `Apply` to apply the changes. Once the changes are applied, *paraview* will re-execute the sphere source to produce a new mesh, as requested. It will then automatically update the view, and you will see the new result rendered.

If you change any of the display properties for the sphere source, such as the properties under the `Display` section of the `Properties` panel (including `Representation` or `Opacity`), the `Apply` button is not affected, the changes are immediately applied, and the view is updated.

The rationale behind this is that, typically, the execution of the source (or filter) is more computationally intensive than the rendering. Changing source (or filter) properties causes that algorithm to re-execute, while changing display properties, in most cases, only triggers a fresh render with an updated graphics state.

Did you know?

For some workflows with smaller data sizes, it may be more convenient if the `Apply` button was automatically applied even after changes are made to the pipeline module properties. You can change this from the application settings dialog, which is accessible from the Edit ⟩ Settings *menu. The setting is called `Auto Apply`. You can also change the `Auto Apply` state using the* ⬡ *button from the toolbar.*

Applying filters

As per the data-flow paradigm, one creates pipelines with filters to transform data. Similar to the Sources menu, which allows us to create new data sources, there's a Filters menu that provides access to the large set of filters that are available in ParaView. If you peruse through the items in this menu, some of them will be enabled, and some of them will be disabled. Filters that can work with the data type being produced by the sphere source are enabled, while others are disabled. You can click on any of the enabled filters to create a new instance of that filter type.

ⓘ Did you know?

To figure out why a particular filter doesn't work with the current source, simply move your mouse over the disabled item in the Filters *menu. On Linux and Windows (not OS X, however), the status bar will provide a brief explanation of why that filter is not available.*

For example, if you click on Filters ≫ Shrink, it will create a filter that shrinks each of the mesh cells by a fixed factor. Exactly as before, when we created the sphere source, we see that the newly-created filter is given a new name, Shrink1, and is highlighted in the Pipeline Browser. The Properties panel is also updated to show the properties for this new filter, and the Apply button is highlighted to request that we accept the properties for the filter so that it can be executed and the result can be rendered. If you click back and forth between the Sphere1 and Shrink1 in the Pipeline Browser, you'll see the Properties panel and toolbars update, reflecting the state of the selected pipeline module. This is an important concept in ParaView. There's a notion of active pipeline module, called the *active source*. Several panels, toolbars, and menus will update based on the active source.

If you click Apply, as was the case before, the shrink filter will be executed and the resulting dataset will be generated and shown in the 3D view. *paraview* will also automatically hide the result from the Sphere1 so that it is not shown in the view. Otherwise, the two datasets will overlap. This is reflected by the change of state for the *eyeball* icons in the Pipeline Browser next to each of the pipeline modules. You can show or hide results from any pipeline module by clicking on the eyeballs.

This simple workflow forms the basis of all the data analysis and visualization in ParaView. The process involves creating sources and filters, changing their parameters, and showing the generated result in one or more views. In the rest of this guide, we will cover various types of filters and data processing that you can do. We will also cover different types of views that can help you produce a wide array of 2D and 3D visualizations, as well as inspect your data and drill down into it.

💣 Common Errors

Beginners often forget to hit the Apply *button after creating sources or filters or after changing properties. This is one of the most common pitfalls for users new to the ParaView workflow.*

1.5 Getting started with pvpython

While this section refers to *pvpython*, everything that we discuss here is applicable to *pvbatch* as well. Until we start looking into parallel processing, the only difference between the two executables is that *pvpython* provides an interactive shell wherein you can type your commands, while *pvbatch* expects the Python script to be specified on the command line argument.

1.5.1 pvpython scripting interface

ParaView provides a scripting interface to write scripts for performing the tasks that you could do using the GUI. The scripting interface can be accessed through Python, which is an interpreted programming language popular among the scientific community for its simplicity and its capabilities. While a working knowledge of Python will be useful for writing scripts with advanced capabilities, you should be able to follow most of the discussion in this book about ParaView scripting even without much Python exposure.

ParaView provides a `paraview` package with several Python modules that expose various functionalities. The primary scripting interface is provided by the `simple` module.

When you start *pvpython*, you should see a prompt in a terminal window as follows (with some platform specific differences).

```
1  Python 2.7.5 (default, Sep  2 2013, 05:24:04)
2  [GCC 4.2.1 Compatible Apple LLVM 5.0 (clang-500.0.68)] on darwin
3  Type "help", "copyright", "credits" or "license" for more information
4  >>>
```

You can now type commands at this prompt, and ParaView will execute them. To bring in the ParaView scripting API, you first need to import the `simple` module from the `paraview` package as follows:

```
1  >>> from paraview.simple import *
```

Common Errors

Remember to hit the `Enter` *or* `Return` *key after every command to execute it. Any Python interpreter will not execute the command until* `Enter` *is hit.*

If the module is loaded correctly, *pvpython* will respond with a text output, which is the ParaView version number.

```
1  >>> from paraview.simple import *
2  paraview version 4.2.0
```

You can consider this as in the same state as when *paraview* was started (with some differences that we can ignore for now). The application is ready to ingest data and start processing.

1.5.2 Understanding the visualization process

Let's try to understand the workflow by looking at the same use-case as we did in Section 1.4.2.

Creating a source

In *paraview*, we created the data source by using the [Sources] menu. In the scripting environment, this maps to simply typing the name of the source to create.

```
1  >>> Sphere()
```

This will create the sphere source with a default set of properties. Just like with *paraview*, as soon as a new pipeline module is created, it becomes the *active source*.

Now, to show the active source in a view, try:

```
1  >>> Show()
2  >>> Render()
```

The Show call will prepare the display, while the Render call will cause the rendering to occur. In addition, a new window will popup, showing the result (Figure 1.5). This is similar to the state after hitting Apply in the UI.

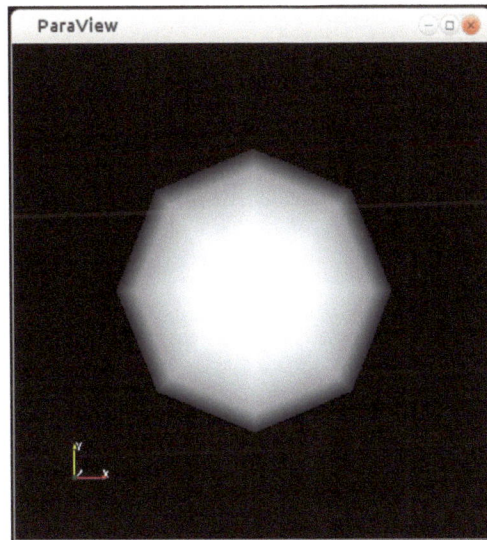

Figure 1.5: Window showing result from the Python code

Changing properties

To change the properties on the sphere source, you can use the SetProperties function.

```
1  # Set a single property on the active source.
2  >>> SetProperties(Radius=1.0)
3
4  # You can also set multiple properties.
5  >>> SetProperties(Center=[1, 0, 0], StartTheta=100)
```

Similar to the Properties panel, SetProperties affects the active source. To query the current value of any property on the active source, use GetProperty.

```
1  >>> radius = GetProperty("Radius")
2  >>> print radius
3  1.0
4  >>> center = GetProperty("Center")
5  >>> print center
6  [1.0, 0.0, 0.0]
```

SetProperties and GetProperty functions serve the same function as the Properties section of the Properties panel – they allow you to set and introspect the pipeline module properties for the active source. Likewise, for the Display section of the panel, or the display properties, we have the SetDisplayProperties and GetDisplayProperty functions.

```
1  >>> SetDisplayProperties(Opacity=0.5)
2
```

```
3  # FIXME: this function is not available yet, but here for completeness.
4  >>> GetDisplayProperty("Opacity")
5  0.5
```

Common Errors

Note how the property names for the SetProperties *and* SetDisplayProperties *functions are not enclosed in double-quotes, while those for the* GetProperty *and* GetDisplayProperty *methods are.*

In *paraview*, every time you hit Apply or change a display property, the UI automatically re-renders the view. In the scripting environment, you have to do this manually by calling the Render function every time you want to re-render and look at the updated result.

.

Applying filters

Similar to creating a source, to apply a filter, you can simply create the filter by name.

```
1   # Create the 'Shrink' filter and connect it to the active source
2   # which is the 'Sphere' instance.
3   >>> Shrink()
4   # As soon as the Shrink filter is created, it will now become the new active
5   # source. All methods acting on active source now act on this filter instance
6   # and not the Sphere instance created earlier.
7
8   # Show the resulting data and render it.
9   >>> Show()
10  >>> Render()
```

If you tried the above script, you'll notice the result isn't exactly what we expected. For some reason, the shrank cells are not visible. This is because we missed one stage: In *paraview*, the UI was smart enough to automatically hide the input dataset for the newly created filter after we hit apply. In the scripting interface, such operations are the user's responsibility. We should have hidden the sphere source from the view. We can use the Hide method, the counter part of Show, to hide the active source. But, now we have a problem – when we created the shrink filter, we changed the active source to be the shrink instance. Luckily, all the functions we discussed so far can take an optional first argument, which is the source or filter instance on which to operate. If provided, that instance is used instead of the active source. The solution is as follows:

```
1   # Get the input property for the active source, i.e. the input for the shrink.
2   >>> shrinksInput = GetProperty("Input")
3
4   # This is indeed the sphere instance we created earlier.
5   >>> print shrinksInput
6   <paraview.servermanager.Sphere object at 0x11d731e90>
7
8   # Hide the sphere instance explicitly.
9   >>> Hide(shrinksInput)
10
11  # Re-render the result.
12  >>> Render()
```

Alternatively, you could also get/set the active source using the `GetActiveSource` and `SetActiveSource` functions.

```
1  >>> shrinkInstance = GetActiveSource()
2  >>> print shrinkInstance
3  <paraview.servermanager.Shrink object at 0x11d731ed0>
4
5  # Get the input property for the active source, i.e. the input
6  # for the shrink.
7  >>> sphereInstance = GetProperty("Input")
8
9  # This is indeed the sphere instance we created earlier.
10 >>> print sphereInstance
11 <paraview.servermanager.Sphere object at 0x11d731e90>
12
13 # Change active source to sphere and hide it.
14 >>> SetActiveSource(sphereInstance)
15 >>> Hide()
16
17 # Now restore the active source back to the shrink instance.
18 >>> SetActiveSource(shrinkInstance)
19
20 # Re-render the result
21 >>> Render()
```

The result is shown in Figure 1.6.

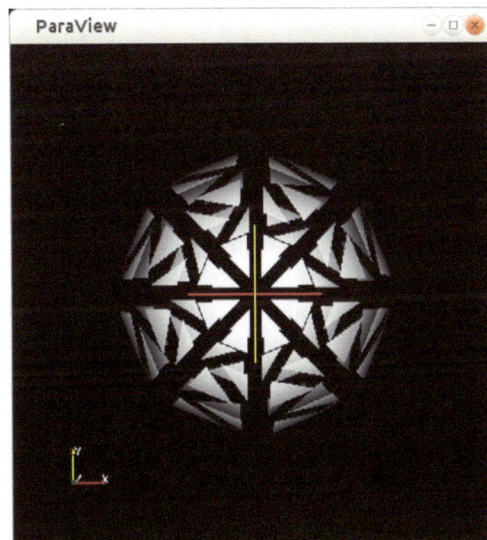

Figure 1.6: Window showing result from the Python code after applying the shrink filter.

`SetActiveSource` has same effect as changing the pipeline module, highlighted in the `Pipeline Browser`, by clicking on a different module.

Alternative approach

Here's another way of doing something similar to what we did in the previous section for those familiar with Python and/or object-oriented programming. It's totally okay to stick with the previous approach.

```
1  >>> from paraview.simple import *
2  >>> sphereInstance = Sphere()
3  >>> sphereInstance.Radius = 1.0
4  >>> sphereInstance.Center[1] = 1.0
5  >>> print sphereInstance.Center
6  [0.0, 1.0, 0.0]
7
8  >>> sphereDisplay = Show(sphereInstance)
9  >>> view = Render()
10 >>> sphereDisplay.Opacity = 0.5
11
12 # Render function can take in an optional view argument, otherwise it
13 # will simply use the active view.
14 >>> Render(view)
15
16 >>> shrinkInstance = Shrink(Input=sphereInstance,
17                            ShrinkFactor=1.0)
18 >>> print shrinkInstance.ShrinkFactor
19 1.0
20 >>> Hide(sphereInstance)
21 >>> shrinkDisplay = Show(shrinkInstance)
22 >>> Render()
```

1.5.3 Updating the pipeline

When changing properties on the `Properties` panel in *paraview*, we noticed that the algorithm doesn't re-execute until you hit `Apply`. In reality, `Apply` isn't what's actually triggering the execution or the updating of the processing pipeline. What happens is that `Apply` updates the parameters on the pipeline module and causes the view to render. If the output of the pipeline module is visible in the view, or if the output of any filter connected to it downstream is visible in the view, ParaView will determine that the data rendered is obsolete and request the pipeline to re-execute. It implies that if that pipeline module (or any of the filters downstream from it) is not visible in the view, ParaView will have no reason to re-execute the pipeline, and the pipeline module will not be be updated. If, later on, you do make this module visible in the view, ParaView will automatically update and execute the pipeline. This is often referred to as *demand-driven pipeline execution*. It makes it possible to avoid unnecessary module executions.

In *paraview*, you can get by without ever noticing this since the application manages pipeline updates automatically. In *pvpython* too, if your scripts are producing renderings in views, you'd never notice this as long as you remember to call `Render`. However, you may want to write scripts to produce transformed datasets or to determine data characteristics. In such cases, since you may never create a view, you'll never be seeing the pipeline update, no matter how many times you change the properties.

Accordingly, you must use the `UpdatePipeline` function. `UpdatePipeline` updates the pipeline connected to the active source (or only until the active source, i.e., anything downstream from it, won't be updated).

```
1  >>> from paraview.simple import *
2  >>> sphere = Sphere()
3
4  # Print the bounds for the data produced by sphere.
5  >>> print sphere.GetDataInformation().GetBounds()
```

```
 6  (1e+299, -1e+299, 1e+299, -1e+299, 1e+299, -1e+299)
 7  # The bounds are invalid -- no data has been produced yet.
 8
 9  # Update the pipeline explicitly on the active source.
10  >>> UpdatePipeline()
11
12  # Alternative way of doing the same but specifying the source
13  # to update explicitly.
14  >>> UpdatePipeline(proxy=sphere)
15
16  # Let's check the bounds again.
17  >>> sphere.GetDataInformation().GetBounds()
18  (-0.48746395111083984, 0.48746395111083984, -0.48746395111083984, 0.48746395111083984,
        -0.5, 0.5)
19
20  # If we call UpdatePipeline() again, this will have no effect since
21  # the pipeline hasn't been modified, so there's no need to re-execute.
22  >>> UpdatePipeline()
23  >>> sphere.GetDataInformation().GetBounds()
24  (-0.48746395111083984, 0.48746395111083984, -0.48746395111083984, 0.48746395111083984,
        -0.5, 0.5)
25
26  # Now let's change a property.
27  >>> sphere.Radius = 10
28
29  # The bounds won't change since the pipeline hasn't re-executed.
30  >>> sphere.GetDataInformation().GetBounds()
31  (-0.48746395111083984, 0.48746395111083984, -0.48746395111083984, 0.48746395111083984,
        -0.5, 0.5)
32
33  # Let's update and see:
34  >>> UpdatePipeline()
35  >>> sphere.GetDataInformation().GetBounds()
36  (-9.749279022216797, 9.749279022216797, -9.749279022216797, 9.749279022216797, -10.0,
        10.0)
```

We will look at the sphere.GetDataInformation API in Section 3.3 in more detail.

For temporal datasets, UpdatePipeline takes in a time argument, which is the time for which the pipeline must be updated.

```
1  # To update to time 10.0:
2  >>> UpdatePipeline(10.0)
3
4  # Alternative way of doing the same:
5  >>> UpdatePipeline(time=10.0)
6
7  # If not using the active source:
8  >>> UpdatePipeline(10.0, source)
9  >>> UpdatePipeline(time=10.0, proxy=source)
```

1.6 Scripting in `paraview`

1.6.1 The `Python shell`

The *paraview* application also provides access to an internal shell, in which you can enter Python commands and scripts exactly as with *pvpython*. To access the Python shell in the GUI, use the [Tools ⟩⟩ Python Shell] menu option. A dialog will pop up with a prompt exactly like *pvpython*. You can try inputting commands from the earlier section into this shell. As you type each of the commands, you will see the user interface update after each command, e.g., when you create the sphere source instance, it will be shown in the `Pipeline Browser`. If you change the active source, the `Pipeline Browser` and other UI components will update to reflect the change. If you change any properties or display properties, the `Properties` panel will update to reflect the change as well!

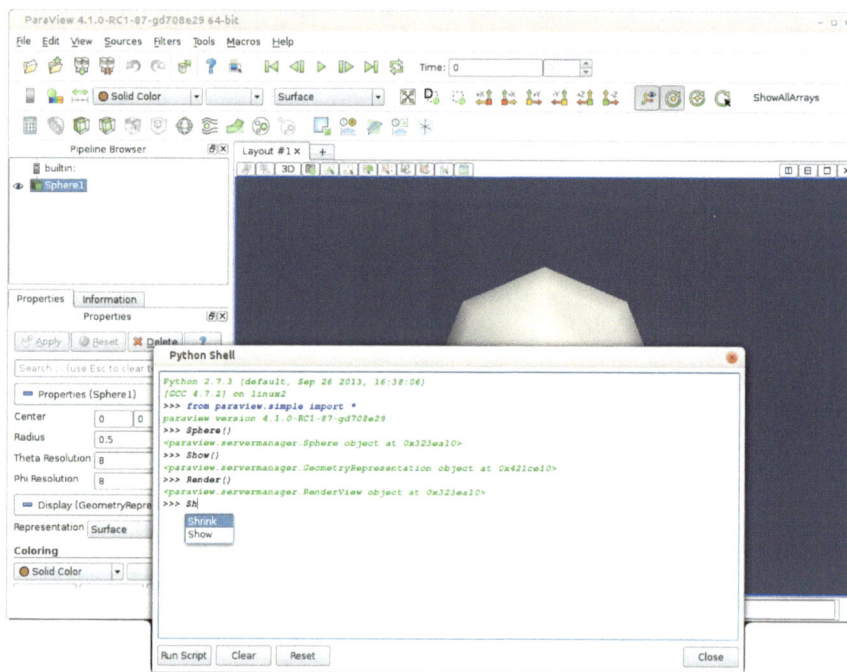

Figure 1.7: Python shell in *paraview* provides access to the scripting interface in the GUI.

Did you know?

The Python shell in paraview supports auto-completion for functions and instance methods. Try hitting the `Tab` *key after partially typing any command (as shown in Figure 1.7).*

1.6.2 Tracing actions for scripting

This guide provides a fair overview of ParaView's Python API. However, there will be cases when you just want to know how to complete a particular action or sequence of actions that you can do with the GUI using a Python script instead. To accomplish this, *paraview* supports tracing your actions in the UI as a Python script. Simply start tracing by clicking on [Tools ⟩⟩ Start Trace]. *paraview* now enters a mode where all your actions (or at least those relevant for scripting) are monitored.

Any time you create a source or filter, open data files, change properties and hit `Apply`, interact with the 3D scene, or save screenshots, etc., your actions will be monitored. Once you are done with the series of actions that you want to script, click Tools ⟩⟩ Stop Trace . *paraview* will then pop up an editor window with the generated trace. This will be the Python script equivalent for the actions you performed. You can now save this as a script to use for batch processing.

LOADING DATA

In a visualization pipeline, data sources bring data into the system for processing and visualization. Sources, such as the `Sphere` source (accessible from the `Sources` menu in *paraview*), programmatically create datasets for processing. Another type of data sources is readers. Readers can read data written out in disk files or other databases and bring it into ParaView for processing. ParaView includes readers that can read several of the commonly used scientific data formats. It's also possible to write plugins that add support for new or proprietary file formats.

ParaView provides several sample datasets for you to get started. You can download an archive with several types of data files from the download page at http://paraview.org.

2.1 Opening data files in `paraview`

To open a data file in *paraview*, you use the `Open File` dialog. This dialog can be accessed from the File〉Open menu or by using the button in the `Main Controls` toolbar. You can also use the keyboard shortcut Ctrl+O (or ⌘+O) to open this dialog.

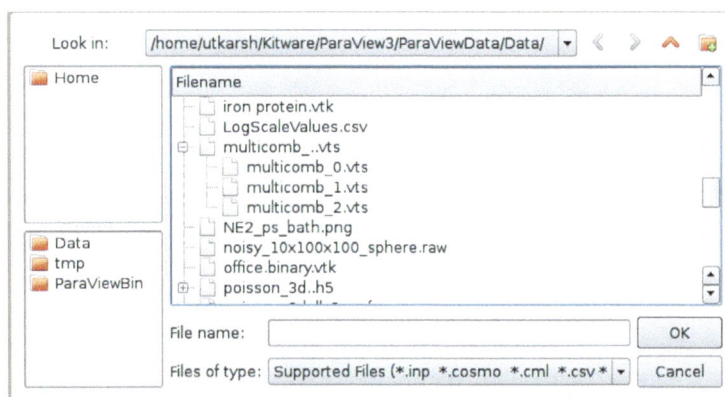

Figure 2.1: `Open File` dialog in *paraview* for opening data (and other) files.

The `Open File` dialog allows you to browse the file system on the data processing nodes. This will become clear when we look at using ParaView for remote visualization. While several of the UI elements in this dialog are obvious such as navigating up the current directory, creating a new directory, and navigating back and forth between directories, there are a few things to note.

- The `Favorites` pane shows some platform-specific common locations such as your home directory and desktop.

- The `Recent Directories` pane shows a few most recently used directories.

You can browse to the directory containing your datasets and either select the file and hit `Ok` or simply double click on the file to open it. You can also select multiple files using the `Ctrl` (or `⌘`) key. This will open each of the selected files separately.

When a file is opened, *paraview* will create a reader instance of the type suitable for the selected file based on its extension. The reader will simply be another pipeline module, similar to the source we created in Chapter 1. From this point forward, the workflow will be the same as we discussed in Section 1.4.2: You adjust the reader properties, if needed, and hit `Apply`. *paraview* will then read the data from the file and render it in the view.

If you selected multiple files using the `Ctrl` (or `⌘`) key, *paraview* will create multiple reader modules. When you hit `Apply`, all of the readers will be executed, and their data will be shown in the view.

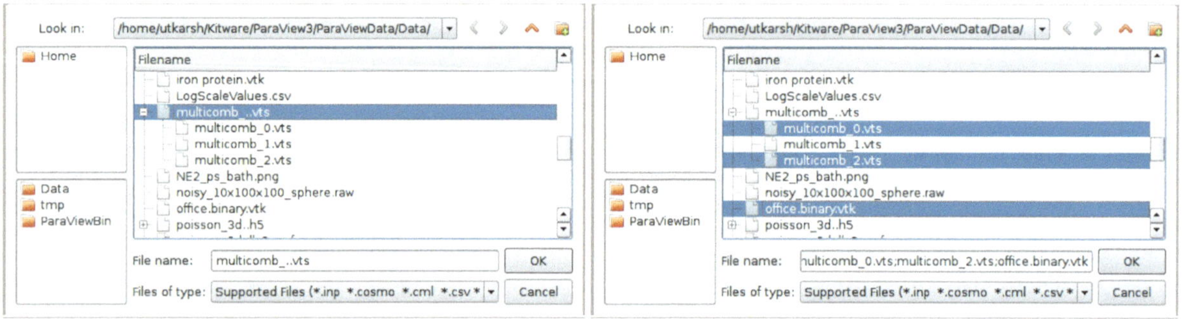

Figure 2.2: The `Open File` dialog can be used to select a temporal file series (left) or select multiple files to open separately (right).

ⓘ Did you know?

This ability to hit the `Apply` button once to accept changes on multiple readers applies to other pipeline modules, including sources and filters. In general, you can change properties for multiple modules in a pipeline, and hit `Apply` to accept all of the changes at once. It is possible to override this behavior from the `Settings` dialog.

2.1.1 Dealing with unknown extensions

On occasion, you will run into situations where a file is named unusually and, despite the fact that ParaView supports reading the file format, *paraview* does not recognize the file, as its extension does not match the expected extension. In this case, *paraview* will pop up the `Open Data With...` dialog, which lists several readers (Figure 2.3). You can then pick the reader for the correct file format from this list and continue. If you picked an incorrect reader, however, you'll get error messages either when the reader module is instantiated or after you hit `Apply`. In either case, you can simply `Delete` the reader module and try opening the file again, this time choosing a different reader.

Error messages in *paraview* are shown in the `Output Messages` window (Figure 2.4). It is accessible from the `Tools` ⟩ ⟩`Output Window` menu. Whenever there's a new error message, *paraview* will automatically pop open this window and raise it to the top.

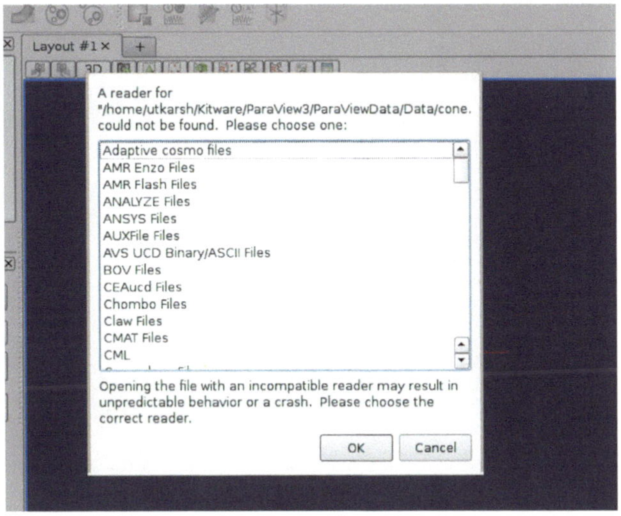

Figure 2.3: `Open Data With...` dialog shown to manually choose the reader to use for a file with an unknown extension.

2.1.2 Handling temporal file series

Most datasets produced by scientific simulation runs are temporal in nature. File formats differ in how this information is saved in the file. While several file formats support saving multiple timesteps in the same file, others save them out as a sequence of files, known as a file series.

The `Open File` dialog automatically detects file series and shows them as a grouped element, as shown in Figure 2.2. To load the file series, simply select the group, and hit `Ok`. You can also open a single file in the series as a regular file. To do so, open the file group and select the file you want to open.

paraview automatically detects several of the commonly-known file naming patterns used for indicating a file series. These include:

- `fooN.vtk`
- `foo_N.vtk`
- `fooN.vtk`
- `foo.N.vtk`
- `Nfoo.vtk`
- `N.foo.vtk`
- `foo.vtk.N`
- `foo.vtksN`

where *foo* could be any filename, *N* is a numeral sequence (with any number of leading zeros), and *vtk* could be any extension.

2.1.3 Dealing with time

When you open a dataset with time, either as a file series or in a file format that natively supports time, *paraview* will automatically setup an animation for you so that you can play through each of the time steps in the dataset by using the

▷ button on the `VCR Controls` toolbar (Figure 7.5). You can change or modify this animation and further customize it, as discussed in Chapter 7.

2.1.4 Reopening previously opened files

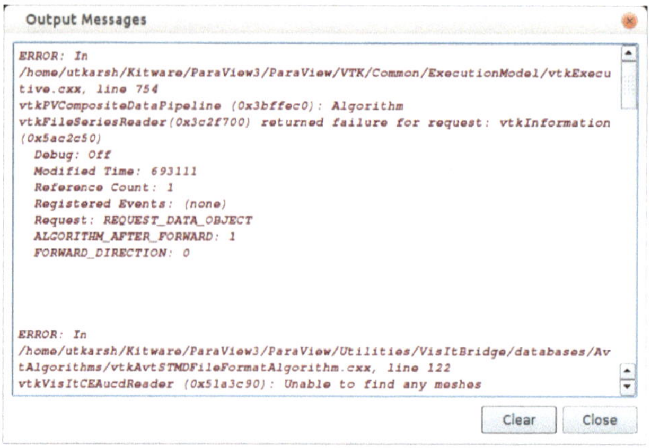

Figure 2.4: The `Output Messages` window is used to show errors, warnings, and other messages raised by the application.

Figure 2.5: `VCR Controls` toolbar for interacting with an animation.

paraview remembers most recently opened files (or file series). Simply use the [File ⟩ Recent Files] menu. *paraview* also remembers the reader type selected for files with unknown extensions or for occasions when multiple reader choices were available. [Recent Files]

2.1.5 Opening files using command line options

paraview provides a command line option that can be used to open datasets on startup.

```
> paraview --data=.../ParaViewData/Data/can.ex2
```

This is equivalent to opening a can.ex2 data file from the `Open File` dialog. The same set of follow-up actions happen. For example, *paraview* will try to locate a reader for the file, create that reader, and wait for you to hit `Apply`.

To open a file series, simply replace the numbers in the file name sequence by a '.' For example, to open a file series named `my0.vtk, my1.vtk...myN.vtk`, use `my..vtk`.

```
> paraview --data=.../ParaViewData/Data/multicomb_.vts
```

2.1.6 Common properties for readers

ParaView uses different reader implementations for different file formats. Each of these have different properties available to you to customize how the data is read and can vary greatly depending on the capabilities of the file format itself or the particular reader implementation. Let's look at some of the properties generally available on readers.

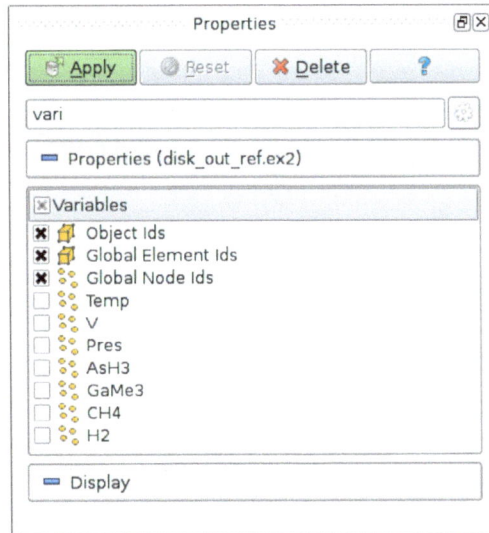

Figure 2.6: Array selection widget for selecting array to load from a data file.

Selecting data arrays

One of the most common properties on readers is one that allows you to select the data arrays (cell centered, point centered, or otherwise, if applicable) to be loaded. Often times, loading only the data arrays you know you are going to use in the visualization will save memory, as well as processing time, since the reader does not have to read in those data arrays, and the filters in the pipeline do not have to process them.

The UI for selecting the arrays to load is simply a list with the names of the arrays and a checkbox indicating whether that array is to be loaded or not (Figure 2.6). Icons, such as 📦 and ⁙ are often used in this widget to give you an indication of whether the array is cell-centered or point-centered, respectively.

If you unselected an array but realize, as you're setting up your visualization pipeline, that you need that data array, you can always go back to the Properties page for the reader by making the reader active in the Pipeline Browser and then changing the array selection. ParaView will automatically re-execute any processing pipeline set up on the reader with this new data array.

💣 Common Errors

§ *Remember to hit* Apply *(or use* Auto Apply*) after changing the array selection for the change to take effect.*

Sometimes this list can get quite large, and it can become cumbersome to find the array for which you are looking. To help with such situations, *paraview* provides a mechanism to search lists. Click inside the widget to make it get the *focus*. Then type `Ctrl`+`F` (or `⌘`+`F`) to get a search widget. Now you can type in the text to search. Matching rows will be highlighted (Figure 2.7).

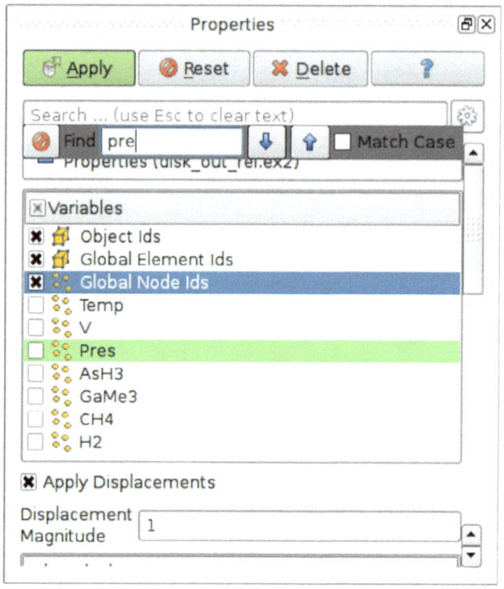

Figure 2.7: To search through large lists in *paraview*, you can use .

🛈 Did you know?

The ability to search for items in an array selection widget also applies to other list and tree widgets in the paraview UI. Whenever you see a widget with a large number of entries in a list, table, or tree fashion, try using `Ctrl` + `F` *(or* `⌘` + `F` *).*

2.2 Opening data files in `pvpython`

To open data files using the scripting interface, ParaView provides the `OpenDataFile` function.

```
1  >>> reader = OpenDataFile("...ParaViewData/Data/can.ex2")
2  >>> if reader:
3  ...    print "Success"
4  ... else:
5  ...    print "Failed"
6  ...
```

`OpenDataFile` will try to determine an appropriate reader based on the file extension, just like *paraview*. If no reader is determined, `None` is returned. If multiple readers can open the file, however, `OpenDataFile` simply picks the first reader. If you explicitly want to create a specific reader, you can always create the reader by its name, similar to other sources and filters.

```
1  >>> reader = ExodusIIReader(FileName="...ParaViewData/Data/can.ex2")
```

To find out information about the reader created and the properties available on it, you can use the `help` function.

```
1  >>> reader = ExodusIIReader(FileName="...ParaViewData/Data/can.ex2")
2  >>> help(reader)
```

```
 3  Help on ExodusIIReader in module paraview.servermanager object:
 4
 5  class ExodusIIReader(ExodusIIReaderProxy)
 6   |   The Exodus reader loads
 7   |   Exodus II files and produces an unstructured grid output.
 8   |   The default file extensions are .g, .e, .ex2, .ex2v2,
 9   |   .exo, .gen, .exoII, .exii, .0, .00, .000, and .0000. The
10   |   file format is described fully at:
11   |   http://endo.sandia.gov/SEACAS/Documentation/exodusII.pdf.
12   |   ...
13   |
14   |   -------------------------------------------------------------
15   |   Data descriptors defined here:
16   |
17   |   AnimateVibrations
18   |       If this flag is on and HasModeShapes is also on, then
19   |       this reader will report a continuous time range [0,1] and
20   |       animate the displacements in a periodic sinusoid. If this
21   |       flag is off and HasModeShapes is on, this reader ignores
22   |       time. This flag has no effect if HasModeShapes is off.
23   |
24   |   ApplyDisplacements
25   |       Geometric locations can include displacements. When this
26   |       option is on, the nodal positions are 'displaced' by the
27   |       standard exodus displacement vector. If displacements are
28   |       turned 'off', the user can explicitly add them by applying
29   |       a warp filter.
30   |   ...
```

ℹ️ **Did you know?**

The help *function can be used to get information about properties available on any source or filter instance. It not only lists the properties, but also provides information about how they affect the pipeline module.* help *can also be used on functions. For example:*

```
1  >>> help(OpenDataFile)
2
3  Help on function OpenDataFile in module paraview.simple:
4
5  OpenDataFile(filename, **extraArgs)
6      Creates a reader to read the given file, if possible.
7      This uses extension matching to determine the best reader
8      possible. If a reader cannot be identified, then this
9      returns None.
```

2.2.1 Handling temporal file series

Unlike *paraview*, *pvpython* does not automatically detect and load file series. You have to explicitly list the filenames in the series and pass that to the OpenDataFile call.

```
1  # Create a list with the names of all the files in the file series in
2  # correct order.
```

```
3 │ >>> files = ["…/Data/multicomb_0.vts",
4 │               "…/Data/multicomb_1.vts",
5 │               "…/Data/multicomb_2.vts"]
6 │ >>> reader = OpenDataFile(files)
```

2.2.2   Dealing with time

Similar to *paraview*, if you open a time series or a file with multiple timesteps, *pvpython* will automatically set up an animation for you to play through the timesteps.

```
 1 │ >>> files = ["…/Data/multicomb_0.vts",
 2 │               "…/Data/multicomb_1.vts",
 3 │               "…/Data/multicomb_2.vts"]
 4 │ >>> reader = OpenDataFile(files)
 5 │ >>> Show()
 6 │ >>> Render()
 7 │
 8 │ # Get access to the animation scene.
 9 │ >>> scene = GetAnimationScene()
10 │ # Now you use the API on the scene when doing things such as playing
11 │ # the animation, stepping through it, etc.
12 │
13 │ # This will simply play through the animation once and stop. Watch
14 │ # the rendered view after you hit 'Enter.'
15 │ >>> scene.Play()
```

2.2.3   Common properties on readers

Selecting data arrays

For those properties on readers that allow you to control what to read in from the file such as point data arrays, cell data arrays, or data blocks, *paraview* uses a selection widget, as seen in Section 2.1.6. Likewise, *pvpython* provides an API that allows you to determine the available options and then select/deselect them.

The name of the property that allows you to make such selections depends on the reader itself. When in doubt, use the tracing capabilities in *paraview* (Section 1.6.2) to figure it out. You can also use help (Section 2.2).

ExodusIIReader has a PointVariables property that can be used to select the point data arrays to load. Let's use this as an example.

```
 1 │ # Open an ExodusII data file.
 2 │ >>> reader = OpenDataFile("…/Data/can.ex2")
 3 │
 4 │ # Alternatively, you can explicitly create the reader instance as:
 5 │ >>> reader = ExodusIIReader(FileName = "…/Data/can.ex2")
 6 │
 7 │ # To query/print the current status for 'PointVariables' property,
 8 │ # we do what we would have done for any other property:
 9 │ >>> print GetProperty("PointVariables")
10 │ ['DISPL', 'VEL', 'ACCL']
11 │
12 │ # An alternative way of doing the same is as follows:
13 │ >>> print reader.PointVariables
```

```
14  ['DISPL', 'VEL', 'ACCL']
15
16  # To set the property, simply set it to list containing the names to
17  # enable, e.g., if we want to read only the 'DISPL' array, we do
18  # the following:
19  >>> SetProperties(PointVariables=['DISPL'])
20
21  # Or using the alternative way for doing the same:
22  >>> reader.PointVariables = ['DISPL']
23
24  # Now, the new value for PointVariables is:
25  >>> print reader.PointVariables
26  ['DISPL']
27
28  # To determine the array available, use:
29  >>> print reader.PointVariables.Available
30  ['DISPL', 'VEL', 'ACCL']
31  # These are the arrays available in the file.
```

Changing PointVariables only changes the value on the property. The reader does not re-execute until a re-execution is requested either by calling Render or by explicitly updating the pipeline using UpdatePipeline.

```
1   >>> reader.PointVariables = ['DISPL', 'VEL', 'ACCL']
2
3   # Assuming that the reader is indeed the active source, let's update
4   # the pipeline:
5   >>> UpdatePipeline()
6
7   # Or you can use the following form if you're unsure of the active
8   # source or just do not want to worry about it.
9   >>> UpdatePipeline(proxy=reader)
10
11  # Print the list of point arrays read in.
12  >>> print reader.PointData[:]
13  [Array: ACCL, Array: DISPL, Array: GlobalNodeId, Array: PedigreeNodeId, Array: VEL]
14
15  # Change the selection.
16  >>> reader.PointVariables = ['DISPL']
17
18  # Print the list of point arrays read in, nothing changes!
19  >>> print reader.PointData[:]
20  [Array: ACCL, Array: DISPL, Array: GlobalNodeId, Array: PedigreeNodeId, Array: VEL]
21
22  # Update the pipeline.
23  >>> UpdatePipeline()
24
25  # Now the arrays read in has indeed changed as we expected.
26  >>> print reader.PointData[:]
27  [Array: DISPL, Array: GlobalNodeId, Array: PedigreeNodeId]
```

We will cover the reader.PointData API in more details in Section 3.3.

UNDERSTANDING DATA

3.1   VTK data model

To use ParaView effectively, you need to understand the ParaView data model. ParaView uses VTK, the Visualization Toolkit, to provide the visualization and data processing model. This chapter briefly introduces the VTK data model used by ParaView. For more details, refer to one of the VTK books.

The most fundamental data structure in VTK is a data object. Data objects can either be scientific datasets, such as rectilinear grids or finite elements meshes (see below), or more abstract data structures, such as graphs or trees. These datasets are formed from smaller building blocks: mesh (topology and geometry) and attributes.

3.1.1   Mesh

Even though the actual data structure used to store the mesh in memory depends on the type of the dataset, some abstractions are common to all types. In general, a mesh consists of vertices (points) and cells (elements, zones). Cells are used to discretize a region and can have various types such as tetrahedra, hexahedra, etc. Each cell contains a set of vertices. The mapping from cells to vertices is called the connectivity. Note that even though it is possible to define data elements such as faces and edges, VTK does not represent these explicitly. Rather, they are implied by a cell's type and by its connectivity. One exception to this rule is the arbitrary polyhedron, which explicitly stores its faces. Figure 3.5 is an example mesh that consists of two cells. The first cell is defined by vertices $(0,1,3,4)$, and the second cell is defined by vertices $(1,2,4,5)$. These cells are neighbors because they share the edge defined by the points $(1,4)$.

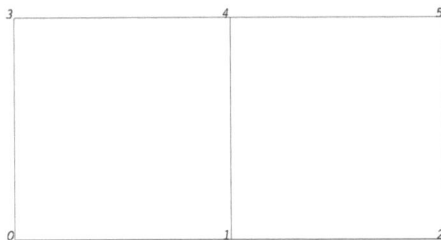

Figure 3.1: Example of a mesh

A mesh is fully defined by its topology and the spatial coordinates of its vertices. In VTK, the point coordinates may be implicit, or they may be explicitly defined by a data array of dimensions ($number\_of\_points \times 3$).

3.1.2 Attributes (fields, arrays)

An attribute (or a data array or field) defines the discrete values of a field over the mesh. Examples of attributes include pressure, temperature, velocity, and stress tensor. Note that VTK does not specifically define different types of attributes. All attributes are stored as data arrays, which can have an arbitrary number of components. ParaView makes some assumptions in regards to the number of components. For example, a 3-component array is assumed to be an array of vectors. Attributes can be associated with points or cells. It is also possible to have attributes that are not associated with either. Figure 3.2 demonstrates the use of a point-centered attribute. Note that the attribute is only defined on the vertices. Interpolation is used to obtain the values everywhere else. The interpolation functions used depend on the cell type. See the VTK documentation for details.

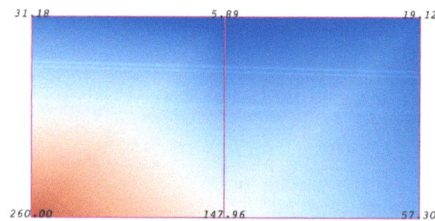

Figure 3.2: Point-centered attribute in a data array or field

Figure 3.3 demonstrates the use of a cell-centered attribute. Note that cell-centered attributes are assumed to be constant over each cell. Due to this property, many filters in VTK cannot be directly applied to cell-centered attributes. It is normally required to apply a Cell Data to Point Data filter. In ParaView, this filter is applied automatically, when necessary.

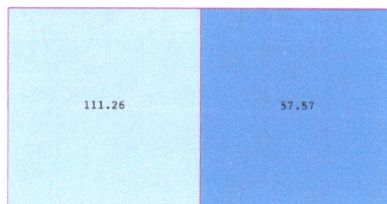

Figure 3.3: Cell-centered attribute

3.1.3 Uniform rectilinear grid (image data)

A uniform rectilinear grid, or image data, defines its topology and point coordinates implicitly (Figure 3.4). To fully define the mesh for an image data, VTK uses the following:

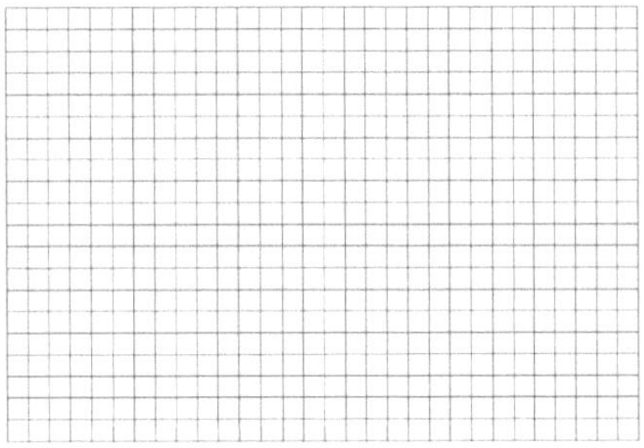

Figure 3.4: Sample uniform rectilinear grid

1. *Extents* - These define the minimum and maximum indices in each direction. For example, an image data of extents $(0,9)$, $(0,19)$, $(0,29)$ has 10 points in the x-direction, 20 points in the y-direction, and 30 points in the z-direction. The total number of points is $10 \times 20 \times 30$.
2. *Origin* - This is the position of a point defined with indices $(0,0,0)$.
3. *Spacing* - This is the distance between each point. Spacing for each direction can defined independently.

The coordinate of each point is defined as follows: $coordinate = origin + index \times spacing$ where coordinate, origin, index, and spacing are vectors of length 3.

Note that the generic VTK interface for all datasets uses a flat index. The (i,j,k) index can be converted to this flat index as follows: $idx\_flat = k \times (npts_x \times npts_y) + j \times nptr_x + i$.

A uniform rectilinear grid consists of cells of the same type. This type is determined by the dimensionality of the dataset (based on the extents) and can either be vertex (0D), line (1D), pixel (2D), or voxel (3D).

Due to its regular nature, image data requires less storage than other datasets. Furthermore, many algorithms in VTK have been optimized to take advantage of this property and are more efficient for image data.

3.1.4 Rectilinear grid

A rectilinear grid, such as Figure 3.5, defines its topology implicitly and point coordinates semi-implicitly. To fully define the mesh for a rectilinear grid, VTK uses the following:

1. *Extents* - These define the minimum and maximum indices in each direction. For example, a rectilinear grid of extents $(0,9)$, $(0,19)$, $(0,29)$ has 10 points in the x-direction, 20 points in the y-direction, and 30 points in the z-direction. The total number of points is $10 \times 20 \times 30$.
2. *Three arrays defining coordinates in the x-, y- and z-directions* - These arrays are of length $npts_x$, $npts_y$, and $npts_z$. This is a significant savings in memory, as the total memory used by these arrays is $npts_x + npts_y + npts_z$ rather than $npts_x \times npts_y \times npts_z$.

The coordinate of each point is defined as follows:

$$coordinate = (coordinate\_array_x(i), coordinate\_array_y(j), coordinate\_array_z(k)).$$

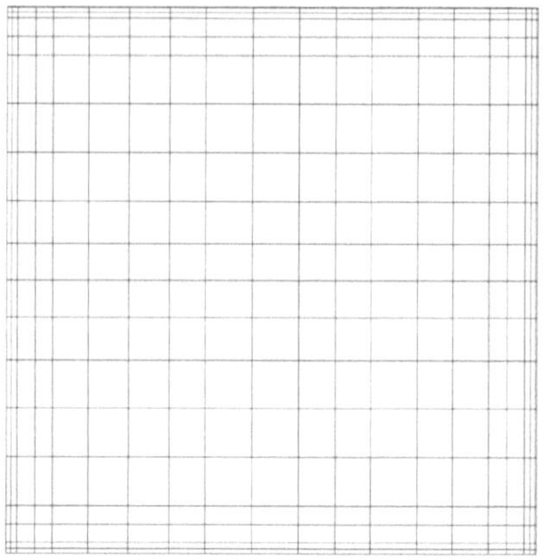

Figure 3.5: Rectilinear grid

Note that the generic VTK interface for all datasets uses a flat index. The (i, j, k) index can be converted to this flat index as follows: $idx\_flat = k \times (npts_x \times npts_y) + j \times nptr_x + i$.

A rectilinear grid consists of cells of the same type. This type is determined by the dimensionality of the dataset (based on the extents) and can either be vertex (0D), line (1D), pixel (2D), or voxel (3D).

3.1.5 Curvilinear grid (structured grid)

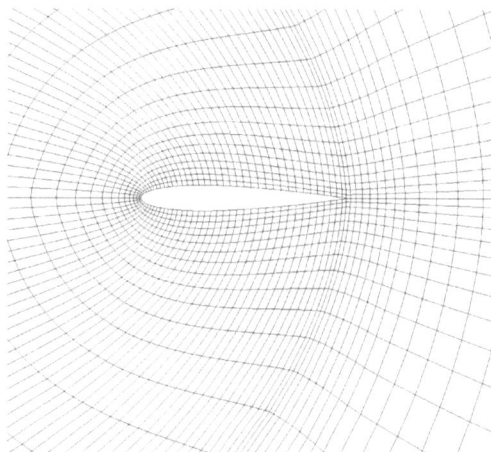

Figure 3.6: Curvilinear or structured grid

A curvilinear grid, such as Figure 3.6, defines its topology implicitly and point coordinates explicitly. To fully define the mesh for a curvilinear grid, VTK uses the following:

1. *Extents* - These define the minimum and maximum indices in each direction. For example, a curvilinear grid of extents $(0, 9)$, $(0, 19)$, $(0, 29)$ has $10 \times 20 \times 30$ points regularly defined over a curvilinear mesh.
2. *An array of point coordinates* - This array stores the position of each vertex explicitly.

The coordinate of each point is defined as follows: $coordinate = coordinate\_array(idx\_flat)$. The (i, j, k) index can be converted to this flat index as follows: $idx\_flat = k \times (npts_x \times npts_y) + j \times npts_x + i$.

A curvilinear grid consists of cells of the same type. This type is determined by the dimensionality of the dataset (based on the extents) and can either be vertex (0D), line (1D), quad (2D), or hexahedron (3D).

3.1.6 AMR dataset

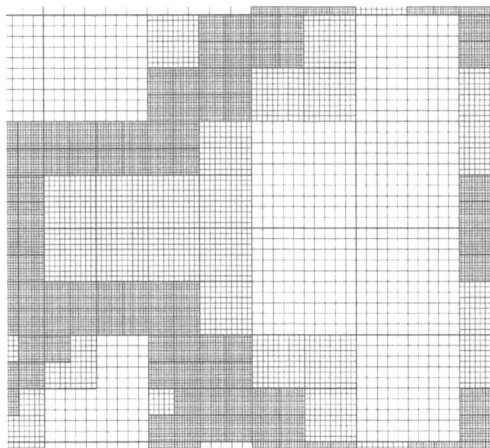

Figure 3.7: AMR dataset

VTK natively supports Berger-Oliger type Adaptive Mesh Refinement (AMR) datasets, as shown in Figure 3.7. An AMR dataset is essentially a collection of uniform rectilinear grids grouped under increasing refinement ratios (decreasing spacing). VTK's AMR dataset does not force any constraint on whether and how these grids should overlap. However, it provides support for masking (blanking) sub-regions of the rectilinear grids using an array of bytes. This allows VTK to process overlapping grids with minimal artifacts. VTK can automatically generate the masking arrays for Berger-Oliger compliant meshes.

3.1.7 Unstructured grid

An unstructured grid, such as Figure 3.8, is the most general primitive dataset type. It stores topology and point coordinates explicitly. Even though VTK uses a memory-efficient data structure to store the topology, an unstructured grid uses significantly more memory to represent its mesh. Therefore, use an unstructured grid only when you cannot represent your dataset as one of the above datasets. VTK supports a large number of cell types, all of which can exist (heterogeneously) within one unstructured grid. The full list of all cell types supported by VTK can be found in the file vtkCellType.h in the VTK source code. Here is the list as of when this document was written:

1. VTK_EMPTY_CELL
2. VTK_VERTEX
3. VTK_POLY_VERTEX
4. VTK_LINE
5. VTK_POLY_LINE
6. VTK_TRIANGLE
7. VTK_TRIANGLE_STRIP
8. VTK_POLYGON
9. VTK_PIXEL
10. VTK_QUAD
11. VTK_TETRA
12. VTK_VOXEL
13. VTK_HEXAHEDRON
14. VTK_WEDGE

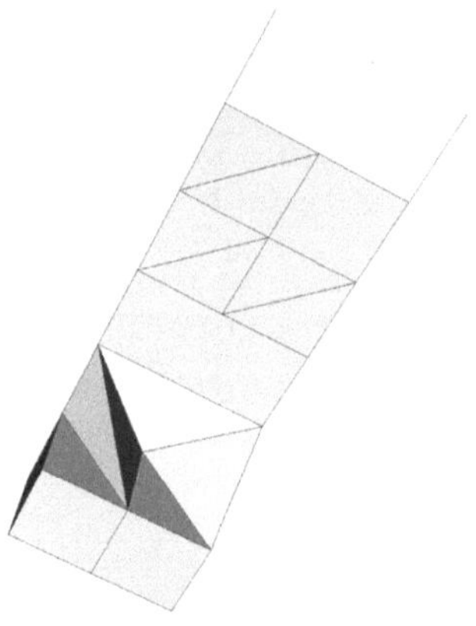

Figure 3.8: Unstructured grid

15. VTK_PYRAMID
16. VTK_PENTAGONAL_PRISM
17. VTK_HEXAGONAL_PRISM
18. VTK_QUADRATIC_EDGE
19. VTK_QUADRATIC_TRIANGLE
20. VTK_QUADRATIC_QUAD
21. VTK_QUADRATIC_TETRA
22. VTK_QUADRATIC
    _HEXAHEDRON
23. VTK_QUADRATIC_WEDGE
24. VTK_QUADRATIC_PYRAMID
25. VTK_BIQUADRATIC_QUAD
26. VTK_TRIQUADRATIC_HEXAHEDRON
27. VTK_QUADRATIC_LINEAR_QUAD
28. VTK_QUADRATIC_LINEAR_WEDGE
29. VTK_BIQUADRATIC_QUADRATIC

    _WEDGE
30. VTK_BIQUADRATIC_QUADRATIC
    _HEXAHEDRON
31. VTK_BIQUADRATIC_TRIANGLE
32. VTK_CUBIC_LINE
33. VTK_CONVEX_POINT_SET
34. VTK_POLYHEDRON
35. VTK_PARAMETRIC_CURVE
36. VTK_PARAMETRIC_SURFACE
37. VTK_PARAMETRIC_TRI_SURFACE
38. VTK_PARAMETRIC_QUAD
    _SURFACE
39. VTK_PARAMETRIC_TETRA
    _REGION
40. VTK_PARAMETRIC_HEX_REGION

Many of these cell types are straightforward. For details, see the VTK documentation.

3.1.8 Polygonal grid (polydata)

A polydata, such as Figure 3.9, is a specialized version of an unstructured grid designed for efficient rendering. It consists of 0D cells (vertices and polyvertices), 1D cells (lines and polylines), and 2D cells (polygons and triangle strips). Certain filters that generate only these cell types will generate a polydata. Examples include the Contour and Slice filters. An unstructured grid, as long as it has only 2D cells supported by polydata, can be converted to a polydata using the `Extract Surface Filter`. A polydata can be converted to an unstructured grid using `Clean to Grid`.

Figure 3.9: Polygonal grid

	Author	Affiliation		Alma Mater	Categories		Age	Coolness
0	Biff	NASA		Ole...	Jazz;	Ro...	27	0.6
1	Bob	Bob's	Supermarket	Ole...	Jazz		54	0.3
2	Baz	Bob's	Supermarket	TVI	Food		16	0.3
3	Bippity	Oil	Changes 'R'	TVI	Food		23	0.2
4	Boppity	Oil	Changes 'R'	Home	Food;	A...	34	0.25
5	Boo	Oil	Changes 'R'	Princeton	Automobiles		27	0.7

Figure 3.10: Table

3.1.9 Table

A table, such as Figure 3.10, is a tabular dataset that consists of rows and columns. All chart views have been designed to work with tables. Therefore, all filters that can be shown within the chart views generate tables. Also, tables can be directly loaded using various file formats such as the comma-separated values format. Tables can be converted to other datasets as long as they are of the right format. Filters that convert tables include Table to Points and Table to Structured Grid.

3.1.10 Multiblock dataset

You can think of a multi-block dataset (Figure 3.11) as a tree of datasets where the leaf nodes are *simple* datasets. All of the data types described above, except AMR , are *simple* datasets. Multi-block datasets are used to group together datasets that are related. The relation between these datasets is not necessarily defined by ParaView. A multi-block dataset can represent an assembly of parts or a collection of meshes of different types from a coupled simulation. Multi-block datasets can be loaded or created within ParaView using the Group filter. Note that the leaf nodes of a multi-block dataset do not all have to have the same attributes. If you apply a filter that requires an attribute, it will be applied only to blocks that have that attribute.

Figure 3.11: Multiblock dataset

3.1.11 Multipiece dataset

Multi-piece datasets, such as Figure 3.12, are similar to multi-block datasets in that they group together simple datasets. There is one key difference. Multi-piece datasets group together datasets that are part of a whole mesh - datasets of the same type and with the same attributes. This data structure is used to collect datasets produced by a parallel simulation without having to append the meshes together. Note that there is no way to create a multi-piece dataset within ParaView. It can only be created by using certain readers. Furthermore, multi-piece datasets act, for the most part, as simple datasets. For example, it is not possible to extract individual pieces or to obtain information about them.

3.2 Getting data information in `paraview`

In the visualization pipeline (Section 1.2), sources, readers, and filters are all producing data. In a VTK-based pipeline, this data is one of the types discussed. Thus, when you create a source or open a data file in *paraview* and hit `Apply`, data is being produced. The `Information` panel and the `Statistics Inspector` panel can be used to inspect the characteristics of the data produced by any pipeline module.

3.2.1 The `Information` panel

The `Information` panel provides summary information about the data produced by the active source. By default, this panel is tucked under a tab below the `Properties` panel. You can toggle its visibility using `View` ≫ `Information`.

The `Information` panel shows the data information for the active source. Thus, similar to the `Properties` panel, it changes when the active source is changed (e.g., by changing the selection in the `Pipeline Browser`). One way to think of this panel is as a panel showing a summary for the data *currently* produced by the active source. Remember that a newly-created pipeline module does not produce any data until you hit `Apply`. Thus, valid information for a newly-created source will be shown on this panel only after that `Apply`. Similarly, if you change properties on the source and hit `Apply`, this panel will reflect any changes in data characteristics. Additionally, for temporal pipelines, this panel shows information for the current timestep alone (except as noted). Thus, as you step through timesteps in a temporal dataset, the information displayed will potentially change, and the panel will reflect those changes.

Figure 3.12: Multipiece dataset

ℹ️ Did you know?

Any text on this panel is copy-able. For example, if want to copy the number of points value to use it as a property value on the `Properties` *panel, simply double-click on the number or click-and-drag to select the number and use the common keyboard shortcut* `Ctrl` + `C` *(or* `⌘` + `C` *) to copy that value to the clipboard. Now, you can paste it in an input widget in* paraview *or any other application, such as an editor, by using* `Ctrl` + `V` *(or* `⌘` + `V` *) or the application-specific shortcut for pasting text from the clipboard. The same is true for numbers shown in lists, such as the* `Data Ranges`.

The panel itself is comprised of several groups of information. Groups may be hidden based on the type of pipeline module or the type of data being produced.

The file `Properties` group is shown for readers with information about the file that is opened. For a temporal file series, as you step through each time step, the file name is updated to point to the name of the file in the series that corresponds to the current time step.

The `Statistics` group provides a summary of the dataset produced including its type, it number of cells and points (or rows and columns in cases of Tabular datasets), and an estimate of the memory used by the dataset. This number only includes the memory space needed to save the data arrays for the dataset. It does not include the memory space used by the data structures themselves and, hence, must only be treated as an estimate.

The `Data Arrays` group lists all of the available point, cells, and field arrays, as well as their types and ranges for the current time step. The `Current data time` field shows the time value for the current timestep as a reference. As with other places in *paraview*, the icons 🔶, ⚫, and 🟨 are used to indicate cell, point, and field data arrays. Since data arrays can have multiple components, the range for each component of the data array is shown.

`Bounds` shows the spatial bounds of the datasets in 3D Cartesian space. This will be unavailable for non-geometric datasets such as tables.

For reader modules, the `Time` group shows the available time steps and corresponding time values provided by the file.

For structured datasets such as uniform rectilinear grids or curvilinear grids, the `Extents` group is shown that displays the structured extents and dimensions of the datasets.

All of the summary information discussed so far provides a synopsis of the entire dataset produced by the pipeline module, including across all ranks (which will become clearer once we look at using ParaView for parallel data processing). In cases of composite datasets, such as mutliblock datasets or AMR datasets, recall that these are datasets that are comprised of other datasets. In such cases, these are summaries over all the blocks in the composite dataset. Every so often, you will notice that the `Data Arrays` table lists an array with the suffix `(partial)` (Figure 3.14). Such arrays are referred to as *partial arrays*. Partial arrays is a term used to refer to arrays that are present on some non-composite blocks or leaf nodes in a composite dataset, but not all. The `(partial)` suffix to indicate partial arrays is also used by *paraview* in other places in the UI.

While summaries over all of the datasets in the composite dataset are useful, you may also want to look at the data information for individual blocks. To do so, you can use the `Data Hierarchy` group, which appears when summarizing composite datasets. The `Data Hierarchy` widget shows the structure or hierarchy of the composite dataset (Figure 3.15). The `Information` panel switches to showing the summaries for the selected sub-tree. By default, the root element will be selected. You can now select any block in the hierarchy to view the summary limited to just that sub-tree.

ⓘ Did you know?

Memory information shown on the `Information` panel and the `Statistics Inspector` should only be used as an approximate reference and does not translate to how much memory the data produced by a particular pipeline module takes. This is due to the following factors:

- *The size does not include the amount of memory needed to build the data structures to store the data arrays. While, in most cases, this is negligible compared to that of the data arrays, it can be nontrivial, especially when dealing with deeply-nested composite datasets.*
- *Several filters such as `Calculator` and `Shrink` simply pass input data arrays through, so there's no extra space needed for those data arrays that are shared with the input. The memory size numbers shown, however, do not take this into consideration.*

If you need an overview of how much physical memory is being used by ParaView in its current state, you can use the `Memory Inspector` (Section 16).

3.2.2 The `Statistics Inspector` panel

The `Information` panel shows data information for the active source. If you need a quick summary of the data produced by all the pipeline modules, you can use the `Statistics Inspector` panel. It's accessible from Views ⟩ Statistics Inspector .

All of the information on this panel is also presented on the `Information` panel, except `Geometry Size`. This corresponds to how much memory is needed for the transformed dataset used for rendering in the active view. For example, to render a 3D dataset as a surface in the 3D view, ParaView must extract the surface mesh as a polydata. `Geometry Size` represents the memory needed for this polydata with the same memory-size-related caveats as with the `Information` panel.

3.3 Getting data information in `pvpython`

When scripting with ParaView, you will often find yourself needing information about the data. While *paraview* sets up filter properties and color tables automatically using the information from the data, when scripting, you have to do that explicitly.

In *pvpython*, for any pipeline module (sources, readers, or filters), you can use the following ways to get information about the data produced.

```
1  >>> from paraview.simple import *
2  >>> reader = OpenDataFile(".../ParaViewData/Data/can.ex2")
3
```

```
4   # We need to update the pipeline. Otherwise, all of the data
5   # information we get will be from before the file is actually
6   # read and, hence, will be empty.
7   >>> UpdatePipeline()
8
9   >>> dataInfo = reader.GetDataInformation()
10
11  # To get the number of cells or points in the dataset:
12  >>> dataInfo.GetNumberOfPoints()
13  10088
14  >>> dataInfo.GetNumberOfCells()
15  7152
16
17  # You can always nest the call, e.g.:
18  >>> reader.GetDataInformation().GetNumberOfPoints()
19  10088
20  >>> reader.GetDataInformation().GetNumberOfCells()
21  7152
22
23  # Use source.PointData or source.CellData to get information about
24  # point data arrays and cell data arrays, respectively.
25
26  # Let's print the available point data arrays.
27  >>> reader.PointData[:]
28  [Array: ACCL, Array: DISPL, Array: GlobalNodeId, Array: PedigreeNodeId, Array: VEL]
29
30  # Similarly, for cell data arrays:
31  >>> reader.CellData[:]
32  [Array: EQPS, Array: GlobalElementId, Array: ObjectId, Array: PedigreeElementId]
```

PointData (and CellData) is a map or dictionary where the keys are the names of the arrays, and the values are objects that provide more information about each of the arrays. In the rest of this section, anything we demonstrate on PointData is also applicable to CellData.

```
1   # Let's get the number of available point arrays.
2   >>> len(reader.PointData)
3   5
4
5   # Print the names for all available point arrays.
6   >>> reader.PointData.keys()
7   ['ACCL', 'DISPL', 'GlobalNodeId', 'PedigreeNodeId', 'VEL']
8
9   >>> reader.PointData.values()
10  [Array: ACCL, Array: DISPL, Array: GlobalNodeId, Array: PedigreeNodeId, Array: VEL]
11
12  # To test if a particular array is present:
13  >>> reader.PointData.has_key("ACCL")
14  True
15
16  >>> reader.PointData.has_key("--non-existent-array--")
17  False
```

From PointData (or CellData), you can get access to an object that provides information for each of the arrays. This object gives us methods to get data ranges, component counts, tuple counts, etc.

```
1
```

```
2   # Let's get information about 'ACCL' array.
3   >>> arrayInfo = reader.PointData["ACCL"]
4   >>> arrayInfo.GetName()
5   'ACCL'
6
7   # To get the number of components in each tuple and the number
8   # of tuples in the data array:
9   >>> arrayInfo.GetNumberOfTuples()
10  10088
11  >>> arrayInfo.GetNumberOfComponents()
12  3
13
14  # Alternative way for doing the same:
15  >>> reader.PointData["ACCL"].GetNumberOfTuples()
16  10088
17  >>> reader.PointData["ACCL"].GetNumberOfComponents()
18  3
19
20  # To get the range for a particular component, e.g. component 0:
21  >>> reader.PointData["ACCL"].GetRange(0)
22  (-4.965284006175352e-07, 3.212448973499704e-07)
23
24  # To get the range for the magnitude in cases of multi-component arrays
25  # use -1 as the component number.
26  >>> reader.PointData["ACCL"].GetRange(-1)
27  (0.0, 1.3329898584157294e-05)
28
29  # To determine the data data type for this array:
30  >>> from paraview import vtk
31  >>> reader.PointData["ACCL"].GetDataType() == vtk.VTK_DOUBLE
32  True
33  # The paraview.vtk module provides access to these constants such as
34  # VTK_DOUBLE, VTK_FLOAT, VTK_INT, etc.
35
36  # Likewise, to test the dataset type, itself:
37  >>> reader.GetDataInformation().GetDataSetType() == \
38                          vtk.VTK_MULTIBLOCK_DATA_SET
39  True
```

Here's a sample script to iterate over all point data arrays and print their magnitude ranges:

```
1
2   >>> def print_point_data_ranges(source):
3   ...     """Prints array ranges for all point arrays"""
4   ...     for arrayInfo in source.PointData:
5   ...         # get the array's name
6   ...         name = arrayInfo.GetName()
7   ...         # get magnitude range
8   ...         range = arrayInfo.GetRange(-1)
9   ...         print "%s = [%.3f, %.3f]" % (name, range[0], range[1])
10
11  # Let's call this function on our reader.
12  >>> print_point_data_ranges(reader)
13  ACCL = [0.000, 0.000]
14  DISPL = [0.000, 0.000]
15  GlobalNodeId = [1.000, 10088.000]
```

```
16  PedigreeNodeId = [1.000,  10088.000]
17  VEL = [0.000,  5000.000]
```

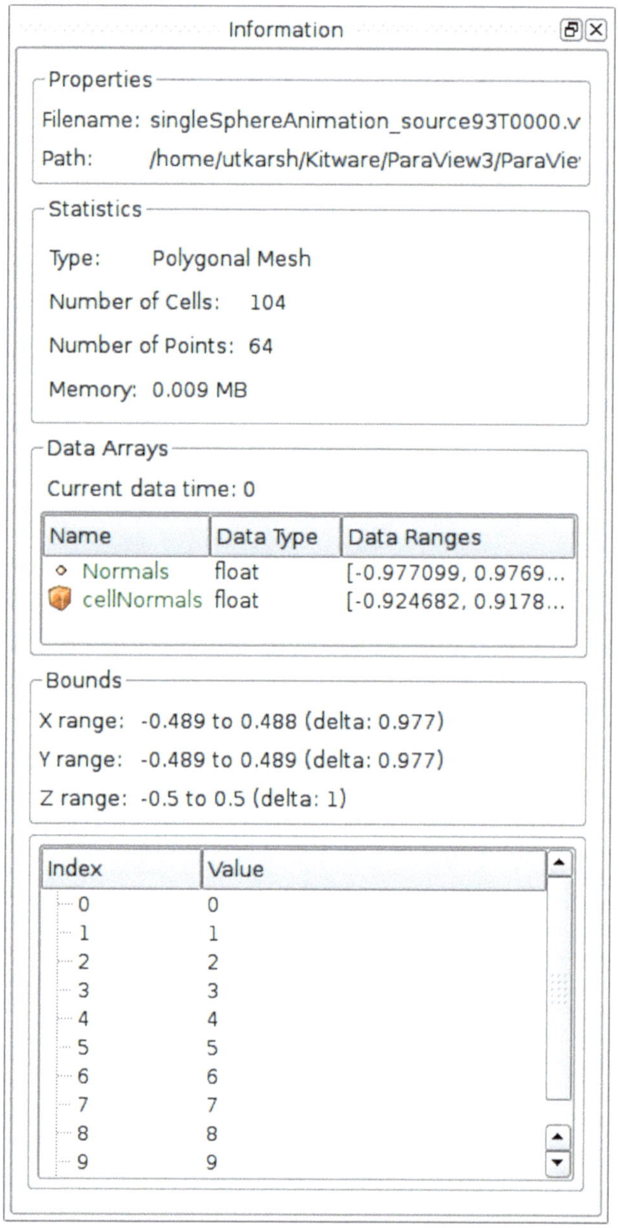

Figure 3.13: The `Information` panel in *paraview* showing data summaries for the active source.

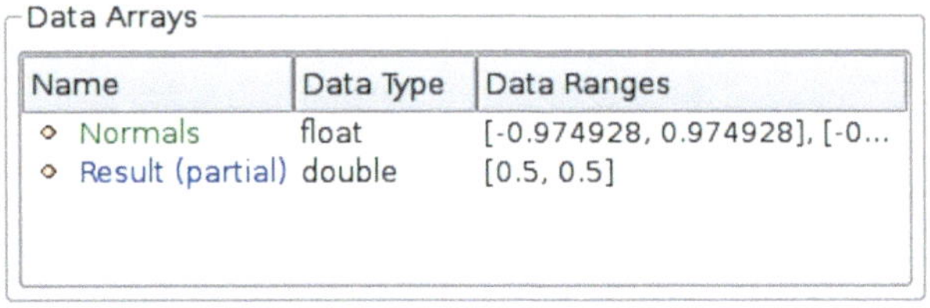
Data Arrays
Name
Data Type
Data Ranges
Normals
float
[-0.974928, 0.974928], [-0...
Result (partial)
double
[0.5, 0.5]

Figure 3.14: The `Data Arrays` section on `Information` panel showing *partial* arrays. Partial arrays are arrays that present on certain blocks in a composite dataset, but not all.

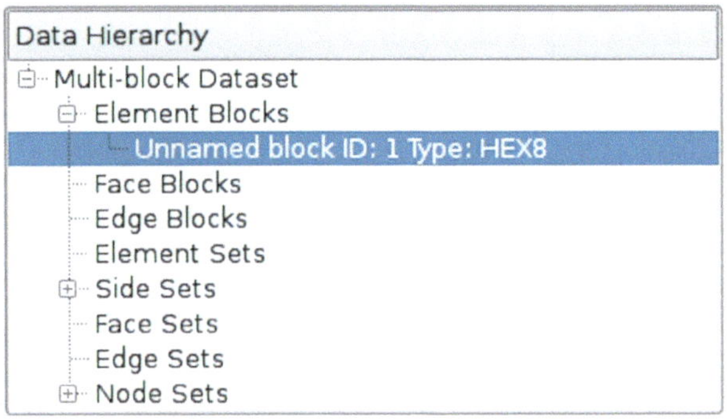
Data Hierarchy
Multi-block Dataset
Element Blocks
Unnamed block ID: 1 Type: HEX8
Face Blocks
Edge Blocks
Element Sets
Side Sets
Face Sets
Edge Sets
Node Sets

Figure 3.15: The `Data Hierarchy` section on the `Information` panel showing the composite data hierarchy. Selecting a particular block or subtree in this widget will result in the reset of the `Information` panel showing summaries for that block or subtree alone.

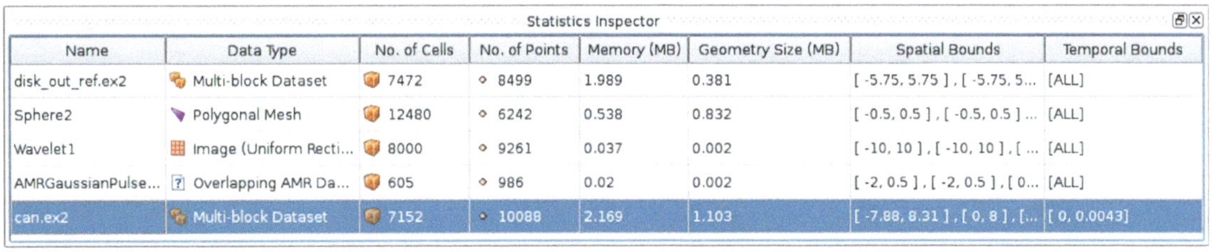
Statistics Inspector
Name
Data Type
No. of Cells
No. of Points
Memory (MB)
Geometry Size (MB)
Spatial Bounds
Temporal Bounds
disk_out_ref.ex2
Multi-block Dataset
7472
8499
1.989
0.381
[-5.75, 5.75], [-5.75, 5...
[ALL]
Sphere2
Polygonal Mesh
12480
6242
0.538
0.832
[-0.5, 0.5], [-0.5, 0.5] ...
[ALL]
Wavelet1
Image (Uniform Recti...
8000
9261
0.037
0.002
[-10, 10], [-10, 10], [...
[ALL]
AMRGaussianPulse...
Overlapping AMR Da...
605
986
0.02
0.002
[-2, 0.5], [-2, 0.5], [0...
[ALL]
can.ex2
Multi-block Dataset
7152
10088
2.169
1.103
[-7.88, 8.31], [0, 8], [...
[0, 0.0043]

Figure 3.16: The `Statistics Inspector` panel in *paraview* showing summaries for all pipeline modules.

DISPLAYING DATA

The goal of any visualization process is to produce visual representations of the data. The visual representations are shown in modules called views. *Views* provide the canvas on which to display such visual representations, as well as to dictate how these representations are generated from the raw data. The role of the visualization pipeline is often to transform the data so that relevant information can be represented in these views.

Referring back to the visualization pipeline from Section 1.2, views are sinks that take in input data but do not produce any data output. (I.e., one cannot connect other pipeline modules such as filters to process the results in a view.) However, views often provide mechanisms to save the results as images or in other formats including PDF, VRML, and X3D.

Different types of views provide different ways of visualizing data. These can be broadly grouped as follows:

- *Rendering Views* are views that render geometries or volumes in a graphical context. The `Render View` is one such view. Other Render View-based views, such as `Slice View` and `Quad View`, extend the basic render view to add the ability to add mechanisms to easily inspect slices or generate orthogonal views.
- *Chart Views* cover a wide array of graphs and plots used for visualizing non-geometric data. These include views such as line charts (`Line Chart View`), bar charts (`Bar Chart View`), bag charts (`Bag Chart View`), parallel co-ordinates (`Parallel Coordinates View`), etc.
- *Comparative Views* are used to quickly generate side-by-side views for parameter study, i.e., to visualize the effects of parameter changes. Comparative variants of `Render View` and several types of the `Chart Views` are available in ParaView.

In this chapter, we take a close look at the various views available in ParaView and how to use these views for displaying data.

4.1 Multiple views

With multiple types of views comes the need for creating and viewing multiple views at the same time. In this section, we look at how you can create multiple views and lay them out.

🛈 Did you know?

> *Multiple views were first supported in ParaView 3.0. Before that, all data was shown in a single 3D render view, including line plots!*

4.1.1 Multiple views in `paraview`

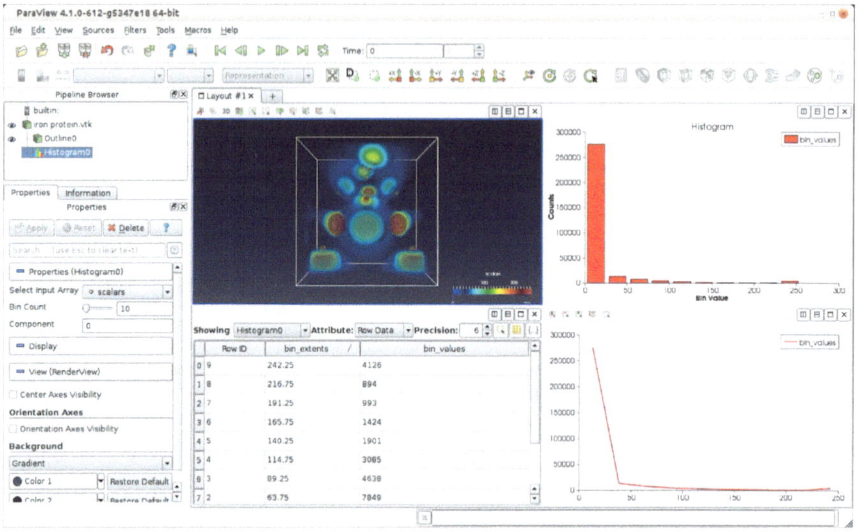

Figure 4.1: Using multiple views in *paraview* to generate different types of visualizations from a dataset.

paraview shows all views in the central part of the application window. When *paraview* starts up, the `Render View` is created and shown in the application window by default.

New views can be created by splitting the view frame using the `Split View` controls at the top-right corner of the view frame. Splitting a view splits the view into two equal parts, either vertically or horizontally, based on the button used for the split. On splitting a view, an empty frame with buttons for all known types of views is shown. Simply click on one of those buttons to create a new view of a chosen type.

You can move views by clicking and dragging the title bar for the view (or empty view frame) and dropping it on the title bar on another view (or empty view frame). This will swap the positions of the two views.

Similar to the notion of active source, there is a notion of *active view*. Several panels, toolbars, and menus will update based on the active view. The `Display` properties section on the `Properties` panel, for example, reflects the display properties of the active source in the active view. Similarly, the eyeball icons in the `Pipeline Browser` show the visibility status of the pipeline module in the active view. Active view is marked in the UI by a blue border around the view frame. Only one view can be active at any time in the application.

Besides being able to create multiple views and laying them out in a pane, *paraview* also supports placing views in multiple layouts under separate tabs. To create new tabs, use the ⊞ button in the tab bar. You can close a tab, which will destroy all views laid out in that tab, by clicking on the ✕ button. To pop out an entire tab as a separate window, use the ▢ button on the tab bar.

The active view is always present in the active tab. Thus, if you change the active tab, the active view will also be changed to be a view in the active tab layout. Conversely, if the active view is changed (by using the `Python Shell`, for example), the active tab will automatically be updated to be the tab that contains the active view.

ⓘ Did you know?

> *You can make the views fullscreen by using* View 》 Fullscreen . *To return back to the normal mode, use the* Esc *key.*

4.1.2 Multiple views in `pvpython`

In *pvpython*, one can create new views using the `CreateView` function or its variants, e.g., `CreateRenderView`.

```
1  >>> from paraview.simple import *
2  >>> view = CreateRenderView()
3  # Alternatively, use CreateView.
4  >>> view = CreateView("RenderView")
```

When a new view is created, it is automatically made active. You can manually make a view active by using the `SetActiveView` function. Several of the functions available in *pvpython* will use the active view when no view is passed as an argument to the function.

```
1  # Create a view
2  >>> view1 = CreateRenderView()
3  # Create a second view
4  >>> view2 = CreateRenderView()
5
6  # Check if view2 is the active view
7  >>> view2 == GetActiveView()
8  True
9
10 # Make view1 active
11 >>> SetActiveView(view1)
12 >>> view1 == GetActiveView()
13 True
```

When using `Python Shell` in *paraview*, if you create a new view, it will automatically be placed in the active tab by splitting the active view. You can manually control the layout and placement of views from Python too, using the layout API.

In Python, each tab that corresponds is referred to as a layout.

```
1  # To get exisiting tabs/layouts
2  >>> layouts = GetLayouts()
3  >>> print layouts
4  {('ViewLayout1', '264'): <paraview.servermanager.ViewLayout object at 0x2e5b7d0>}
5
6  # To get layout corresponding to a particular view
7  >>> print GetLayout(view)
8  <paraview.servermanager.ViewLayout object at 0x2e5b7d0>
9
10 # If view is not specified, active view is used
11 >>> print GetLayout()
12 <paraview.servermanager.ViewLayout object at 0x2e5b7d0>
13
14 # To create a new tab
15 >>> new_layout = servermanager.misc.ViewLayout(registrationGroup="layouts")
16
17 # To split the cell containing the view, either horizontally or vertically
18 >>> view = GetActiveView()
19 >>> layout = GetLayout(view)
20 >>> locationId = layout.SplitViewVertical(view=view,
21                                           fraction=0.5)
22 # fraction is optional, if not specified the frame is split evenly.
23
```

```
24  # To assign a view to a particular cell.
25  >>> view2 = CreateRenderView()
26  >>> layout.AssignView(locationId, view2)
```

4.2 View properties

Just like parameters on pipeline modules, such as readers and filters, views provide parameters that can be used for customizing the visualization such as changing the background color for rendering views and adding title texts for chart views. These parameters are referred to as `View Properties` and are accessible from the `Properties` panel in *paraview*.

4.2.1 View properties in `paraview`

Similar to properties on pipeline modules like sources and readers, view properties are accessible from the `Properties` panel. These are grouped under the `View` section. When the active view is changed, the `Properties` panel updates to show the view properties for the active view. Unlike pipeline modules, however, when you change the view properties, they affect the visualization immediately, without use of the `Apply` button.

> **Did you know?**
>
> *It may seem odd that `View` and `Display` properties on the `Properties` panel don't need to be `Apply`-ed to take effect, while properties on pipeline modules like sources, readers and filter require you to hit the `Apply` button. To understand the reasoning behind that, we need to understand why the `Apply` action is needed in the first place. Generally, executing a data processing filter or reader is time consuming on large datasets. If the pipeline module keeps on executing as you are changing the parameter, the user experience will quickly deteriorate, since the pipeline will keep on executing with intermediate (and potentially invalid) property values. To avoid this, we have the `Apply` action. This way, you can set up the pipeline properties to your liking and then trigger the potentially time consuming execution.*
>
> *Since the visualization process in general focuses on reducing data to generate visual representations, the rendering (broadly speaking) is less time-intensive than the actual data processing. Thus, changing properties that affect rendering are not as compute-intensive as transforming the data itself. (E.g., changing the color on a surface mesh is not as expensive as generating the mesh in the first place.) Hence, the need to `Apply` such properties becomes less relevant. At the same time, when changing display properties such as opacity, you may want to see the result as you change the property to decide on the final value. Hence, it is desirable to see the updates immediately.*
>
> *Of course, you can always enable `Auto Apply` to have the same immediate update behavior for all properties on the `Properties` panel.*

4.2.2 View properties in `pvpython`

In *pvpython*, once you have access to the view, you can directly change view properties on the view object. There are several ways to get access to the view object.

```
1  # 1. Save reference when a view is created
2  >>> view = CreateView("RenderView")
3
4  # 2. Get reference to the active view.
5  >>> view = GetActiveView()
```

The properties available on the view will change based on the type of the view. You can use the `help` function to discover available properties.

```
1  >>> view = CreateRenderView()
2  >>> help(view)
3
4    Help on RenderView in module paraview.servermanager object:
5
6  class RenderView(Proxy)
7   |  View proxy for a 3D interactive render
8   |  view.
9   |
10  |  ----------------------------------------------------------------
11  |  Data descriptors defined here:
12  |
13  |  CenterAxesVisibility
14  |      Toggle the visibility of the axes showing the center of
15  |      rotation in the scene.
16  |
17  |  CenterOfRotation
18  |      Center of rotation for the interactor.
19  |
20  ...
```

Once you have a reference to the view, you can then get/set the properties.

```
1  # Get the current value
2  >>> print view.CenterAxesVisibility
3  1
4
5  # Change the value
6  >>> view.CenterAxesVisibility = 0
```

4.3 Display properties

Display properties refers to available parameters that control how data from a pipeline module is displayed in a view, e.g., choosing to view the output mesh as a wireframe, coloring the mesh using a data attribute, and selecting which attributes to plot in chart view. A set of display properties is associated with a particular pipeline module and view. Thus, if the data output from a source is shown in two views, there will be two sets of display properties used to control the appearance of the data in each of the two views.

4.3.1 Display properties in `paraview`

Display properties are accessible from the `Display` section on the `Properties` panel. When the active source or active view changes, this section updates to show the display properties for the active source in the active view, if available. If the active source produces data that cannot be shown (or has never been shown) in the view, then the `Display` properties section may be empty.

Similar to view properties, display property changes are immediately applied, without requiring the use of the `Apply` button.

4.3.2 Display properties in `pvpython`

To access display properties in *pvpython*, you can use `SetDisplayProperties` and `GetDisplayProperty` methods.

```
1
2  # Using SetDisplayProperties/GetDisplayProperties to access the display
3  # properties for the active source in the active view.
4
5  >>> print GetDisplayProperties("Opacity")
6  1.0
7
8  >>> SetDisplayProperties(Opacity=0.5)
```

Alternatively, you can get access to the display properties object using `GetDisplayProperties` and then changing properties directly on the object.

```
1  # Get display properties object for the active source in the active view.
2  >>> disp = GetDisplayProperties()
3
4  # You can also save the object returned by Show.
5  >>> disp = Show()
6
7  # Now, you can directly access the properties
8  >>> print disp.Opacity
9  0.5
10
11 >>> disp.Opacity = 0.75
```

As always, you can use the `help` method to discover available properties on a display object.

```
1  >>> disp = Show()
2
3  >>> help(disp)
4  >>> help(a)
5  Help on GeometryRepresentation in module paraview.servermanager object:
6
7  class GeometryRepresentation(SourceProxy)
8   |  ParaView's default representation for showing any type of
9   |  dataset in the render view.
10  |
11  |  Method resolution order:
12  |      GeometryRepresentation
13  |      SourceProxy
14  |      Proxy
15  |      __builtin__.object
16  |
17  |  ----------------------------------------------------------------
18  |  Data descriptors defined here:
19  |
20  |  ...
21  |
22  |  CenterStickyAxes
23  |      Keep the sticky axes centered in the view window.
24  |
25  |  ColorArrayName
26  |      Set the array name to color by. Set it to empty string
```

```
27  |        to use solid color.
28  |
29  |   ColorAttributeType
30  |   ...
```

4.4 Render View

`Render View` is the most commonly used view in ParaView. It is used to render geometries and volumes in a 3D scene. This is the view that you typically think of when referring to 3D visualization. The view relies on techniques to map data to graphics primitives such as triangles, polygons, and voxels, and it renders them in a scene.

Most of the scientific datasets discussed in Section 3.1 are comprised of meshes. These meshes can be mapped to graphics primitives using several of the established visualization techniques. (E.g., you can compute the outer surface of these meshes and then render that surface as filled polygons, you can just render the edges, or you can render the data as a nebulous blob to get a better understanding of the internal structure in the dataset.) Plugins, like `Surface LIC`, can provide additional ways of rendering data using advanced techniques that provide more insight into the data.

If the dataset doesn't represent a mesh, e.g., a table (Section 3.1.9), you cannot directly show that data in this view. However, in such cases, it may be possible to construct a mesh by mapping columns in the table to positions to construct a point cloud, for example.

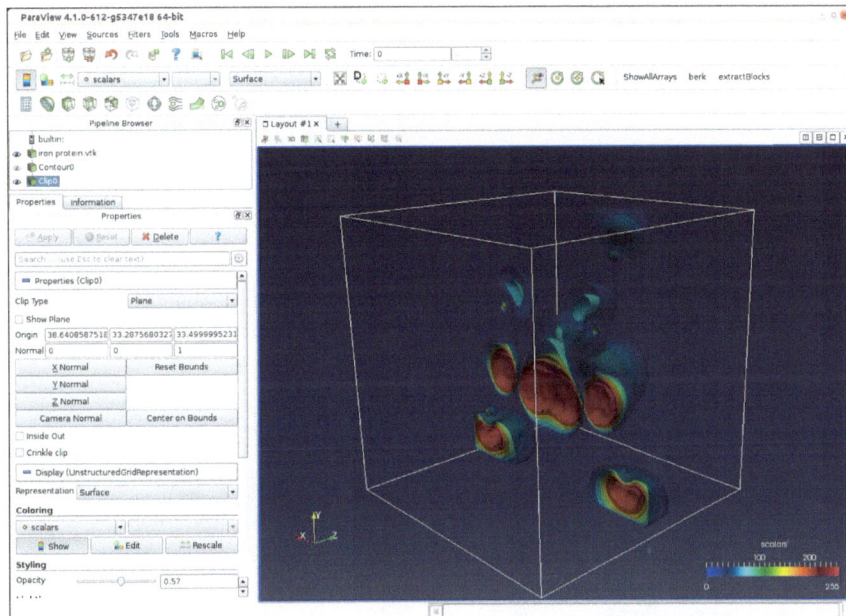

Figure 4.2: *paraview* using `Render View` to generate 3D visualizations from a dataset.

4.4.1 Understanding the rendering process

`Render View` uses data processing techniques to map raw data to graphics primitives, which can then be rendered in a 3D scene. These mapping techniques can be classified as follows:

- *Surface rendering* methods provide general rendering by rendering a surface mesh for the dataset. For polygonal datasets (Section 3.1.8), this is simply the raw data. In cases of other datasets including structured (Sections 3.1.3, 3.1.4, 3.1.5) and unstructured (Section 3.1.7) grids, this implies extracting a surface mesh for all external faces in the dataset and then rendering that mesh. The surface mesh itself can then be rendered as a filled surface or as a wireframe simply showing the edges, etc.
- *Slice* rendering is available for uniform rectilinear grid datasets (Section 3.1.3) where the visualization is generated by simply rendering an orthogonal slice through the dataset. The slice position and alignment can be selected using the display properties.
- *Volume* rendering generates rendering by tracing a ray through the dataset and accumulating intensities based on the color and opacity transfer functions set.

Each of these techniques are referred to as *representations*. When available, you can change the representation type from the display properties on the `Properties` panel or using the `Representation Toolbar`.

4.4.2 Render View in `paraview`

Creating a Render View

Unless you changed the default setting, a new `Render View` will be created when *paraview* starts up or connects to a new server. To create a `Render View` in *paraview*, split or close a view, and select the `Render View` button. You can also convert a view to a Render View (or any other type) by right-clicking on the view's title bar and picking from the `Convert To` sub-menu. It simply closes the chosen view and creates a selected view type in its place.

You can use the `Pipeline Browser` to control the visibility of datasets produced by pipeline modules in this view. The eyeball icons reflect the visibility state. Clicking on the eyeball icon will toggle the visibility state. If no eyeball icon is shown, it implies that the pipeline module doesn't produce a data type that can be directly shown in the active view, e.g., if the module produced a table, then when `Render View` is active, there will not be any eyeball icon next to that module.

Interactions

You can interact with the Render View to move the camera in the scene for exploring the visualization and setting up optimal viewing angles. Each of the three mouse buttons, combined with keyboard modifier keys (Ctrl or ⌘, and ⇧), move the camera differently. The interaction mode can be changed from the `Camera` tab in the `Settings` dialog, which is accessible from Tools ⟩ Settings (or ParaView ⟩ Preferences on OS X).

The default interactions options are as follows:

Modifier	Left Button	Middle Button	Right Button
	Rotate	Pan	Zoom
⇧	Roll	Rotate	Pan
Ctrl or ⌘	Zoom	Rotate	Zoom

Generally, you are interacting with a 3D scene, however, there are cases when you are working with a 2D dataset such as a slice plane or a 2D image. In such cases, *paraview* provides a separate set of interaction options suitable for 2D interactions. You can toggle between the default 3D interaction options and 2D interaction options by clicking the 2D or 3D button in the view toolbar. The default interaction options for 2D interactions are as follows:

Modifier	Left Button	Middle Button	Right Button
	Pan	Roll	Zoom
⇧	Zoom	Zoom	Zoom
Ctrl or ⌘	Roll	Pan	Rotate

View properties

Several of the view properties in Render View control the annotations shown in the view (Figure 4.3).

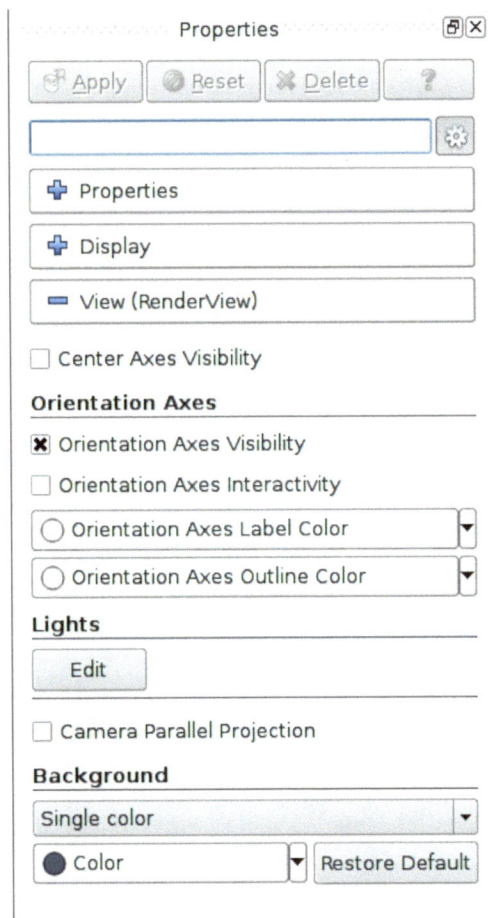

Figure 4.3: The Properties panel showing view properties for Render View.

The *Center axes* refers to axes rendered in the scene positioned as the center of rotation, i.e., the location is space around which the camera revolves during Rotate camera interaction. Center Axes Visibility controls the visibility of the center axes.

The *Orientation axes* is the widget shown at the lower-left corner by default, which is used to get a sense for the orientation of the scene. The properties grouped under the Orientation Axes group allow you to toggle the visibility and the interactivity of this widget. When interactivity is enabled, you can click and drag this widget to the location of your choosing in the scene.

You can also change the Background used for this view. You can either set it as a Single color or as a Gradient comprised of two colors, or you can select an Image (or texture) to use as the background.

Display properties

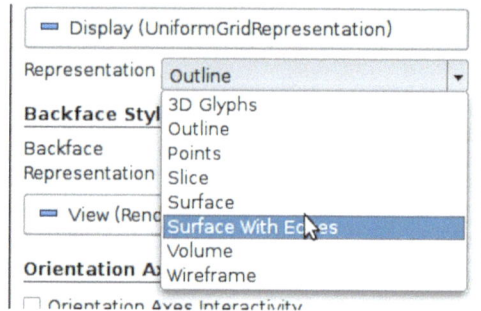

One of the first (and probably the most often used) display properties is Representation. Representation allows you to pick one of the *mapping* modes. The options available depend on the data type, as well as the plugins loaded. While all display properties are accessible from the advanced view for the Properties panel, certain properties may be shown/hidden from the default view based on the chosen representation type.

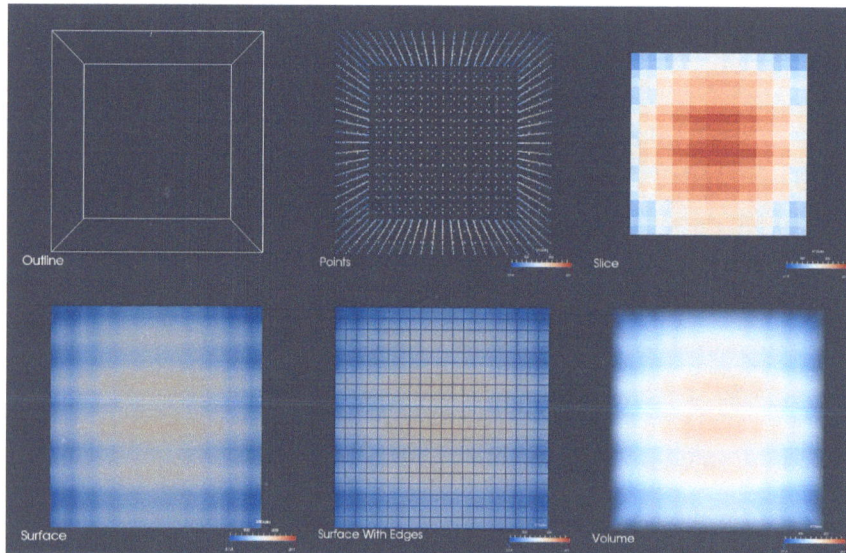

Figure 4.4: Different renderings generated by rendering data produced by the Wavelet source as outline, points, slice, surface, surface with edges, and volume.

Outline representation can be used to render an outline for the dataset. This is arguably the fastest way of rendering the dataset since only the bounding box is rendered. Scalar coloring options, i.e., selecting an array with which to color, has no effect on this representation type. You can still, however, change the Solid Color to use as well as the Opacity. To change the color, select Solid Color in the combo-box under Coloring, and then click Edit to pick the color to use. To change the opacity, simply change the Opacity slider. 0 implies total transparency and, hence, invisiblity, while 1 implies totally opacity.

ℹ Did you know?

Rendering translucent data generally adds computational costs to the rendering process. Thus, when rendering large datasets, you may want to leave changing opacities to anything less than 1 to the very end, after having set up the visualization. In doing so, you avoid translucent geometries during exploration, but use them for generating images or screenshots for presentations and publications.

Points, Surface, Surface With Edges, and Wireframe rely on extracting the surface mesh from the dataset and then rendering that either as a collection of points, as solid surface, as solid surface with cell boundaries highlighted, or as a wireframe of cell boundaries with empty cells. You can either set a single solid color to use, as with Outline, or select a data array to use for scalar coloring (also known as pseudocoloring).

Next, we will cover each of the property groups available under Display properties. Several of these are marked as advanced. Accordingly, you may need to either toggle the panel to show advanced properties using the ⚙ button or search for it by name using the search box.

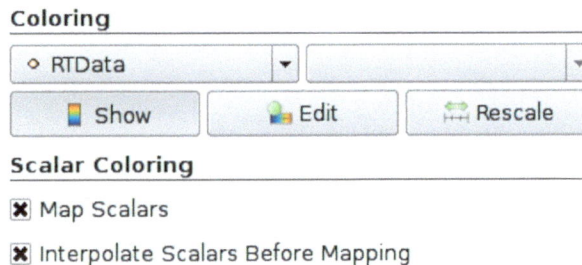

Display properties under Coloring allow you to set how the dataset is colored. To select a single solid color to use to fill the surface or with which to color wireframe or points, select Solid Color in the combo-box, and then click Edit. That will pop up the standard color chooser dialog, allowing you to pick a color to use. If, instead, you want to pseudocolor using an attribute array available on the dataset, select that array name from the combo-box. For multi-component arrays, you can pick a particular component or Magnitude to use for scalar coloring. ParaView will automatically setup a color transfer function to use to map the data array to colors. The default range for the transfer function is set up based on the application Settings. To reset the transfer function range to the current data range, you can use the Rescale button. Remember that, despite the fact that you can set the scalar array with which to color when rendering as Outline, the outline itself continues to use the specified solid color. Scalar Coloring properties are only relevant when you have selected a data array with which to pseudocolor. The Map Scalars checkbox affects whether a color transfer function should be used (Figure 4.5). If unchecked, and the data array can directly be interpreted as colors, then those colors are used directly. If not, the color transfer function will be used. A data array can be interpreted as colors if, and only if, it is an unsigned char array with two, three, or four components. Interpolate Scalars Before Mapping controls how color interpolation happens across rendered polygons. If on, scalars will be interpolated within polygons, and color mapping will occur on a per-pixel basis. If off, color mapping occurs at polygon points, and colors are interpolated, which is generally less accurate. Refer to the Kitware blog[10] for a detailed explanation of this option.

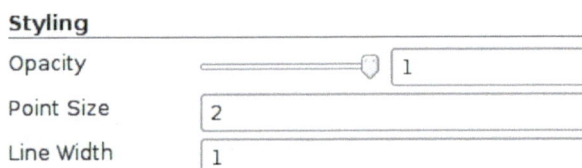

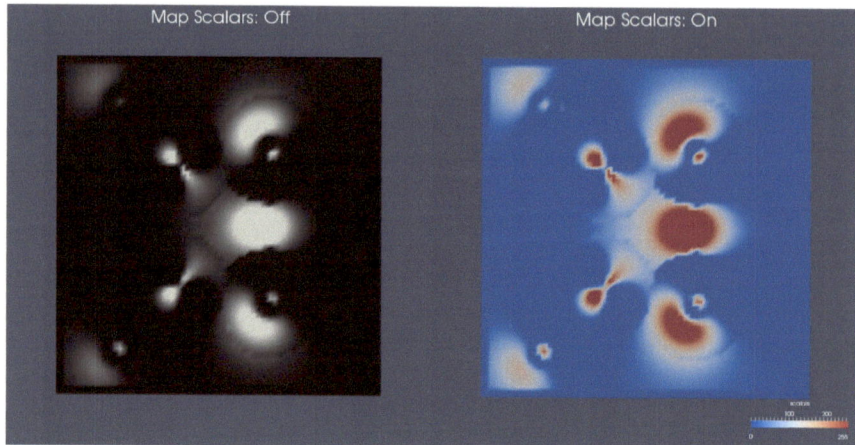

Figure 4.5: The `Map Scalars` property can be used to avoid using a transfer function and directly interpreting the array values as colors, if possible.

`Styling` properties include `Opacity` (useful when rendering translucent geometries), `Point Size` (used to control size of points rendered with using `Points` representation), and `Line Width` (used to control the thickness of lines when rendering as `Wireframe` or that of the edges when rendering as `Surface With Edges`.

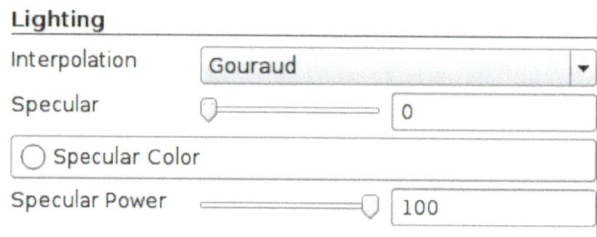

`Lighting` properties affect the shading for rendered surfaces. `Interpolation` allows you to pick between `Flat` and `Gouraud` shading. `Specular`, together with `Specular Color` and `Specular Power`, affects the shininess of the surface. Set this to a non-zero value to render shiny, metallic surfaces.

Common Errors

Specular highlights can lead to misinterpretation of scalar values when using scalar coloring, since the color shown on the shiny part of the surface will not correspond to any color on the color transfer function. Hence, it is generally advisable to use specular highlights on surfaces colored with a single solid color and not on those using scalar coloring (or pseduocoloring).

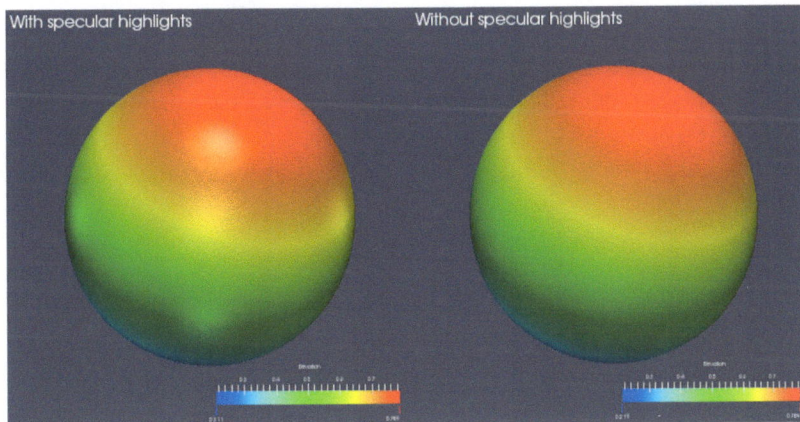

Edge Styling

⬤ Edge Color ▾

Edge Styling allows you to set the Edge Color with which to color the edges when using Surface With Edges representation.

Backface Styling

Backface Representation	Follow Frontface ▾
◯ Backface Ambient Color	
◯ Backface Diffuse Color	
Backface Opacity	1

Backface Styling provides advanced controls to fine-tune the rendering by controlling front and back faces. A front face is any mesh face facing the camera, while a back face is the one facing away from the camera. By choosing to Cull Frontface or Cull Backface, or by selecting a specific representation type to use for the backface, you can customize your visualizations.

Transforming

Translation	0	0	0
Scale	1	1	1
Orientation	0	0	0
Origin	0	0	0

`Transforming` properties can be used to transform the rendered data in the scene without affecting the raw data itself. Thus, if you apply filters on the data source, it will indeed be working with the untransformed data. To transform the data itself, you should use the `Transform` filter.

Miscellaneous

☒ Pickable

Texture   None ▼

Nonlinear
Subdivision Level   —○—— 1

Properties under the `Miscellaneous` group include `Pickable`. Uncheck this if you want the dataset to be ignored when making selections. If the dataset has a texture coordinates array, you can apply a texture to the dataset surface using the `Texture` combo-box. Choose `Load` to load a texture or apply a previously loaded texture listed in the combo-box. If your dataset doesn't have texture coordinates, you can create them by applying one of `Texture Map to Cylinder`, `Texture Map to Sphere`, or `Texture Map To Plane` filters. The `Nonlinear Subdivision Level` is used when rendering datasets with higher-order elements. Use this to set the subdivision level for triangulating higher order elements. The higher the value, the smoother the edges. This comes at the cost of more triangles and, hence, potentially, increased rendering time.

Cube Axes

☐ Show Axis   [Edit]

`Cube Axes` refers to an annotation axis rendered around the dataset (Figure 4.6). You use the `Show Axis` checkbox to show/hide this axis. To control the axis formatting, labels, etc., click on the `Edit` button, which is enabled when the axis is shown. That will pop up a dialog where you can configure the cube axes.

Volume Rendering

Volume Rendering
Mode   Smart ▼

☐ Shade

`Volume Rendering` options are available if the data can be volume rendered. You can pick a specific type of `Volume Rendering Mode`, although the default (`Smart`) should work in most cases, since it attempts to pick a volume rendering mode suitable for your data and graphics setup. To enable gradient-based shading, check `Shade`, if available.

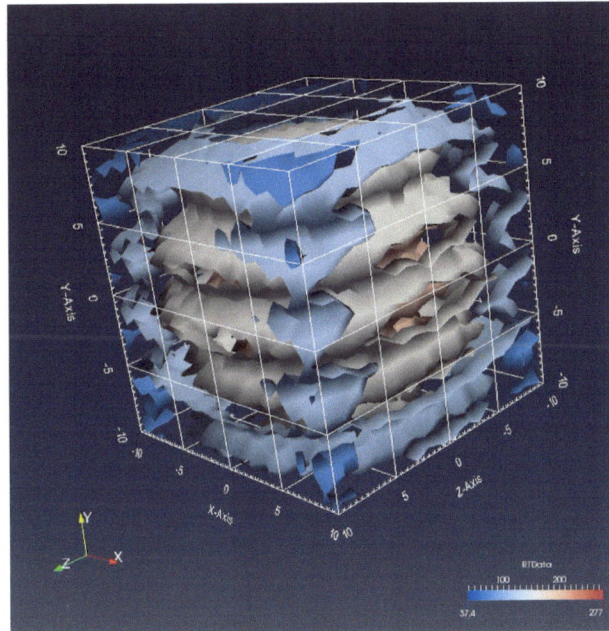

Figure 4.6: `Cube Axes` is used to annotate data bounds in `Render View`.

`Slicing` properties are available when the `Slice` representation type is present. These allow you to pick the orthogonal slice plane orientation and slice offset using `Slice Direction` and the `Slice` slider.

4.4.3 Render View in `pvpython`

Creating a Render View

You use `CreateRenderView` or `CreateView` functions to create a new instance of a render view.

```
1 >>> from paraview.simple import *
2 >>> view = CreateRenderView()
3 # Alternatively, use CreateView.
4 >>> view = CreateView("RenderView")
```

You use `Show` and `Hide` to show or hide data produced by a pipeline module in the view.

```
1 >>> source = Sphere()
2 >>> view = CreateRenderView()
3
4 # Show active source in active view.
5 >>> Show()
6
```

```
7   # Or specify source and view explicitly.
8   >>> Show(source, view)
9
10  # Hide source in active view.
11  >>> Hide(source)
```

Interactions

Since *pvpython* is designed for scripting and batch processing, it currently does not support direct interaction with the view. You can, however, programmatically change the camera as follows:

```
1   # Get camera from the active view, if possible.
2   >>> camera = GetActiveCamera()
3
4   # or, get the camera from a specific render view.
5   >>> camera = view.GetActiveCamera()
6
7   # Now, you can use methods on camera to move it around the scene.
8
9   # Divide the camera's distance from the focal point by the given dolly value.
10  # Use a value greater than one to dolly-in toward the focal point, and use a
11  # value less than one to dolly-out away from the focal point.
12  >>> camera.Dolly(10)
13
14  # Set the roll angle of the camera about the direction of projection.
15  >>> camera.Roll(30)
16
17  # Rotate the camera about the view up vector centered at the focal point. Note
18  # that the view up vector is whatever was set via SetViewUp, and is not
19  # necessarily perpendicular to the direction of projection. The result is a
20  # horizontal rotation of the camera.
21  >>> camera.Aziumth(30)
22
23  # Rotate the focal point about the view up vector, using the camera's position
24  # as the center of rotation. Note that the view up vector is whatever was set
25  # via SetViewUp, and is not necessarily perpendicular to the direction of
26  # projection. The result is a horizontal rotation of the scene.
27  >>> camera.Yaw(10)
28
29  # Rotate the camera about the cross product of the negative of the direction
30  # of projection and the view up vector, using the focal point as the center
31  # of rotation. The result is a vertical rotation of the scene.
32  >>> camera.Elevation(10)
33
34  # Rotate the focal point about the cross product of the view up vector and the
35  # direction of projection, using the camera's position as the center of
36  # rotation. The result is a vertical rotation of the camera.
37  >>> camera.Pitch(10)
```

Alternatively, you can explicitly set the camera position, focal point, view up, etc,. to explicitly place the camera in the scene.

```
1   >>> camera.SetFocalPoint(0, 0, 0)
2   >>> camera.SetPosition(0, 0, -10)
3   >>> camera.SetViewUp(0, 1, 0)
```

```
4   >>> camera.SetViewAngle(30)
5   >>> camera.SetParallelProjection(False)
6
7   # If ParallelProjection is set to True, then you'll need
8   # to specify parallel scalar as well i.e. the height of the viewport in
9   # world-coordinate distances. The default is 1. Note that the 'scale'
10  # parameter works as an 'inverse scale'      larger numbers produce smaller
11  # images. This method has no effect in perspective projection mode.
12  >>> camera.SetParallelScale(1)
```

View properties

In *pvpython*, view properties are directly accessible on the view object returned by
CreateRenderView or GetActiveView.

Once you get access to the view properties objects, you can then set properties on it similar to properties on pipeline
modules such as sources, filters, and readers.

```
1   >>> view = GetActiveView()
2
3   # Set center axis visibility
4   >>> view.CenterAxesVisibility = 0
5
6   # Or you can use this variant to set the property on the active view.
7   >>> SetViewProperties(CenterAxesVisibility=0)
8
9   # Another way of doing the same
10  >>> SetViewProperties(view, CenterAxesVisibility=0)
11
12  # Similarly, you can change orientation axes related properties
13  >>> view.OrientationAxesVisibility = 0
14  >>> view.OrientationAxesLabelColor = (1, 1, 1)
```

Display properties

Similar to view properties, display properties are accessible from the display properties object or using the
SetDisplayProperties function.

```
1
2   >>> displayProperties = GetDisplayProperties(source, view)
3   # Both source and view are optional. If not specified, the active source
4   # and active view will be used.
5
6   # Now one can change properties on this object
7   >>> displayProperties.Representation = "Outline"
8
9   # Or use the SetDisplayProperties API.
10  >>> SetDisplayProperties(source, view, Representation=Outline)
11
12  # Here too, source and view are optional and when not specified,
13  # active source and active view will be used.
```

You can always use the help function to get information about available properties on a display properties object.

4.5   Line Chart View

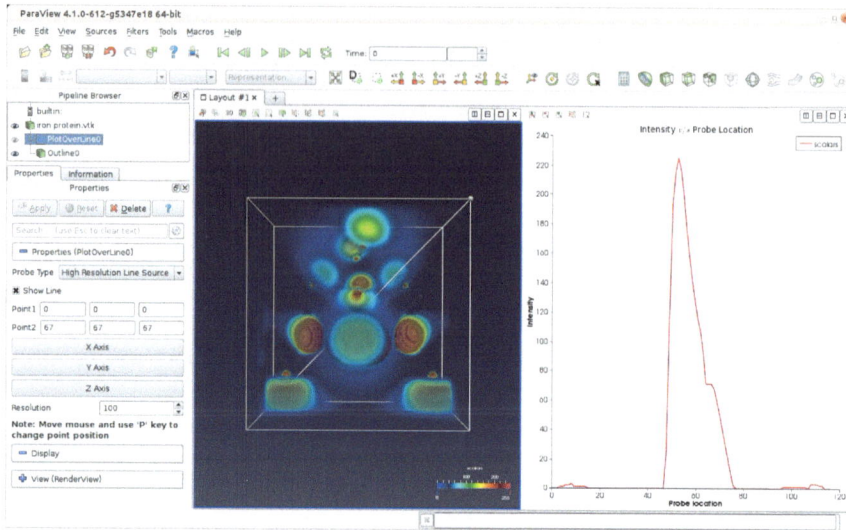

Figure 4.7: *paraview* using `Line Chart View` to plot data values probed along a line through the dataset using `Plot Over Line` filter.

`Line Chart View` can be used to plot data as a line plot representing changes in dependent variables against an independent variable. Using display properties, you can also show scatter plots in this view. This view and other charting views in ParaView follow a similar design, where you pick attribute arrays to plot using display properties, and they are plotted in the view. How those values get plotted depends on the type of the view: `Line Chart View` draws a line connecting sample points, `Bar Chart View` renders bars at each sample point, etc.

One of the most common ways of showing a line plot is to apply the `Plot Over Line` filter to any dataset. This will probe the dataset along the probe line specified. You then plot the sampled values in the `Line Chart View`. Alternatively, if you have a tabular dataset (i.e. vtkTable), then you can directly show the data in this view.

> ℹ️ **Did you know?**
> *You can plot any arbitrary dataset, even those not producing vtkTable outputs, by using the `Plot Data` filter. Remember, however, that for extremely large datasets, while `Render View` may use parallel rendering strategies to improve performance and reduce memory requirements, chart views rarely, if ever, support such parallel strategies.*

4.5.1   Understanding plotting

`Line Chart View` plots data arrays. For any dataset being shown in the view, you first select which data array is to be treated as the independent variable and plotted along the x-axis. Then, you select which arrays to plot along the Y-axis. You can select multiple of these and setup properties for each of the series so they are rendered with different colors and line styles. Since data arrays in VTK datasets are associated with cells or points, and the two are not directly comparable to one another, you can only pick arrays associated with one type of attribute at any time.

4.5.2 Line Chart View in `paraview`

Creating a Line Chart View

Similar to creating `Render View`, you can split the viewport or convert an existing view to `Line Chart View`. `Line Chart View` will also be automatically created if you apply a filter that needs this view, e.g., the `Plot Over Line` filter.

Interactions

Interactions with the chart view result in changing the plotted axes ranges. You can left-click and drag to pan, i.e., change the origin. To change the range on either of the axes, you can right-click and drag vertically and/or horizontally to change the scale on the vertical axes and/or horizontal axes, respectively.

You can also explicitly specify the axes range using view properties.

View properties

The view properties for `Line Chart View` are grouped as properties that affect the view and those that affect each of the potential four axes.

Title

Chart Title	
Chart Title Alignment	Center ▼

Legend

☒ Show Legend

Legend Location	TopRight ▼

To set a title, use `Chart Title`. To toggle the visibility of the legend, use `Show Legend`. While you cannot interactively place the legend in this view, you can use `Legend Location` to place it at one of the corners.

Left Axis

Left Axis Title	

Left Axis Range

☐ Left Axis Log Scale

☐ Left Axis Use Custom Range

There are four axes possible in this view: left, bottom, top, and right. The top and right axes are shown only when some series is set to use those. (We will cover this in the *Display properties* subsection.) For each of the axes, you can set a title (e.g., `Left Axis Title`, `Bottom Axis Title`, etc.).

Next, you can customize the axes ranges. You can always simply interact with the mouse to set the axes ranges. To precisely set the range, check the `Axis Use Custom Range` for the appropriate axis, e.g., `Bottom Axis Use Custom Range` for fixing the bottom axis range, and then specify the data values to use for the min and the max.

The labels on the axes are, by default, automatically determined to avoid visual clutter. You can override the default labelling strategy for any of the axes separately and, instead, specify the locations to label explicitly. This can be done by checking `Axis Use Custom Labels` for a particular axis, e.g., `Bottom Axis Use Custom Labels`. When checked, a list widget will be shown in which you can manually add values at which to place labels.

For generating log plots, simply check the corresponding `Axis Use Log Scale`, e.g., `Left Axis Use Log Scale` to use log scale for Y-axis (Figure 4.8). Note that log scale should only be used for an axis with a non-zero positive range, since the log of a number less than or equal to 0 is undefined.

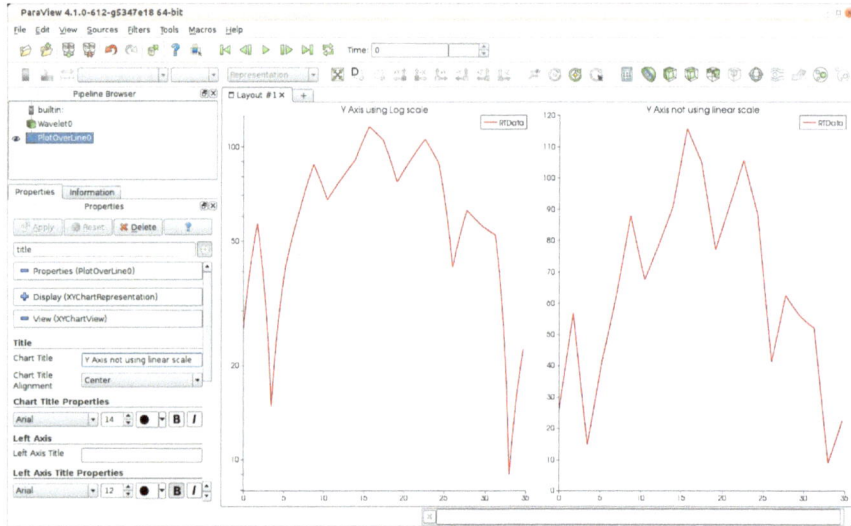

Figure 4.8: Differences between line charts when using log scale for the Y-axis.

Display properties

Display properties allow you to setup which series or data arrays are plotted in this view. You start by picking the `Attribute Type`. Select the attribute type that has the arrays of interest. (E.g., if you are plotting arrays associated with points, then you should pick `Point Data`.) Arrays with different associations cannot be plotted together. You may need to apply filters such as `Cell Data to Point Data` or `Point Data to Cell Data` to convert arrays between different associations for that.

Properties under `X Axis Parameters` allow you to select the independent variable plotted on the X axis by choosing the `X Array Name`. If none of the arrays are appropriate, you can choose to use the element index in the array as the X axis by checking `Use Index for XAxis`.

Series Parameters control series or data arrays plotted on the Y-axis. All available data arrays are lists in the table widget that allows you to check/uncheck a series to plot in the first column. The second column in the table shows the associated color used to plot that series. You can double-click the color swatch to change the color to use. By default, ParaView will try to pick a palette of discrete colors. The third column shows the label to use for that series in the legend. By default, it is set to be the same as the array name. You can double-click to change the name to your choice, e.g., to add units.

Other series parameters include Line Thickness, Line Style, and Marker Style. To change any of these, highlight a row in the Series Parameters widget, and then change the associated parameter to affect the highlighted series. You can change properties for multiple series and can select multiple of them by using the [Ctrl] (or [⌘]) and [⇧] keys.

Using Chart Axes, you can change which axes on which a series is shown. The default is Bottom-Left, but you can change it to be Bottom-Right, Top-Left, or Top-Right to accommodate series with widely different ranges in the same plot.

4.5.3 Line Chart View in pvpython

The principles involved in accessing Line Chart View from *pvpython* are similar to those with Render View. You work with the view properties and display properties objects to change views and display properties, respectively. The thing that changes is the set of available properties.

The following script demonstrates the typical usage:

```
 1  >>> from paraview.simple import *
 2
 3  # Create a data source to probe into.
 4  >>> Wavelet()
 5  <paraview.servermanager.Wavelet object at 0x1156fd810>
 6
 7  # We update the source so that when we create PlotOverLine filter
 8  # it has input data  available to determine good defaults. Otherwise,
 9  # we will have to manually set the defaults up.
10  >>> UpdatePipeline()
11
12  # Now, create the PlotOverLine filter. It will be initialized using
13  # defaults based on the input data.
14  >>> PlotOverLine()
15  <paraview.servermanager.PlotOverLine object at 0x1156fd490>
```

```
16
17  # Show the result.
18  >>> Show()
19  <paraview.servermanager.XYChartRepresentation object at 0x1160a6a10>
20
21  # This will automatically create a new Line Chart View if the
22  # the active view is no a Line Chart View since PlotOverLine
23  # filter indicates it as the preferred view. You can also explicitly
24  # create it by using CreateView() function.
25
26  # Display the result.
27  >>> Render()
28
29  # Access display properties object.
30  >>> dp = GetDisplayProperties()
31  >>> print dp.SeriesVisibility
32  ['arc_length', '0', 'RTData', '1']
33
34  # This is  list with key-value pairs where the first item is the name
35  # of the series, then its visibility and so on.
36  # To toggle visibility, change this list e.g.
37  >>> dp.SeriesVisibility = ['arc_length', '1', 'RTData', '1']
38
39  # Same is true for other series parameters including series color,
40  # line thickness etc.
41
42  # For series color, the value consists of 3 values: red, green, and blue
43  # color components.
44  >>> print dp.SeriesColor
45  ['arc_length', '0', '0', '0', 'RTData', '0.89', '0.1', '0.11']
46
47  # For series labels, value is the label to use.
48  >>> print dp.SeriesLabel
49  ['arc_length', 'arc_length', 'RTData', 'RTData']
50
51  # e.g. to change RTData's legend label, we can do something as follows:
52  >>> dp.SeriesLabel[3] = 'RTData -- new label'
53
54  # Access view properties object.
55  >>> view = GetActiveView()
56  # or
57  >>> view = GetViewProperties()
58
59  # To change titles
60  >>> view.ChartTitle = "My Title"
61  >>> view.BottomAxisTitle = "X Axis"
62  >>> view.LeftAxisTitle = "Y Axis"
```

4.6 Bar Chart View

Bar Chart View is very similar to Line Chart View when it comes to creating the view, view properties, and display properties. One difference is that, instead of rendering lines for each series, this view renders bars. In addition, under the display properties, the Series Parameters like Line Style and Line Thickness are not available, since they are not

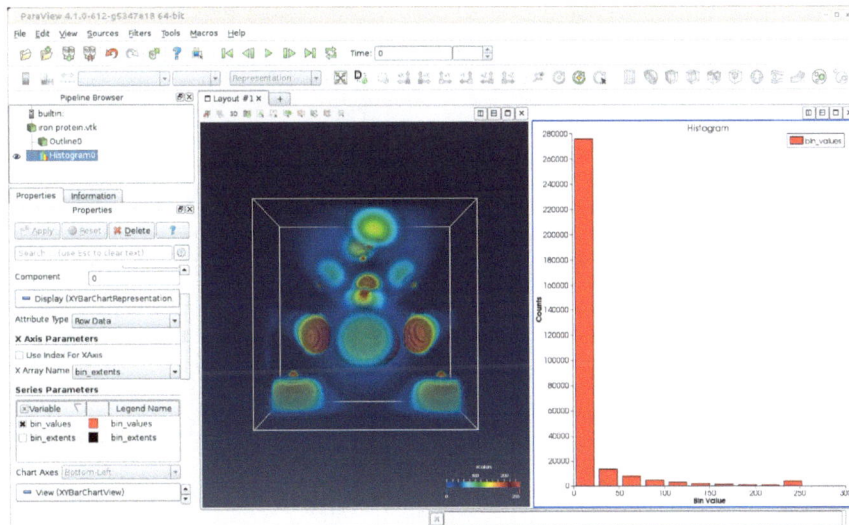

Figure 4.9: *paraview* using `Bar Chart View` to plot the histogram for a dataset using the `Histogram` filter.

applicable to bars.

4.7 Plot Matrix View

`Plot Matrix View` is a chart view that renders a scatter plot matrix. It allows you to spot patterns in the small scatter plots, change focus to those plots of interest, and perform basic selection. The principle is that, for all selected arrays or series to be plotted, the view generates a scatter plot for each pair. You can activate a particular scatter plot, in which case the active plot is re-drawn at a bigger scale to make it easier to for inspection. Additionally, the view shows a histogram for each plotted variable or series.

The view properties allow you to set colors to use for active plot, histograms, etc., while the display properties allow you to pick which series are plotted.

4.7.1 Interactions

You can click on any of the plots (except the histograms) in the matrix to make it active. Once actived, the active plot will show that plot. You can then interact with the active plot exactly like `Line Chart View` or `Bar Chart View` for panning and zoom.

4.7.2 View properties

View properties on this view allow you to pick styling parameters for the rendering ranging from title (`Chart Title`) to axis colors (`Active Plot Axis Color`, `Active Plot Grid Color`). You can also control the visibility of the histrogram plots, the active plot, the axes labels, the grids, and so on.

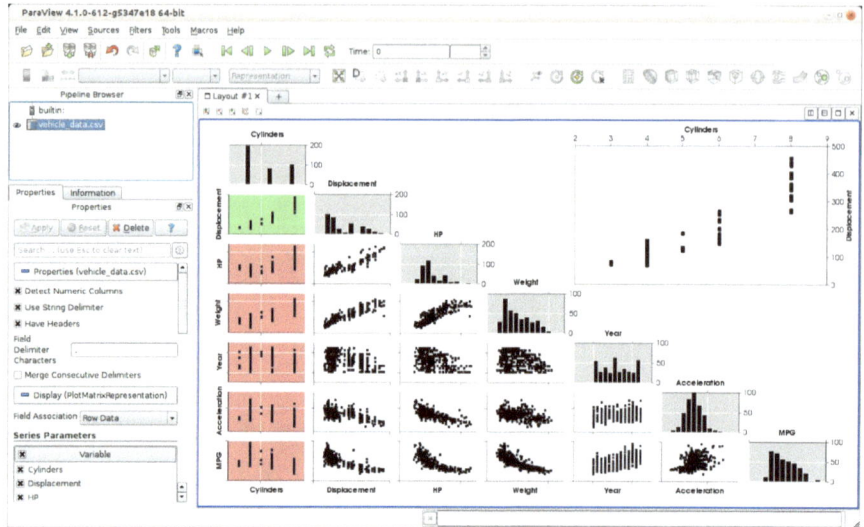

Figure 4.10: *paraview* using `Plot Matrix View` to generate a scatter plot matrix to understand correlations between variables.

4.7.3 Display properties

Similar to `Line Chart View`, you select the `Attribute Type` and then the arrays to plot. Since, in a scatter plot matrix, the order in which the selected series are rendered can make it easier to understand correlations, you can change the order by clicking and dragging the rows in the `Series Parameters` table.

4.8 Parallel Coordinates View

Like `Plot Matrix View`, `Parallel Coordinates View` is also used to visualize correlations between data arrays.

4.9 Spreadsheet View

`SpreadSheet View` is used to inspect raw data values in a tabular form. Unlike most other views, this view is primarily intended to be used in the *paraview* user interface and, hence, is not available in *pvpython*.

To use this view, simply create this view and show the dataset produced by any pipeline module in it by using the `Pipeline Browser`. `SpreadSheet View` can only show one dataset at a time. Therefore, showing a new dataset will automatically hide the previously shown dataset.

The view's toolbar provides quick access to several of this view's capabilities. Use the `Showing` widget on the view toolbar to view as well as to change the dataset being shown. The `Attribute` field allows you to pick which types of elements to show, e.g., `Cell Data`, `Point Data`, `Field Data`, etc. `Precision` can be utilized to change the precision used when displaying floating point numbers. The ⊞ button enables you to select columns to show. Click on the button to get a popup menu in which you check/uncheck the columns to show/hide. If showing `Cell Data`, the {...} button, when checked, enables you to see the point ids that form each of the cells.

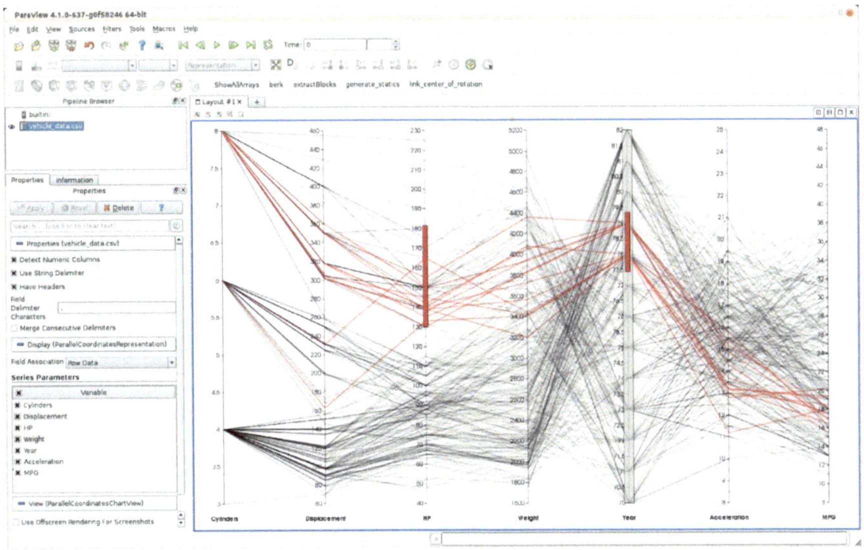

Figure 4.11: *paraview* using `Parallel Coordinates View` to plot correlations between columns in a table.

section 6.1 discusses how selections can be made in views to select elements of interest. Use the [icon] button to make the view show only selected elements. Now, as you make selections in other views, this `SpreadSheet View` will update to only show the values of the selected elements (as long as the dataset selected in are indeed being shown in the view).

4.10 Slice View

`Slice View` is special type of `Render View` that can be used to view orthogonal slices from any dataset. Any dataset shown in the view will be sliced in axis-aligned slices based on the locations specified on the view. The slice locations along the three orthogonal axis planes can be specified by using the frame decoration around the view window.

4.10.1 Interactions

Since this view is a type of `Render View`, the camera interactions are same as that of `Render View`. Additionally, you can interact with the frame decoration to manipulate slice locations along the three axis planes.

- Double-click the left mouse button in the region between the axis border and the view to add a new slice.
- You can click-and-drag a marker to move the slice location.
- To remove a slice, double-click with the left mouse button on the marker corresponding to that slice.
- To toggle visibility of the slice, you can right-click on the marker.

4.10.2 Slice View in `pvpython`

```
1  # To create a slice view in use:
2  >>> view = CreateView("MultiSlice")
3
4  # Use properties on view to set/get the slice offsets.
```

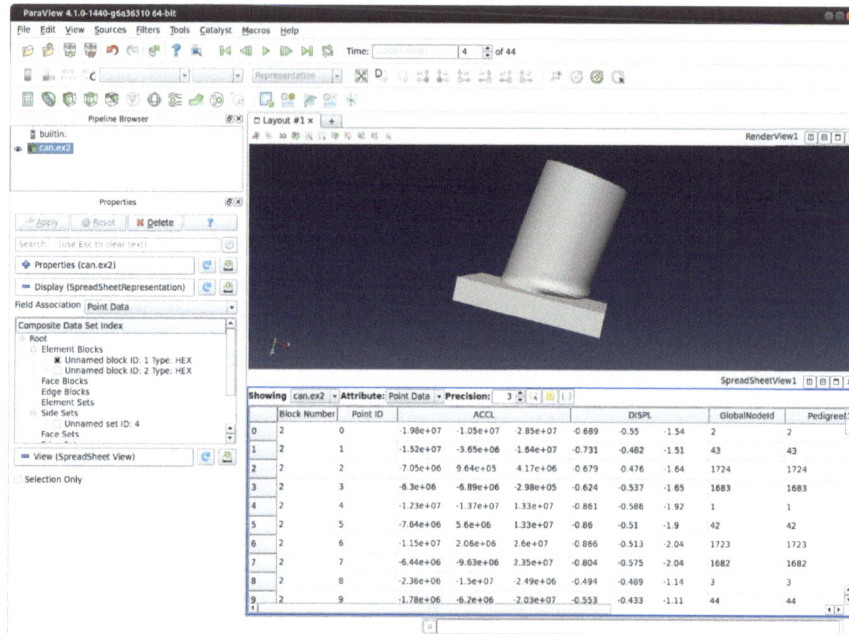

Figure 4.12: *paraview* using `SpreadSheet View` to plot raw data values for the *can.ex*2 dataset.

```
5  >>> view.XSliceValues = [-10, 0, 10]
6  >>> print view.XSliceValues
7  [-10, 0, 10]
8
9  # Similar to XSliceValues, you have YSliceValues and ZSliceValues.
10 >>> view.YSliceValues = [0]
11 >>> view.ZSliceValues = []
```

4.11 Python View

Some Python libraries, such as matplotlib, are widely used for making publication-quality plots of data. The `Python View` provides a way to display plots made in a Python script right within *paraview*.

The `Python View` has a single property, a Python script that generates the image to be displayed in the viewport. All the Python bindings for ParaView and VTK that are available in the Python scripting module are available from within this script, making it possible to plot any array from just about any dataset that can be loaded into ParaView. The Python script for the view is evaluated in a unique Python environment so that global variables defined in the script do not clobber global variables in other Python scripts (either in other instances of the `Python View` or in the Python interpreter). This environment is reset each time the script is evaluated, so data cannot be saved between evaluations.

The `Python View` requires that the Python script where the plotting occurs define two functions. In the first function, you request which arrays you would like to transfer to the client for rendering. At present, all rendering in this view takes place on the client, even in client-server mode. These arrays can be point data, cell data, field data, and table row data. This function runs only on data-server processes. It provides access to the underlying data object on the server so that you can query any aspect of the data using the Python-wrapped parts of VTK and ParaView.

The second function is where you put Python plotting or rendering commands. This function runs only on the ParaView

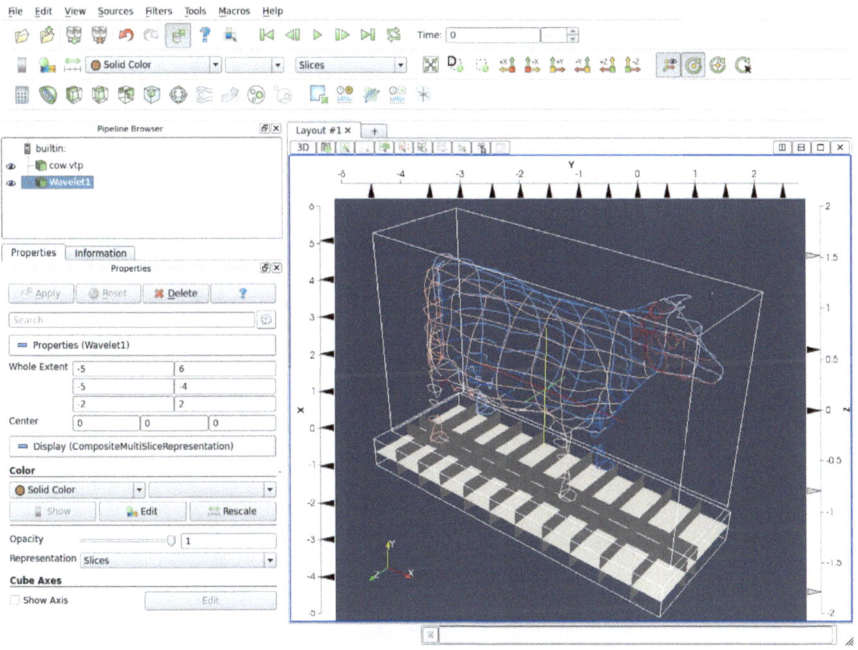

Figure 4.13: `Slice View` can be used to show orthogonal slices from datasets.

client. It has access to the complete data object gathered from the data server nodes, but only has access to the arrays requested in the first function. This function will typically set up objects from a plotting library, convert data from VTK to a form that can be passed to the plotting library, plot the data, and convert the plot to an image (a `vtkImageData` object) that can be displayed in the viewport.

4.11.1 Selecting data arrays to plot

All the rendering in the `Python View` occurs in the client, so the client must get the data from the server. Because the dataset residing on the ParaView server may be large, transferring all the data to the client may not be possible or practical. For that reason, we have provided a mechanism to select which data arrays in a data object on the server to transfer to the client. The overall structure of the data object, however, (including cell connectivity, point positions, and hierarchical block structure) is always transferred to the client. By default, no data arrays are selected for transfer from the server.

The Python script for the view must define a function called `setup_data(view)`. The `view` argument is the VTK object for the `Python View`. The current datasets loaded into ParaView may be accessed through the view object.

Here's an example of this function that was used to generate the image in Figure 4.14:

```
1  def setup_data(view):
2    # Iterate over visible data objects
3    for i in xrange(view.GetNumberOfVisibleDataObjects()):
4      # You need to use GetVisibleDataObjectForSetup(i)
5      # in setup_data to access the data object.
6      dataObject = view.GetVisibleDataObjectForSetup(i)
7
8      # The data object has the same data type and structure
9      # as the data object that sits on the server. You can
```

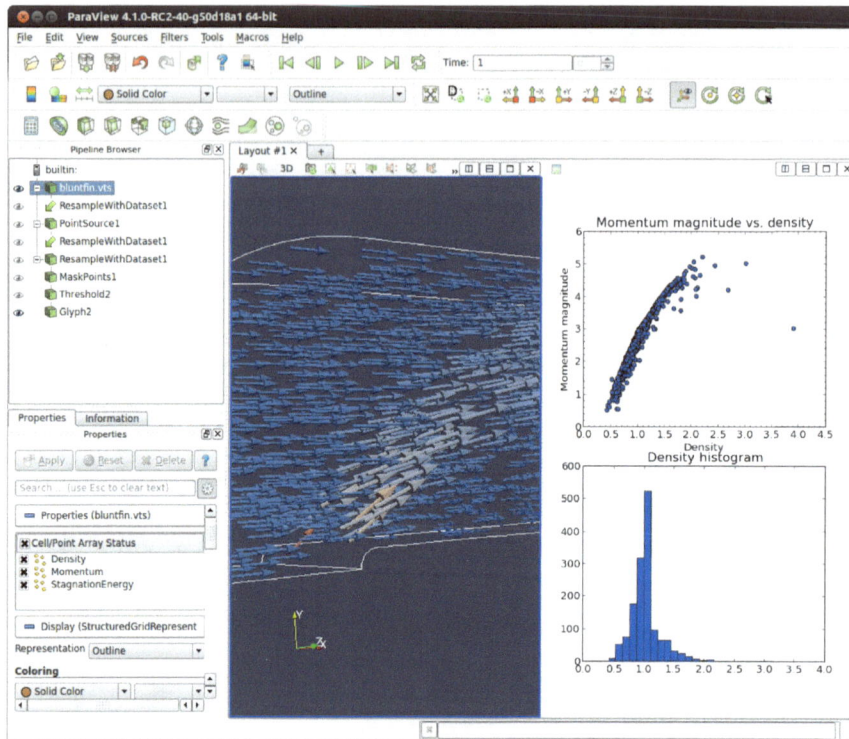

Figure 4.14: *paraview* using `Python View` with matplotlib to display a scatterplot of momentum magnitude versus density (upper right) and a histogram of density (lower right) in the bluntfin.vts dataset.

```
10    # query the size of the data, for instance, or do anything
11    # else you can do through the Python wrapping.
12    print "Memory size:", dataObject.GetActualMemorySize(), "kilobytes"
13
14    # Clean up from previous calls here. We want to unset
15    # any of the arrays requested in previous calls to this function.
16    view.DisableAllAttributeArrays()
17
18    # By default, no arrays will be passed to the client.
19    # You need to explicitly request the arrays you want.
20    # Here, we'll request the Density point data array
21    view.SetAttributeArrayStatus(i, vtkDataObject.POINT, "Density", 1)
22    view.SetAttributeArrayStatus(i, vtkDataObject.POINT, "Momentum", 1)
23
24    # Other attribute arrays can be set similarly
25    view.SetAttributeArrayStatus(i, vtkDataObject.FIELD, "fieldData", 1)
```

The `vtkPythonView` class passed in as the `view` argument to `setup_data(view)` defines several methods useful for specifying which data arrays to copy:

- `GetNumberOfVisibleDataObjects()` - This returns the number of visible data objects in the view. If an object is not visible, it should not show up in the rendering, so all the methods provided by the view deal only with visible objects.

- GetVisibleDataObjectForSetup(visibleObjectIndex) - This returns the visibleObjectIndex'th visible data object in the view. (The data object will have an open eye next to it in the pipeline browser.)

- GetNumberOfAttributeArrays(visibleObjectIndex, attributeType) - This returns the number of attribute arrays for the visibleObjectIndex'th visible object and the given attributeType (e.g., vtkDataObject.POINT, vtkDataObject.CELL, etc.).

- GetAttributeArrayName(visibleObjectIndex, attributeType, arrayIndex) - This returns the name of the array of the given attribute type at the given array index for the visibleObjectIndex'th object.

- SetAttributeArrayStatus(visibleObjectIndex, vtkDataObject.POINT, "Density", 1) -

  This sets the array status of an attribute array. The first argument is the visible object index, the second object is the attribute association of the array, the third argument is the name of the array, and the last argument specifies if the array is to be copied (1) or not (0).

- GetAttributeArrayStatus(visibleObjectIndex, vtkDataObject.POINT, "Density") - This retrieves the array status for the object with the given visible index with a given attribute association (second argument) and a name (last argument).

- EnableAllAttributeArrays() - This sets all arrays to be copied.

- DisableAllAttributeArrays() - This sets all arrays to not be copied.

The methods GetNumberOfVisibleDataObjects(), GetVisibleDataObjectForSetup(...), GetNumberOfAttributeArrays(...), and GetAttributeArrayName(...) are all convenient methods for obtaining information about visible data objects in the view that could otherwise be accessed with existing view and representation methods. The last four methods are valid only from within the setup_data(view) function.

4.11.2 Plotting data in Python

After the setup_data(view) function has been called, ParaView will transfer the data object and selected arrays to the client. When that is done, it will call the render(view, width, height) function you have defined in your script.

The view argument to the render(view, width, height) function is the vtkPythonView object on the client. The width and height arguments are the width and height of the viewport, respectively. The render(view, width, height) function uses the data available through the view, along with the width and height, to generate a vtkImageData object that will be displayed in the viewport. This vtkImageData object must be returned from the render(view, width, height) function. If no vtkImageData is returned, the viewport will be black. If the size of the image does not match the size of the viewport, the image will be stretched to fit the viewport.

Putting it all together, here is a simple example that generates a solid red image to display in the viewport.

```
1  def render(view, width, height):
2    from paraview.vtk import vtkImageData
3    image = vtkImageData()
4    image.SetDimensions(width, height, 1)
5    from paraview.numeric import VTK_UNSIGNED_CHAR
6    image.AllocateScalars(VTK_UNSIGNED_CHAR, 4)
7    pixel_array = image.GetPointData().GetArray(0)
8    pixel_array.FillComponent(0, 255.0)
9    pixel_array.FillComponent(1, 0.0)
10   pixel_array.FillComponent(2, 0.0)
```

```
11    pixel_array.FillComponent(3, 0.0)
12
13    return image
```

This example does not produce an interesting visualization, but serves as a minimal example of how the `render(view, width, height)` function should be implemented. Typically, we expect that the Python plotting library you use has some utilities to expose the generated plot image pixel data. You need to copy that pixel data to the `vtkImageData` object returned by the `render(view, width, height)` function. Exactly how you do this is up to you, but ParaView comes with some utilities to make this task easier for matplotlib.

Set up a matplotlib Figure

The `Python View` comes with a Python module, called `python_view`, that has some utility functions you can use. To import it, use:

```
1  from paraview import python_view
```

This module has a function, called `matplotlib_figure(view, width, height)`, that returns a `matplotlib.figure.Figure` given `width` and `height` arguments. This figure can be used with matplotlib plotting commands to plot data as in the following:

```
1  def render(view, width, height):
2    figure = python_view.matplotlib_figure(width, height)
3
4    ax = figure.add_subplot(1,1,1)
5    ax.minorticks_on()
6    ax.set_title('Plot title')
7    ax.set_xlabel('X label')
8    ax.set_ylabel('Y label')
9
10   # Process only the first visible object in the pipeline browser
11   dataObject = view.GetVisibleDataObjectForRendering(0)
12
13   x = dataObject.GetPointData().GetArray('X')
14
15   # Convert VTK data array to numpy array for plotting
16   from paraview.numpy_support import vtk_to_numpy
17   np_x = vtk_to_numpy(x)
18
19   ax.hist(np_x, bins=10)
20
21   return python_view.figure_to_image(figure)
```

This definition of the `render(view, width, height)` function creates a histogram of a point data array named `X` from the first visible object in the pipeline browser. Note the conversion function, `python_view.figure_to_image(figure)`, in the last line. This converts the matplotlib `Figure` object created with `python_view.matplotlib_figure(width, height)` into a `vtkImageData` object suitable for display in the viewport.

4.12 Comparative Views

`Comparative Views`, including `Render View (Comparative)`, `Line Chart View (Comparative)`, and `Bar Chart View (Comparative)`, are used for generating comparative visualization from parameter studies. We will cover these views in Chapter 12.

FILTERING DATA

Visualization can be characterized as a process of transforming raw data produced from experiments or simulations until it takes a form in which it can be interpreted and analysed. The visualization pipeline introduced in Section 1.2 formalizes this concept as a data flow paradigm where a pipeline is set up of sources, filters, and sinks (collectively called pipeline modules or algorithms). Data *flows* through this pipeline, being transformed at each node until it is in a form where it can be consumed by the sinks. In previous chapters, we saw how to ingest data into ParaView (Chapter 2) and how to display it in views (Chapter 4). If the data ingested into ParaView already has all the relevant attribute data, and it is in the form that can be directly represented in one the existing views, then that is all you would need. The true power of the visualization process, however, comes from leveraging the various visualization techniques such as slicing, contouring, clipping, etc., which are available as filters. In this chapter, we look at constructing pipelines to transform data using such filters.

5.1 Understanding filters

In ParaView, filters are pipeline modules or algorithms that have inputs and outputs. They take in data on their inputs and produce transformed data or results on their outputs. A filter can have multiple input and output ports. The number of input and output ports on a filter is fixed. Each input port accepts input data for a specific purpose or role within the filter. (E.g., the `Resample With Dataset` filter has two input ports. The one called `Input` is the input port through which the dataset providing the attributes to interpolate is ingested. The other, called `Source`, is the input port through which the dataset used as the mesh on which to re-sample is accepted.)

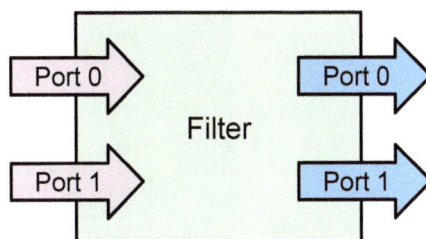

Figure 5.1: A filter is a pipeline module comprised of inputs and outputs. Data enters a filter through the inputs. The filter transforms the data and produces the resulting data on its outputs. A filter can have one or more input and output ports. Each input port can, optionally, accept multiple input connections.

An input port itself can, optionally, accept multiple input connections, e.g., the `Append Datasets` filter, which appends multiple datasets to create a single dataset only has one input port (named `Input`). However, that port can accept multiple connections for each of the datasets to be appended . Filters define whether a particular input port can accept one or many input connections.

Similar to readers, the properties on the filter allow you to control the filtering algorithm. The properties available depend on the filter itself.

5.2 Creating filters in `paraview`

All available filters in *paraview* are listed under the | Filters | menu. These are organized in various categories. To create a filter to transform the data produced by a source or a reader, you select the source in the `Pipeline Browser` to make it active, and then click on the corresponding menu item in the | Filters | menu. If a menu item is disabled, it implies that the active source does not produce data that can be transformed by this filter.

ℹ️ Did you know?

If a menu item in the | Filters | menu is disabled, it implies that the active source(s) is not producing data of the expected type or the characteristics needed by the filter. On Windows and Linux machines, if you hover over the disabled menu item, the status bar will show the reason why the filter is not available.

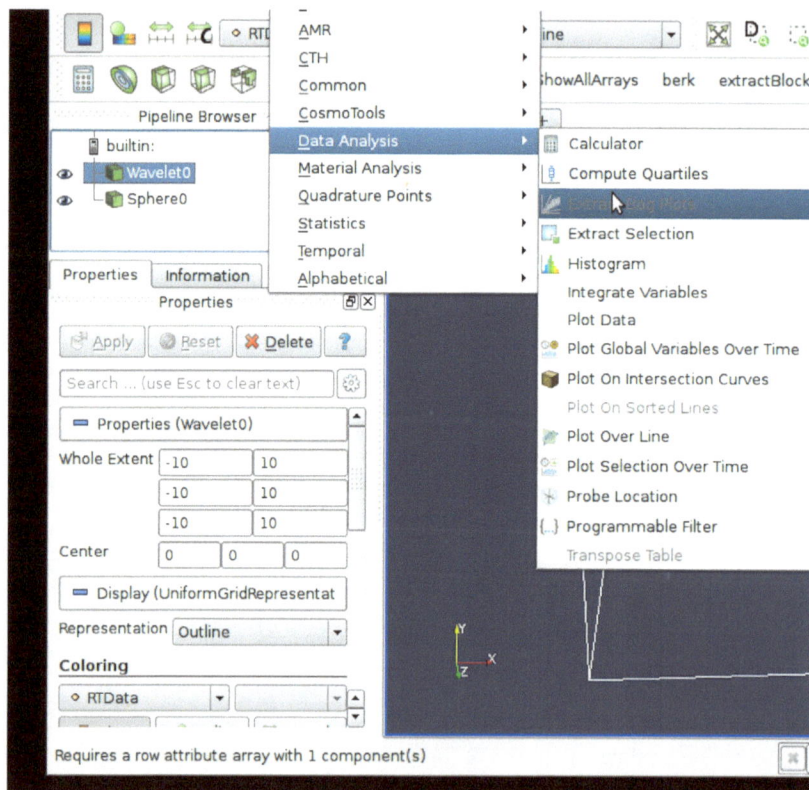

5.2.1   Multiple input connections

When you create a filter, the active source is connected to the first input port of the filter. Filters like Append Datasets can take multiple input connections on that input port. In such a case, to pass multiple pipeline modules as connections on a single input port of a filter, select all the relevant pipeline modules in the Pipeline Browser. You can select multiple items by using the Ctrl (or ⌘) and ⇧ key modifiers. When multiple pipeline modules are selected, only the filters that accept multiple connections on their input ports will be enabled in the Filters menu.

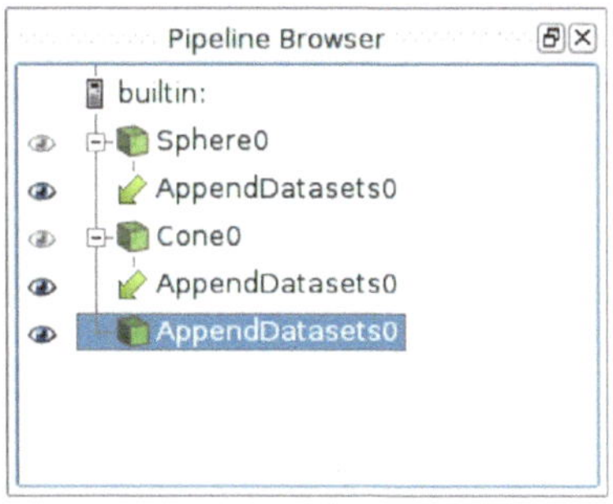

Figure 5.2: The Pipeline Browser showing a pipeline with multiple input connections. The Append Datasets filter has two input connections on its only input port, Sphere0 and Cone0.

5.2.2   Multiple input ports

Most filters have just one input port. Hence, as soon as you click on the filter name in the Filters menu, it will create a new filter instance and that will show up in the Pipeline Browser. Certain filters, such as Resample With Dataset, have multiple inputs that must be set up before the filter can be created. In such a case, when you click on the filter name, the Change Input Dialog will pop up, as seen in Figure 5.4. This dialog allows you to select the pipeline modules to be connected to each of the input ports. The active source(s) is connected by default to the first input port. You are free to change those as well.

5.2.3   Changing input connections

paraview allows you to change the inputs to a filter after the filter has been created. To change inputs to a filter, right-click on the filter in the Pipeline Browser to get the context menu, and then select Change Input.... This will pop up the same Change Input Dialog as when creating a filter with multiple input ports. You can use this dialog to set new inputs for this filter.

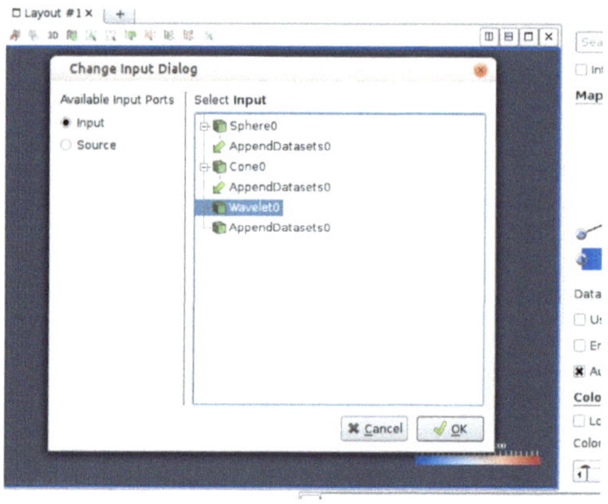

Figure 5.3: The `Change Input Dialog` is shown to allow you to pick inputs for each of the input ports for a filter with multiple input ports. To use this dialog, first select the `Input Port` you want to edit on the left side, and select the pipeline module(s) that are to be connected to this input port. Repeat the step for the other input port(s). If an input port can accept multiple input connections, you can select multiple modules, just like in the `Pipeline Browser`.

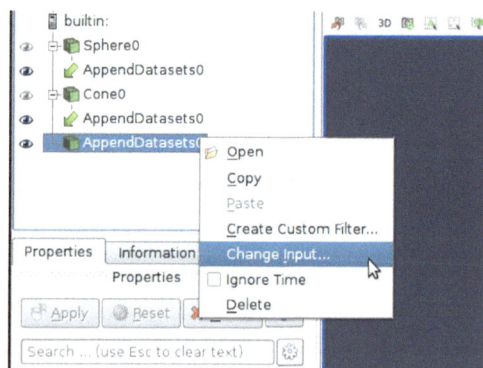

Figure 5.4: The context menu in the `Pipeline Browser` showing the option to change inputs for a filter.

ⓘ Did you know?

While the Filters *menu is a handy way to create new filters, with the long list of filters available in ParaView, manually finding a particular filter in this menu can be very challenging. To make it easier, ParaView incorporates a quick launch mechanism. When you want to create a new filter (or a source), simply hit* Ctrl + Space *,* Alt + Space *, or* ⌘ + Space *. This will pop up the quick-launch dialog. Now, start typing the name of the filter you want. As you type, the dialog will update to show the filters and sources that match the typed text. You can use the arrow keys to navigate and use the* Enter *key to create the selected filter (or source). Note that filters may be disabled, as was the case in the* Filters *menu. Therefore, hitting* Enter *will have no effect. You can use* Esc *to clear the text you have typed so far. Hit the* Esc *a second time, and the dialog will close without creating any new filter.*

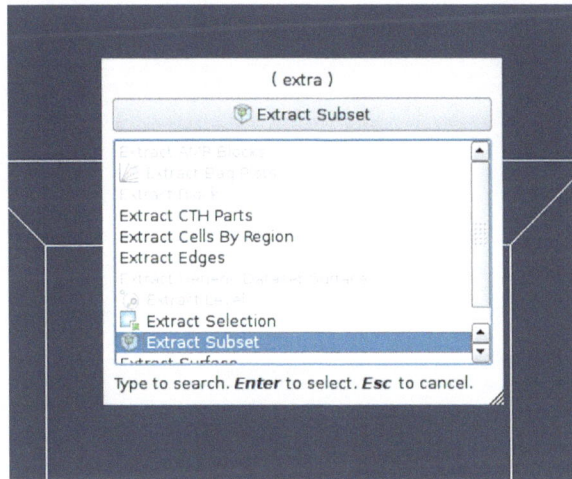

5.3 Creating filters in pvpython

To create a filter in *pvpython*, you simply create the object by using its name as a constructor function.

```
1 >>> from paraview.simple import *
2     ...
3 >>> filter = Shrink()
```

Similar to *paraview*, the filter will use the active source(s) as the input. Additionally, you can explicitly specify the input in the function arguments.

```
1 >>> reader = OpenDataFile(...)
2     ...
3 >>> shrink = Shift(Input=reader)
```

5.3.1 Multiple input connections

To setup multiple input connections, you can specify the connections as follows:

```
1 >>> sphere = Sphere()
2 >>> cone = Cone()
```

```
3
4   # Simply pass the sources as a list to the constructor function.
5   >>> appendDatasets = AppendDatasets(Input=[sphere, cone])
6   >>> print appendDatasets.Input
7   [<paraview.servermanager.Sphere object at 0x6d75f90>, <paraview.servermanager.Cone
        object at 0x6d75c50>]
```

5.3.2 Multiple input ports

Setting up connections to multiple input ports is similar to the multiple input connections, except that you need to ensure that you name the input ports properly.

```
1   >>> sphere = Sphere()
2   >>> wavelet = Wavelet()
3
4   >>> resampleWithDataSet = ResampleWithDataset(Input=sphere, Source=wavelet)
```

5.3.3 Changing input connections

Changing inputs in Python is as simple as setting any other property on the filter.

```
1   # For filter with single input connection
2   >>> shrink.Input = cone
3
4   # for filters with multiple input connects
5   >>> appendDatasets.Input = [reader, cone]
6
7   # to add a new input.
8   >>> appendDatasets.Input.append(sphere)
9
10  # to change multiple ports
11  >>> resampleWithDataSet.Input = wavelet2
12  >>> resampleWithDataSet.Source = cone
```

5.4 Changing filter properties in `paraview`

Filters provide properties that you can change to control the processing algorithm employed by the filter. Changing and viewing properties on filters is the same as with any other pipeline module, including readers and sources. You can view and change these properties, when available, using the `Properties` panel. Chapter 9 covers how to effectively use the `Properties` panel. Since this panel only shows the properties present on the *active source*, you must ensure that the filter you are interested in is active. To make the filter active, use the `Pipeline Browser` to click on the filter and select it.

5.5 Changing filter properties in `pvpython`

With *pvpython*, the available properties are accessible as properties on the filter object, and you can get or set their values by name (similar to changing the input connections (Section 5.3.3)).

```
1
2   # You can save the object reference when it's created.
3   >>> shrink = Shrink()
4
5   # Or you can get access to the active source.
6   >>> Shrink() # <-- this will make the Shrink the active source.
7   >>> shrink = GetActiveSource()
8
9   # To figure out available properties, you can always use help.
10  >>> help(shrink)
11  Help on Shrink in module paraview.servermanager object:
12
13  class Shrink(SourceProxy)
14   |   The Shrink filter
15   |   causes the individual cells of a dataset to break apart
16   |   from each other by moving each cell's points toward the
17   |   centroid of the cell. (The centroid of a cell is the
18   |   average position of its points.) This filter operates on
19   |   any type of dataset and produces unstructured grid
20   |   output.
21   |   ----------------------------------------------------------------
22   |   Data descriptors defined here:
23   |
24   |   Input
25   |       This property specifies the input to the Shrink
26   |       filter.
27   |
28   |   ShrinkFactor
29   |       The value of this property determines how far the points
30   |       will move. A value of 0 positions the points at the centroid of the
31   |       cell; a value of 1 leaves them at their original
32   |       positions.
33   ....
34
35  # To get the current value of a property:
36  >>> sf = shrink.ShrinkFactor
37  >>> print sf
38  0.5
39
40  # To set the value
41  >>> shrink.ShrinkFactor = 0.75
```

In the rest of this chapter, we will discuss some of the commonly used filters in detail. They are grouped under categories based on the type of operation that they perform.

5.6 Filters for sub-setting data

These filters are used for extracting subsets from an input dataset. How this subset is defined and how it is extracted depends on the type of the filter.

5.6.1 Clip

Clip is used to clip any dataset using either an implicit function (such as a plane, sphere, or a box) or using values of a scalar data array in the input dataset. A scalar array is a point or cell attribute array with a single component. Clipping involves iterating over all cells in the input dataset and then removing those cells that are considered *outside* of the space defined by the implicit function or that have an attribute values less than the selected value. For cells that straddle the clipping surface, these are *clipped* to pass through the part of the cell that is truly inside the specified implicit function (or greater than the scalar value).

This filter converts any dataset into an unstructured grid (Section 3.1.7) or a multi-block of unstructured grids (Section 3.1.10) in the case of composite datasets.

Clip in paraview

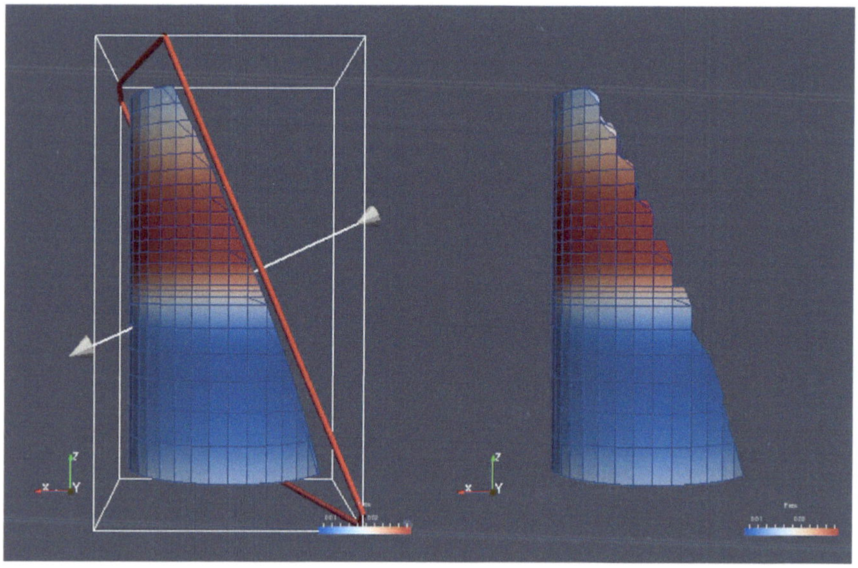

Figure 5.5: Comparison between results produced by the Clip filter with Crinkle Clip unchecked (left) and checked (right) when clipping with an implicit plane. The image on the left also shows the 3D widget used to interactivly place the implicit plane for the clipping operation.

To create the Clip filter, you can use the [Filters ⟩ Common] or the [Filters ⟩ Alphabetical] menu. This filter is also accessible from the Common filters toolbar. You can click the ⬡ button to create this filter.

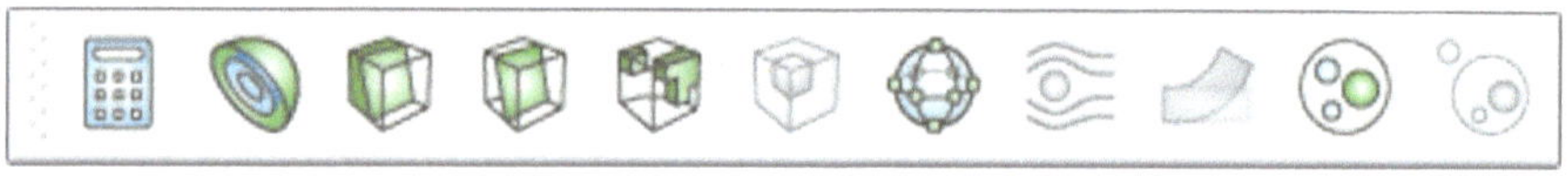

Figure 5.6: The Common filters toolbar in *paraview* for quick access to the commonly used filters.

On the Properties panel, you will see the available properties for this filter. One of the first things that you should select is the Clip Type. Clip Type is used to specify the type of implicit function to use for the clipping operations. The available options include Plane, Box, Sphere, and Scalar. Selecting any one of these options will update the panel to show properties that are used to define the implicit function, e.g., the `Origin` and the `Normal` for the `Plane` or the `Center` and the `Radius` for the `Sphere`. If you select `Scalar`, the panel will let you pick the data array and the value with which to clip. Remember, cells with the data value greater than or equal to the selected value are considered *in* and are passed through the filter.

> (i) Did you know?
>
> *When clipping with implicit functions, ParaView renders widgets in the active view that you can use to interactively control the implicit function, called* `3D widgets`. *As you interact with the 3D widget, the panel will update to reflect the current values. The 3D widget is considered as an aid and not as a part of the actual visualization scene. Thus, if you change the active source and the* `Properties` *panel navigates away from this filter, the 3D widget will automatically be hidden.*

The `Inside Out` option can be used to invert the behavior of this filter. Basically, it flips the notion of what is considered inside and outside of the given clipping space.

Check `Crinkle Clip` if you don't want this filter to truly clip cells on the boundary, but want to preserve the input cell structure and to pass the entire cell on through the boundary (Figure 5.5). This option is not available when clipping by `Scalar`.

Clip in *pvpython*

This following script demonstrates various aspects of using the `Clip` filter in *pvpython*.

```
1
2  # Create the Clip filter.
3  >>> clip = Clip(Input=...)
4
5  # Specify a 'ClipType' to use.
6  >>> clip.ClipType = 'Plane'
7
8  # You can also use the SetProperties API instead.
9  >>> SetProperties(clip, ClipType='Plane')
10
11 >>> print clip.GetProperty('ClipType').GetAvailable()
12 ['Plane', 'Box', 'Sphere', 'Scalar']
13
14 # To set the plane origin and normal
15 >>> clip.ClipType.Origin = [0, 0, 0]
16 >>> clip.ClipType.Normal = [1, 0, 0]
17
18 # If you want to change to Sphere and set center and
19 # radius, you can do the following.
20 >>> clip.ClipType = 'Sphere'
21 >>> clip.ClipType.Center = [0, 0, 0]
22 >>> clip.ClipType.Radius = 12
23
24 # Using SetProperties API, the same looks like
25 >>> SetProperties(clip, ClipType='Sphere')
26 >>> SetProperties(clip.ClipType, Center=[0, 0, 0],
27                                  Radius = 12)
28
29 # To set Crinkle clipping.
```

```
30  >>> clip.Crinkleclip = 1
31
32  # For clipping with scalar, you pick the scalar array
33  # and then the value as follows:
34  >>> clip.ClipType = 'Scalar'
35  >>> clip.Scalars = ('POINTS', 'Temp')
36  >>> clip.Value = 100
37
38  # To get available values, use
39  >>> clip.GetProperty('Scalars').GetAvailable()
40
41  # As always, to get the list of available properties on
42  # the clip filter, use help()
43  >>> help(clip)
44  Help on Clip in module paraview.servermanager object:
45
46  class Clip(SourceProxy)
47   |   The Clip filter
48   |   cuts away a portion of the input data set using an
49   |   implicit plane. This filter operates on all types of data
50   |   sets, and it returns unstructured grid data on
51   |   output.
52   |
53   |   -------------------------------------------------------------------
54   |   Data descriptors defined here:
55   |
56   |   ClipType
57   |       This property specifies the parameters of the clip
58   |       function (an implicit plane) used to clip the dataset.
59   |
60   |   Crinkleclip
61   |       This parameter controls whether to extract entire cells
62   |       in the given region or clip those cells so all of the output one stay
63   |       only inside that region.
64   |
65   |   Input
66   |       This property specifies the dataset on which the Clip
67   |       filter will operate.
68   |
69   |   InsideOut
70   |       If this property is set to 0, the clip filter will
71   |       return that portion of the dataset that lies within the clip function.
72   |       If set to 1, the portions of the dataset that lie outside the clip
73   |       function will be returned instead.
74  ...
75
76  # To get help on a specific implicit function type, make it the active
77  # ClipType and then use help()
78  >>> clip.ClipType = 'Plane'
79  >>> help(clip.ClipType)
80  Help on Plane in module paraview.servermanager object:
81
82  class Plane(Proxy)
83   ...
```

> ⚠ **Common Errors**
>
> *It is very easy to forget that clipping a structured dataset such as image data can dramtically increase the memory requirements, since this filter will convert the structured dataset into an unstructured grid due to the nature of the clipping operation itself. For structured dataset, think about using `Slice` or `Extract Subset` filters instead, whenever appropriate. Those are not entirely identical operations, but they are often sufficient.*

5.6.2 Slice

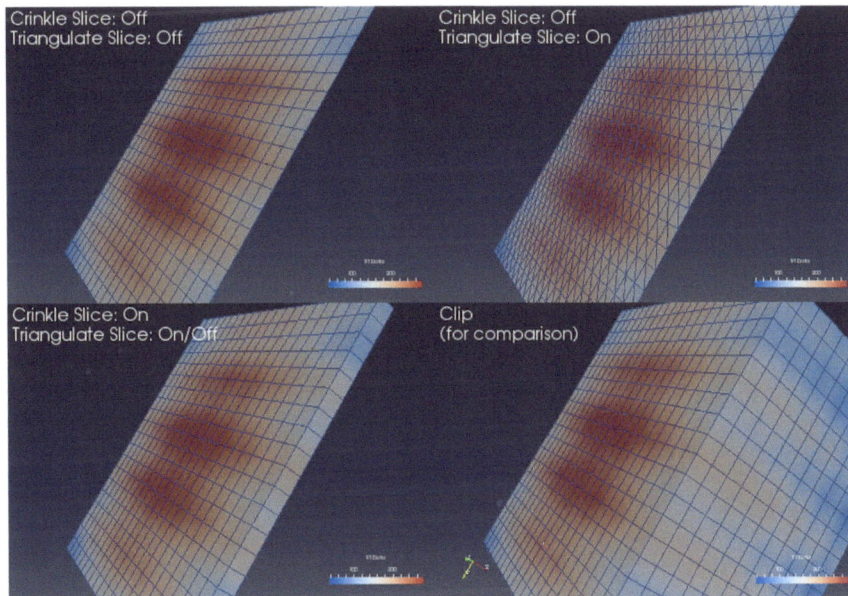

Figure 5.7: Comparison between results produced by the `Slice` filter when slicing image data with an implicit plane with different options. The lower-left image shows the output produced by the `Clip` filter when clipping with the same implicit function, for contrast.

The `Slice` filter slices through the input dataset with an implicit function such as a plane, a sphere, or a box. Since this filter returns data elements along the implicit function boundary, this is a dimensionality reducing filter (except when crinkle slicing is enabled), i.e., if the input dataset has 3D elements like tetrahedrons or hexahedrons, the output will have 2D elements, line triangles, and quads, if any. While slicing through a dataset with 2D elements, the result will be lines.

The properties available on this filter, as well as the way of setting this filter up, is very similar to the `Clip` filter with a few notable differences. What remains similar is the set up of the implicit function – you have similar choices: `Plane`, `Sphere`, and `Box`, as well as the option to toggle `Crinkle slice` (i.e., to avoid cutting through cells, pass complete cells from the input dataset that intersects the implicit function).

What is different includes the lack of slicing by `Scalar` (for that, you can use the `Contour` filter) and a new option, `Triangulate the slice`. Figure 5.7 shows the difference in the generated meshes when various slice properties are changed.

In *paraview*, this filter can be created using the button on the `Common` filters toolbar, besides the `Filters` menu.

5.6.3 Extract Subset

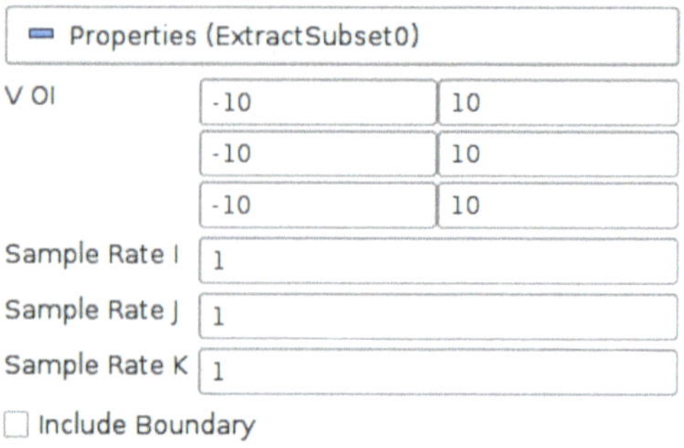

Figure 5.8: The `Properties` panel for the `Extract Subset` filter showing all available properties (including the advanced properties).

For structured datasets such as image datasets (Section 3.1.3), rectilinear grids (Section 3.1.4), and curvilinear grids (Section 3.1.5), `Extract Subset` filter can be used to extract a region of interest or a subgrid. The region to extract is specified using structured coordinates, i.e., the i, j, k values. Whenever possible, this filter should be preferred over `Clip` or `Slice` for structured datasets, since it preserves the input data type. Besides extracting a subset, this filter can also be used to resample the dataset to a coarser resolution by specifying the sample rate along each of the structured dimensions.

Extract Subset in `paraview`

This is one of the common filters available on the `Common` filters toolbar ⬚. To specify the region of interest, you use the `VOI` property. The values are specified as min and max values for each of the structured dimensions (i, j, k,) in each row. `Sample Rate I`, `Sample Rate J`, and `Sample Rate K` specify the sub-sampling rate. Set it to a value greater than one to sub-sample. `Include Boundary` is used to determine if the boundary slab should be included in the extracted result, if the sub-sampling rate along that dimension is greater than 1, and the boundary slab would otherwise have been skipped.

5.6.4 Threshold

The `Threshold` filter extracts the portions of the input dataset whose scalars lie within the specified range. This filter operates on either point-centered or cell-centered data. This filter operates on any type of dataset and produces an unstructured grid output. To use this filter, you select the `Scalars` with which to threshold, and then specify the range through which to pass. When thresholding with cell data, all cells that have scalars within the specified range will be passed through the filter. When thresholding with point data, cells with *all* points with scalar values within the range are passed through if `All Scalars` is checked; otherwise, cells with *any* point that passes the thresholding criteria are passed through.

Threshold in `paraview`

This filter is represented as ⬚ on the `Common` filters toolbar. After selecting the `Scalars` with which to threshold from the combo-box, you select the `Minimum` and `Maximum` values to specify the range. If the range shown by the sliders is not sufficient, you can manually type the values in the input boxes. The values are deliberately not clamped to the current data

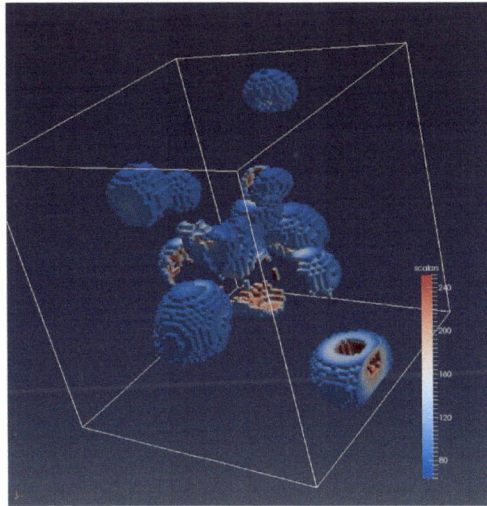

Figure 5.9: Results from using the `Threshold` filter on the *iron_protein.vtk* dataset from ParaView data.

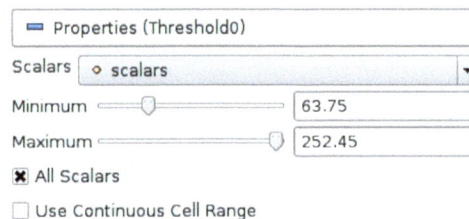

Figure 5.10: The `Properties` panel for the `Threshold` filter.

range. The `Scalars` combo-box uses icons to help you differentiate between point data arrays and cell data arrays .

Threshold in `pvpython`

```
1  # To create the filter (if Input is not specified, the active source will be
2  # used as the input.
3  >>> threshold = Threshold(Input=...)
4
5  # Here's how to select a scalar array,
6  >>> threshold.Scalars = ("POINTS", "scalars")
7
8  # The value is a tuple with first value as the association:
9  # either "POINTS" or "CELLS" and the second value is the name of the selected
10 array.
11
12 >>> print threshold.Scalars
13 ['POINTS', 'scalars']
14
```

```
15 │ >>>> print threshold.Scalars.GetArrayName()
16 │ 'scalars'
17 │
18 │ >>> print threshold.Scalars.GetAssociation()
19 │ 'POINTS'
20 │
21 │ # The threshold range is specified as:
22 │ >>> threshold.ThresholdRange = [63.75, 252.45]
```

To determine the types of arrays available in the input dataset, and their ranges, refer to the discussion on data information in Section 3.3.

5.6.5 Iso Volume

The `Iso Volume` filter is similar to `Threshold` in that you use this to create an output dataset from an input where the cells that satisfy the specified range are scalar values. In fact, the filter is identical to `Threshold` when the cell data scalars are selected. For point data scalars, however, this filter acts similar to the `Clip` filters when clipping with scalars, in that cells are clipped along the iso-surface formed the scalar range.

5.6.6 Extract Selection

`Extract Selection` is a general-purpose filter to extract selected elements from a dataset. There are several ways of making selections in ParaView. Once you have made the selection, this filter allows you to extract the selected elements as a new dataset for further processing. We will cover this filter in more detail when looking at selections in ParaView in Section 6.5.

5.7 Filters for geometric manipulation

These filters are used to transform the geometry of the dataset without affecting its topology or its connectivity.

5.7.1 Transform

The `Transform` can be used to arbitrarily translate, rotate, and scale a dataset. The transformation is applied by scaling the dataset, rotating it, and then translating it based on the values specified.

As this is a geometric manipulation filter, this filter does not affect connectivity in the input dataset. While it tries to preserve the input dataset type, whenever possible, there are cases when the transformed dataset can no longer be represented in the same data type as the input. For example, with image data (Section 3.1.3) and rectilinear grids (Section 3.1.4), due to the ability of rotating the dataset, the output dataset can be non-axis aligned and, hence, cannot be represented as either data types. In such cases, the dataset is converted to an unstructured grid (Section 3.1.7). Since unstructured grids are not as compact as data structured as the other two, this implies a considerable increase in the memory footprint.

5.7.2 Transform in `paraview`

You can create a new `Transform` from the `Filters ⟩ Alphabetical` menu. Once created, you can set the transform as the translation, rotation, and scale to use utilizing the `Properties` panel. Similar to `Clip`, this filter also supports using a 3D widget to interactively set the transformation.

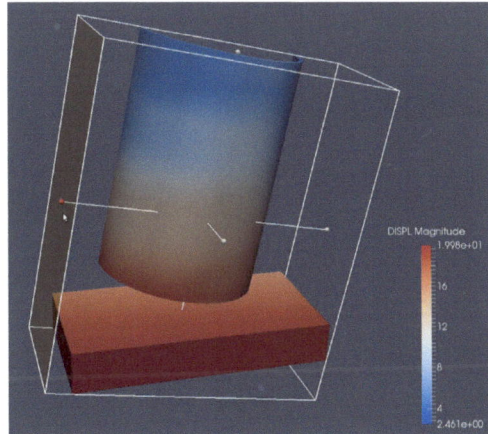

Figure 5.11: The `Transform` filter showing the 3D widget that can be used to interactively set the transform.

5.7.3 Transform in `pvpython`

```
1  # To create the filter(if Input is not specified, the active source will be
2  # used as the input).
3  >>> transform = Transform(Input=...)
4
5  # Set the transformation properties.
6  >>> transform.Translate.Scale = [1, 2, 1]
7  >>> transform.Transform.Translate = [100, 0, 0]
8  >>> transform.Transform.Rotate = [0, 0, 0]
```

5.7.4 Reflect

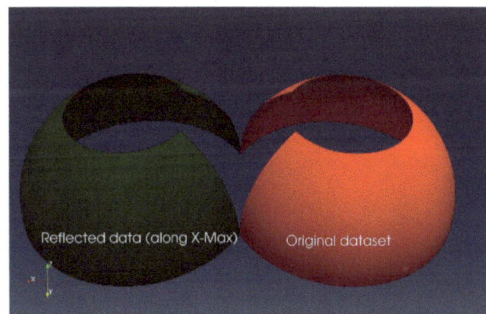

Figure 5.12: The `Reflect` filter can be used to reflect a dataset along a specific axis plane.

`Reflect` can be used to reflect any dataset across an axis plane. You can pick the axis plane to be one of the planes formed by the bounding box of the dataset. For that, set `Plane` as `X Min`, `X Max`, `Y Min`, `Y Max`, `Z Min`, or `Z Max`. To reflect across an arbitrary axis plane, select `X`, `Y`, or `Z` for the `Plane` property, and then set the `Center` to the plane offset from the origin.

This filter reflects the input dataset and produces an unstructured grid (Section 3.1.7). Thus, the same caveats for `Clip` and `Threshold` filter apply here when dealing with structured datasets.

5.7.5 Warp By Vector

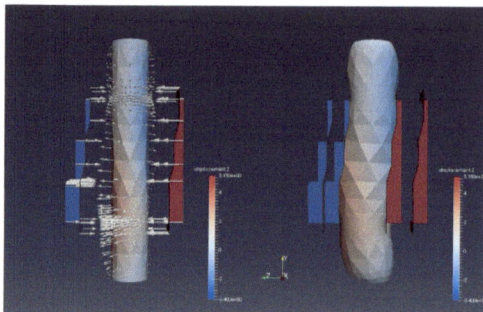

Figure 5.13: The `Warp By Vector` filter can be used to displace points in original data shown on the left, using the *displacement* vectors (indicated by arrow glyphs5.7.8) to produce the result shown on the right.

`Warp By Vector` can be used to displace point coordinates in an input mesh using vectors in the dataset itself. You select the vectors to use utilizing the `Vectors` property on the `Properties` panel. `Scale Factor` can be used to scale the displacement applied.

5.7.6 Warp By Scalar

`Warp By Scalar` is similar to `Warp By Vector` in the sense that it warps the input mesh. However, it does so using a scalar array in the input dataset. The direction of displacement can either be explicitly specified using the `Normal` property, or you can check `Use Normal` to use normals at the point locations.

5.7.7 Filters for sampling

These filters compute new datasets that represent some essential features from the datasets that they take as input.

5.7.8 Glyph

`Glyph` is used to place markers or glyphs at point locations in the input dataset. The glyphs can be oriented or scaled based on vector and scalar attributes on those points.

To create this filter in *paraview*, you can use the Filters menu, as well as the ⬡ button on the `Common` filters toolbar. You first select the type for the glyph using one of the options in `Glyph Type`. The choices include `Arrow`, `Sphere`, `Cylinder`, etc. Next, you select the point arrays to treat as the `Scalars` and the `Vectors`. This selection is then used when scaling or orienting the glyphs. To orient the glyphs using the selected `Vectors`, check the `Orient` checkbox.

The `Scale Mode` controls how the glyphs are scaled. The options are as follows:

- `off`: This disables scaling on glyphs based on point arrays.
- `scalar`: This scales the glyphs using the point array selected using `Scalars`.
- `vector`: This scales the glyphs using the magnitude for the point array selected for `Vectors`.

- `vector_components`: This is similar to `vector`; however, instead of scaling the glyph in all three directions using the magnitude of the vectors, the scale factor for each direction is obtained from the point array by treating each component individually.

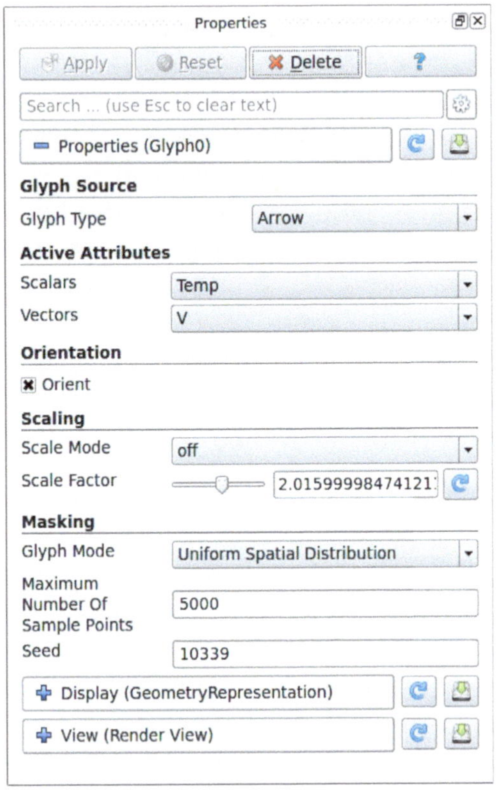

Figure 5.14: The `Properties` panel for the `Glyph` filter.

The `Scale Factor` is used to apply a constant scaling to all the glyphs, independent of the `Scale Mode`. Choosing a good scale factor depends on several things including the bounds on the input dataset, the `Scale Mode` selected, and the range for the array that would affect the glyph scaling based on `Scale Mode`. You can use the ⟳ button next to the `Scale Factor` widget to have *paraview* pick a scale factor value based on the current dataset and selections.

The `Masking` properties allow you to control which points from the input dataset get glyphed. The `Glyph Mode` controls how points are selected to be glyphs (Figure 5.15). The available options are as follows:

- `All Points`: This selects all points in the input dataset for glyphing. Use this mode with caution and only when the input dataset has relatively few points. Since all points in the input dataset are glyphed, this can not only cause visual clutter, but also clog up memory and take a long to time to generate and render the glyphs.
- `Every Nth Points`: This elects every n^{th} point in the input dataset for glyphing, where n can be specified using `Stride`. Setting `Stride` to 1 will have the same effect as `All Points`.
- `Uniform Spatial Distribution`: This selects a random set of points. The algorithm works by first computing up to `Maximum Number of Sample Points` in the space defined by the bounding box of the input dataset. Then, points in the input dataset that are close to the point in this set of sample points are glyphed. The `Seed` is used to seed the random number generator used to generate the sample points. This ensures that the random sample points are reproducible and consistent.

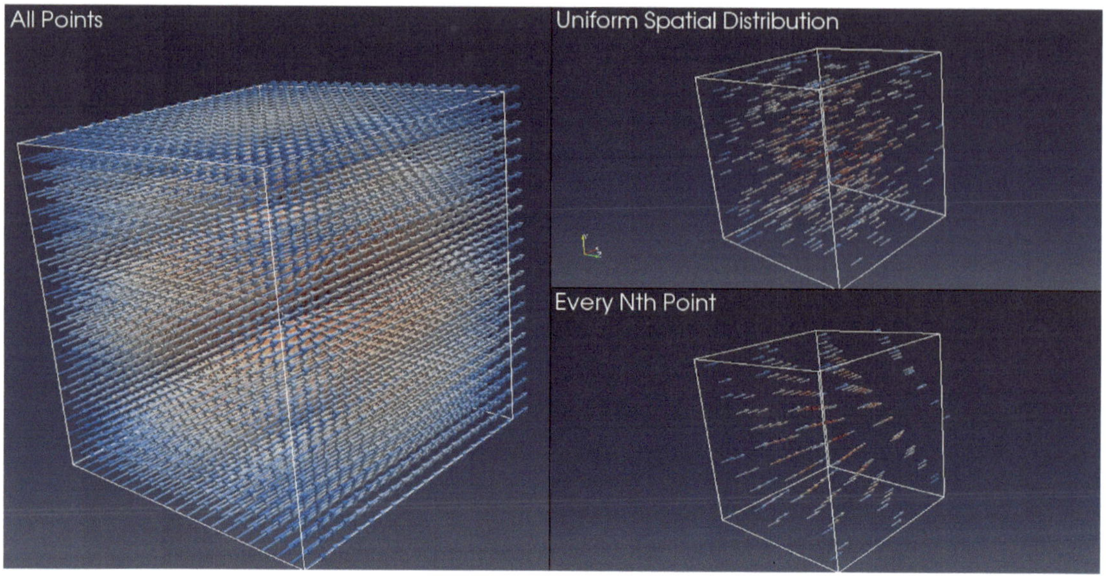

Figure 5.15: Comparison between various `Glyph Modes` when applied to the same dataset generated by the `Wavelet` source.

5.7.9 Glyph With Custom Source

`Glyph With Custom Source` is the same as `Glyph`, except that instead of a limited set of `Glyph Type`, you can select any data source producing a polygonal dataset (Section 3.1.8) available in the `Pipeline Browser`.

5.7.10 Stream Tracer

The `Stream Tracer` filter is used to generate streamlines for vector fields. In visualization, streamlines refer to curves that are instanteneously tangential to the the vector field in the dataset. They provide an indication of the direction in which the particles in the dataset would travel at that instant in time. The algorihm works by taking a set of points, known as *seed* points, in the dataset and then inegrating the streamlines starting at these seed points.

In *paraview*, you can create this filter using the Filters menu, as well as the button on the `Common` filters toolbar. To use this filter, you first select the attribute array to use as the `Vectors` for generaing the streamline. `Integration Parameters` let you fine tune the streamline integeration by specifying the direction to integrate, `Integration Direction`, as well as the type of integeration algorithm to use, `Integrator Type`. Advanced integration parameters are available in the advanced view of the `Properties` panel that let you further tune the integration, including specifying the step size and others. You use the `Maximum Streamline Length` to limit the maximum length for the streamline – the longer the length, the longer the generated streamlines.

`Seeds` group lets you set how the seed points for generating the streamlines are produced. You have two options: `Point Source`, which produces a point clound around the user-specified `Point` based on the parameters specified, and `High Resolution Line Source`, which produces seed points along the user-specified line. You can use the 3D widgets shown in the active `Render View` to interactively place the center for the point cloud or for defining the line.

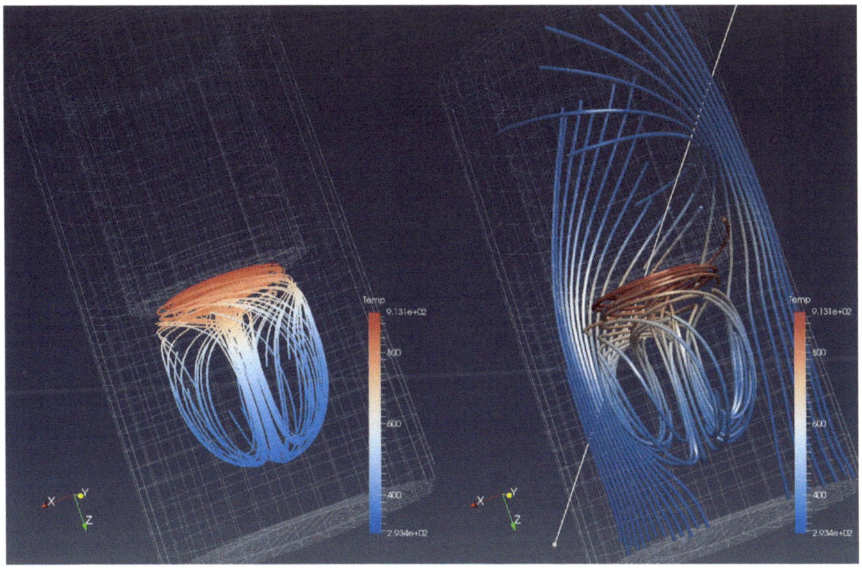

Figure 5.16: Streamlines generated from the `disk_out_ref.ex2` dataset using the `Point Source` (left) and the `High Resolution Line Source` (right). On the left, we also added the `Tube` filter to the output of the `Stream Tracer` filter to generate 3D tubes rather than 1D polygonal lines, which can be hard to visualize due to lack of shading.

ⓘ Did you know?

The `Stream Tracer` filter produces a polydata with 1D lines for each of the generated streamlines. Since 1D lines cannot be shaded like surfaces in the `Render View`, you can get visualizations where it is hard to follow the streamlines. To give the streamlines some 3D structure, you can apply the `Tube` filter to the output of the streamlines. The properties on the `Tube` filter let you control the thickness of the tubes. You can also vary the thickness of the tubes based on data array, e.g., the magnitude of the vector field at the sample points in the streamline!

A script using the `Stream Tracer` filter in *paraview* typically looks like this:

```
1  # find source
2  >>> disk_out_refex2 = FindSource('disk_out_ref.ex2')
3
4  # create a new 'Stream Tracer'
5  >>> streamTracer1 = StreamTracer(Input=disk_out_refex2,
6                                    SeedType='Point Source')
7  >>> streamTracer1.Vectors = ['POINTS', 'V']
8
9  # init the 'Point Source' selected for 'SeedType'
10 >>> streamTracer1.SeedType.Center = [0.0, 0.0, 0.07999992370605469]
11 >>> streamTracer1.SeedType.Radius = 2.015999984741211
12
13 # show data in view
14 >>> Show()
15
16 # create a new 'Tube'
17 >>> tube1 = Tube(Input=streamTracer1)
18
```

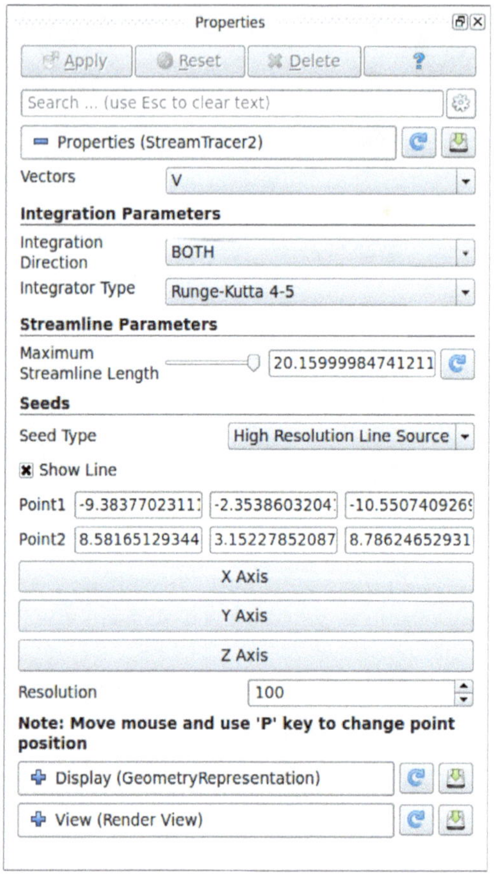

Figure 5.17: The `Properties` panel showing the default properties for the `Stream Tracer` filter.

```
19  # Properties modified on tube1
20  >>> tube1.Radius = 0.1611409378051758
21
22  # show the data from tubes in view
23  >>> Show()
```

5.7.11 Stream Tracer With Custom Source

`Stream Tracer` allows you to specify the seed points either as a point cloud or as a line source. However, if you want to provide your own seed points from a another data producer, use the `Stream Tracer With Custom Source`. Similar to `Glyph With Custom Source`, this filter allows you to pick a second input connection to use as the seed points.

5.7.12 Probe

`Probe` samples the input dataset at a specific point location to obtain the cell data attributes for the cell containing the point as well as the interpolated point data attributes. You can either use the `SpreadSheet View` or the `Information`

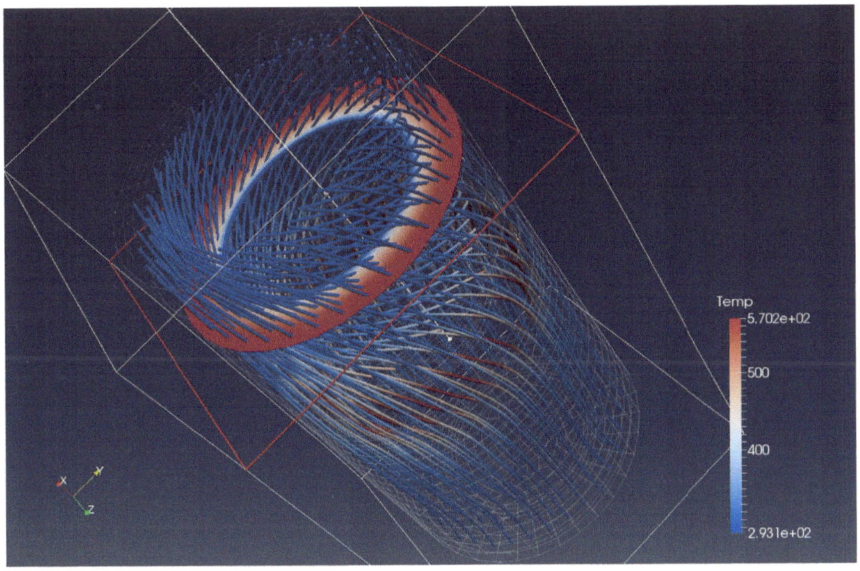

Figure 5.18: Streamlines generated from the `disk_out_ref.ex2` dataset using the output of the `Slice` filter as the `Source` for seed points.

panel to inspect the probed values. The probe location can be specified using the interactive 3D widget shown in the active `Render View`.

5.7.13   Plot over line

`Plot Over Line` will sample the input dataset along the specified line and then plot the results in `Line Chart View`. Internally, this filter uses the same mechanism as the `Probe` filter, probing along the points in the line to get the containing cell attributes and interpolated point attributes.

Using the `Resolution` property on the `Properties` panel, you can control the number of sample points along the line.

5.8   Filters for attribute manipulation

The filters covered in this section are used to add new attribute arrays to the dataset, which are typically used to add derived quantities to use in pipelines for further processing.

5.8.1   Calculator

The `Calculator` filter computes a new data array or new point coordinates as a function of existing input arrays. If point-centered arrays are used in the computation of a new data array, the resulting array will also be point-centered. Similarly, computations using cell-centered arrays will produce a new cell-centered array. If the function is computing point coordinates (requested by checking the `Coordinate Results` property on the `Properties` panel) , the result of the function must be a three-component vector. The `Calculator` interface operates similarly to a scientific calculator. In creating the function to evaluate, the standard order of operations applies. Each of the calculator functions is described below. Unless otherwise noted, enclose the operand in parentheses using the (and) buttons.

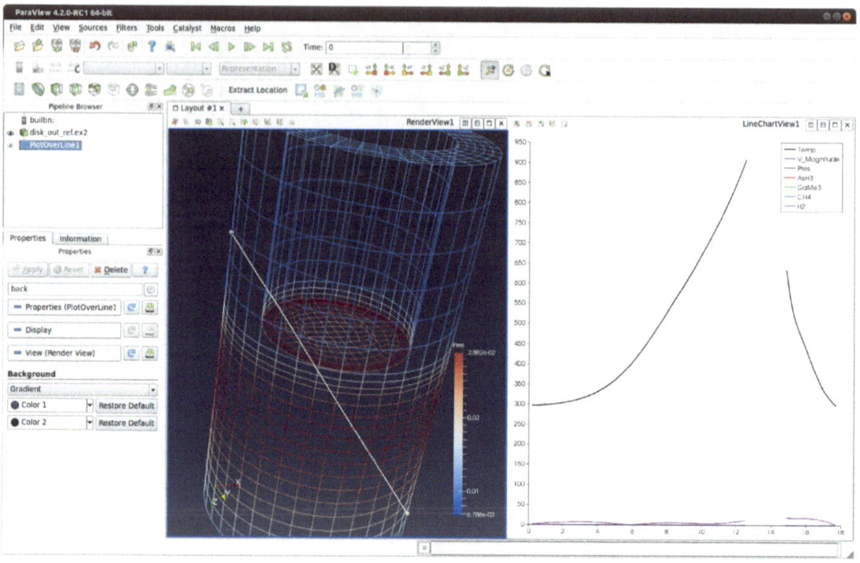

Figure 5.19: The `Plot Over Line` filter applied to the `disk_out_ref.ex2` dataset to plot values at sampled locations along the line. Gaps in the line correspond to the locations in the input dataset where the line falls outside the dataset.

- `Clear`: Erase the current function.
- `/`: Divide one scalar by another. The operands for this function are not required to be enclosed in parentheses.
- `*`: Multiply two scalars, or multiply a vector by a scalar (scalar multiple). The operands for this function are not required to be enclosed in parentheses.
- `-`: Negate a scalar or vector (unary minus), or subtract one scalar or vector from another. The operands for this function are not required to be enclosed in parentheses.
- `+`: Add two scalars or two vectors. The operands for this function are not required to be enclosed in parentheses.
- `sin`: Compute the sine of a scalar.
- `cos`: Compute the cosine of a scalar.
- `tan`: Compute the tangent of a scalar.
- `asin`: Compute the arcsine of a scalar.
- `acos`: Compute the arccosine of a scalar.
- `atan`: Compute the arctangent of a scalar.
- `sinh`: Compute the hyperbolic sine of a scalar.
- `cosh`: Compute the hyperbolic cosine of a scalar.
- `tanh`: Compute the hyperbolic tangent of a scalar.
- `min`: Compute minimum of two scalars.
- `max`: Compute maximum of two scalars.
- $x\hat{y}$: Raise one scalar to the power of another scalar. The operands for this function are not required to be enclosed in parentheses.
- `sqrt`: Compute the square root of a scalar.
- $e\hat{x}$: Raise e to the power of a scalar.
- `log10`: Compute the logarithm of a scalar to the base 10.
- `ln`: Compute the logarithm of a scalar to the base e.
- `ceil`: Compute the ceiling of a scalar.
- `floor`: Compute the floor of a scalar.
- `abs`: Compute the absolute value of a scalar.
- `v1.v2`: Compute the dot product of two vectors. The operands for this function are not required to be enclosed in

parentheses. `cross`: Compute cross product of two vectors. `mag`: Compute the magnitude of a vector. `norm`: Normalize a vector. The operands are described below. The digits 0 - 9 and the decimal point are used to enter constant scalar values.

- `iHat`, `jHat`, and `kHat` are vector constants representing unit vectors in the X, Y, and Z directions, respectively.

The `Scalars` menu lists the names of the scalar arrays and the components of the vector arrays of either the point-centered or cell-centered data. The `Vectors` menu lists the names of the point-centered or cell-centered vector arrays. The function will be computed for each point (or cell) using the scalar or vector value of the array at that point (or cell). The filter operates on any type of data set, but the input data set must have at least one scalar or vector array. The arrays can be either point-centered or cell-centered. The `Calculator` filter's output is of the same data set type as the input.

A common use-case is to convert three input scalars into a vector array. For that, the `Function` would look something like: $scalar_x * iHat + scalar_y * jHat + scalar_z * kHat$.

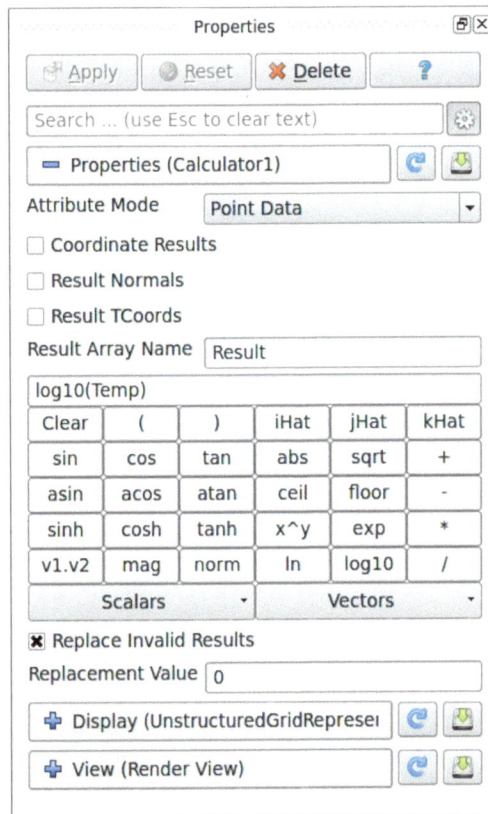

Figure 5.20: The `Properties` panel for the `Calculator` filter showing the advanced properties.

The `Properties` panel provides access to several options for this filter. Checking `Coordinate Results`, `Result Normals`, or `Result TCoords` will set the computed array as the point coordinates, normals, or texture coordinates, respectively. `Result Array Name` is used to specify a name for the computed array. The default is `Result`.

Sometimes, the expression can yield invalid values. To replace all invalid values with a specific value, check the `Replace Invalid Results` checkbox and then enter the value to use to replace invalid values using the `Replacement Value`.

5.8.2 Python calculator

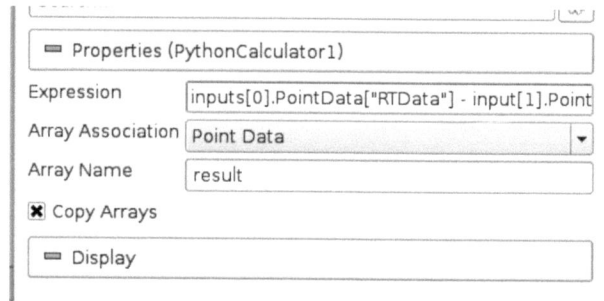

Figure 5.21: The Properties Panel for Python Calculator

The `Python Calculator` is similar to `Calculator` in that it processes one or more input arrays based on an expression provided by the user to produce a new output array. However, it uses Python (and *numpy*) to do the computation. Therefore, it provides more expressive expression capabilities.

Specify the `Expression` to use, the `Array Association` to indicate the array association (`Point Data` or `Cell Data`), the name of output array (`Array Name`), and a toggle that controls whether the input arrays are copied to the output (`Copy Array`).

Basic tutorial

Start by creating a Sphere source and applying the Python Calculator to it. As the first expression, use the following and apply:

```
1 | 5
```

This should create an array name *result* in the output point data. Note that this is an array that has a value of 5 for each point. When the expression results in a single value, the calculator will automatically make a constant array. Next, try the following:

```
1 | Normals
```

Now, the *result* array should be the same as the input array Normals. As described in detail later, various functions are available through the calculator. For example, the following is a valid expression:

```
1 | sin(Normals) + 5
```

It is very important to note that the Python Calculator has to produce one value per point or cell depending on the Array Association parameter. Most of the functions described here apply individually to all point or cell values and produce an array the same dimensions as the input. However, some of them (such as min() and max()) produce single values.

Accessing data

There are several ways of accessing input arrays within expressions. The simplest way is to access it by name:

```
1 | sin(Normals) + 5
```

This is equivalent to:

```
1 │ sin(inputs[0].PointData['Normals']) + 5
```

The example above requires some explanation. Here, inputs[0] refer to the first input (dataset) to the filter. Python Calculator can accept multiple inputs. Each input can be accessed as inputs[0], inputs[1], ... You can access the point or cell data of an input using the .PointData or .CellData qualifiers. You can then access individual arrays within the point or cell data containers using the [] operator. Make sure to use quotes or double-quotes around the array name. Arrays that have names with certain characters (such as space, +, -, *, /) can only be accessed using this method.

Certain functions apply directly on the input mesh. These filters expect an input dataset as argument. For example,

```
1 │ area(inputs[0])
```

For data types that explicitly define the point coordinates, you can access the coordinates array using the .Points qualifier. The following extracts the first component of the coordinates array:

```
1 │ inputs[0].Points[:,0]
```

Note that for certain data types, mainly image data (uniform rectilinear grids) and rectilinear grids, point coordinates are defined implicitly and cannot be accessed as an array.

Comparing multiple datasets

The Python Calculator can be used to compare multiple datasets, as shown by the following example.

- Go to the Menu Bar, and select File ¿ Disconnect to clear the Pipeline.

- Select Source > Mandelbrot, and then click Apply, which will set up a default version of the Mandelbrot Set. The data for this set are stored in a 251×251 scalar array.

- Select Source > Mandelbrot again, and then go to the Properties panel and set the Maximum Number of Iterations to 50. Click Apply, which will set up a different version of the Mandelbrot Set, represented by the same size array.

- Hold the Shift key down and select both of the Mandelbrot entries in the Pipeline Inspector, and then go to the Menu Bar, and select Filter ¿ Python Calculator. The two Mandelbrot entries will now be shown as linked, as inputs, to the Python Calculator.

- In the Properties panel for the Python Calculator filter, enter the following into the Expression box:

  ```
  1 │   inputs[1].PointData['Iterations'] - inputs[0].PointData['Iterations']
  ```

  This expression specifies the difference between the second and the first Mandelbrot arrays. The result is saved in a new array called 'results'. The prefixes in the names for the array variables, inputs[1] and inputs[0], refer to the first and second Mandelbrot entries, respectively, in the Pipeline. PointData specifies that the inputs contain point values. The quoted label 'Iterations' is the local name for these arrays. Click Apply to initiate the calculation.

Click the Display tab in the Properties panel for the Python Calculator, and go to the first tab to the right of the *Color by* label. Select the item results in that tab, which will cause the display window to the right to show the results of the expression we entered in the Python Calculator. The scalar values representing the difference between the two Mandelbrot arrays are represented by colors that are set by the current color map (see Edit Color Map... for details).

There are a few things to note:

- Python Calculator will always copy the mesh from the first input to its output.

- All operations are applied point-by-point. In most cases, this requires that the input meshes (topology and geometry) are the same. At the least, it requires that the inputs have the same number of points and cells.

- In parallel execution mode, the inputs have to be distributed exactly the same way across processes.

Basic Operations

The Python calculator supports all of the basic arithmetic operations using the $+$, $-$, $*$ and $/$ operators. These are always applied element-by-element to point and cell data including scalars, vectors, and tensors. These operations also work with single values. For example, the following adds 5 to all components of all Normals.

```
1  Normals + 5
```

The following adds 1 to the first component, 2 to the second component, and 3 to the third component:

```
1  Normals + [1,2,3]
```

This is specially useful when mixing functions that return single values. For example, the following normalizes the Normals array:

```
1  (Normals - min(Normals))/(max(Normals) - min(Normals))
```

A common use case in a calculator is to work on one component of an array. This can be accomplished with the following:

```
1  Normals[:, 0]
```

The expression above extracts the first component of the Normals vector. Here, ':' is a placeholder for "all elements". One element can be extracted by replacing ':' with an index. For example, the following creates a constant array from the first component of the normal of the first point:

```
1  Normals[0, 0]
```

Alternatively, the following assigns the normal of the first point to all points:

```
1  Normals[0, :]
```

It is also possible to merge multiple scalars into an array using the hstack() function:

```
1  hstack([velocity_x, velocity_y, velocity_z]) # Note the square brackets ([]).
```

> ⓘ *Did you know?*
>
> *Under the cover, the Python Calculator uses NumPy. All arrays in the expression are compatible with NumPy arrays and can be used where NumPy arrays can be used. For more information on what you can do with these arrays, consult with the NumPy references.[9]*

Functions

The following is a list of functions available in the Python Calculator. Note that this is a partial list, since most of the NumPy and SciPy functions can be used in the Python Calculator. Many of these functions can take single values or arrays as argument.

- *abs (x)* : Returns the absolute value(s) of x.
- *add (x, y)*: Returns the sum of two values. x and y can be single values or arrays. This is the same as x+y.
- *area (dataset)* : Returns the surface area of each cell in a mesh.
- *aspect (dataset)* : Returns the aspect ratio of each cell in a mesh.
- *aspect_gamma (dataset)* : Returns the aspect ratio gamma of each cell in a mesh.
- *condition (dataset)* : Returns the condition number of each cell in a mesh.

- *cross (x, y)* : Returns the cross product for two 3D vectors from two arrays of 3D vectors.
- *curl (array)*: Returns the curl of an array of 3D vectors.
- *divergence (array)*: Returns the divergence of an array of 3D vectors.
- *divide (x, y)*: Element-by-element division. x and y can be single values or arrays. This is the same as $\frac{x}{y}$.
- *det (array)* : Returns the determinant of an array of 2D square matrices.
- *determinant (array)* : Returns the determinant of an array of 2D square matrices.
- *diagonal (dataset)* : Returns the diagonal length of each cell in a dataset.
- *dot (a1, a2)*: Returns the dot product of two scalars/vectors of two array of scalars/vectors.
- *eigenvalue (array)* : Returns the eigenvalue of an array of 2D square matrices.
- *eigenvector (array)* : Returns the eigenvector of an array of 2D square matrices.
- *exp (x)*: Returns e^x.
- *global_max(array)*: Returns the maximum value of an array of scalars, vectors, or tensors among all process. This is not yet supported for multi-block and AMR datasets.
- *global_mean (array)* : Returns the mean value of an array of scalars, vectors, or tensors among all processes. This is not yet supported for multi-block and AMR datasets.
- *global_min(array)*: Returns the minimum value of an array of scalars/vectors/tensors among all process. This is not yet supported for multi-block and AMR datasets.
- *gradient(array)*: Returns the gradient of an array of scalars or vectors.
- *inv (array)* : Returns the inverse an array of 2D square matrices.
- *inverse (array)* : Returns the inverse of an array of 2D square matrices.
- *jacobian (dataset)* : Returns the jacobian of an array of 2D square matrices.
- *laplacian (array)* : Returns the jacobian of an array of scalars.
- *ln (array)* : Returns the natural logarithm of an array of scalars/vectors/tensors.
- *log (array)* : Returns the natural logarithm of an array of scalars/vectors/tensors.
- *log10 (array)* : Returns the base 10 logarithm of an array of scalars/vectors/tensors.
- *max (array)*: Returns the maximum value of the array as a single value. Note that this function returns the maximum within a block for AMR and multi-block datasets, not across blocks/grids. Also, this returns the maximum within each process when running in parallel.
- *max_angle (dataset)* : Returns the maximum angle of each cell in a dataset.
- *mag (a)* : Returns the magnigude of an array of scalars/vectors.
- *mean (array)* : Returns the mean value of an array of scalars/vectors/tensors.
- *min (array)* : Returns the minimum value of the array as a single value. Note that this function returns the minimum within a block for AMR and multi-block datasets, not across blocks/grids. Also, this returns the minimum within each process when running in parallel.
- *min_angle (dataset)* : Returns the minimum angle of each cell in a dataset.
- *mod (x, y)*: Same as remainder (x, y).
- *multiply (x, y)*: Returns the product of x and y. x and y can be single values or arrays. Note that this is an element-by-element operation when x and y are both arrays. This is the same as $x \times y$.
- *negative (x)*: Same as -x.
- *norm (a)* : Returns the normalized values of an array of scalars/vectors.
- *power (x, a)*: Exponentiation of x with a. Here, both x and a can either be a single value or an array. If x and y are both arrays, a one-by-one mapping is used between two arrays.
- *reciprocal (x)*: Returns $\frac{1}{x}$.
- *remainder (x, y)*: Returns $x - y \times floor(\frac{x}{y})$. x and y can be single values or arrays.
- *rint (x)*: Rounds x to the nearest integer(s).
- *shear (dataset)* : Returns the shear of each cell in a dataset.
- *skew (dataset)* : Returns the skew of each cell in a dataset.
- *square (x)*: Returns $x * x$.
- *sqrt (x)*: Returns $\sqrt[2]{x}$.
- *strain (array)* : Returns the strain of an array of 3D vectors.

- *subtract (x, y)*: Returns the difference between two values. x and y can be single values or arrays. This is the same as $x - y$.
- *surface_normal (dataset)* : Returns the surface normal of each cell in a dataset.
- *trace (array)* : Returns the trace of an array of 2D square matrices.
- *volume (dataset)* : Returns the volume normal of each cell in a dataset.
- *vorticity(array)*: Returns the vorticity/curl of an array of 3D vectors.
- *vertex_normal (dataset)* : Returns the vertex normal of each point in a dataset.

Trigonometric Functions

Below is a list of supported trigonometric functions:

- *sin (x)*
- *cos (x)*
- *tan (x)*
- *arcsin (x)*
- *arccos (x)*
- *arctan (x)*
- *hypot (x1, x2)*
- *sinh(x)*
- *cosh (x)*
- *tanh (x)*
- *arcsinh (x)*
- *arccosh (x)*
- *arctanh (x)*

5.8.3   Gradient

There are two filters that can compute gradients:

- `Gradient`: This is designed for efficiently computing gradients of point data arrays on a uniform rectilinear grid (Section 3.1.3).
- `Gradient of Unstructured DataSet`: This computes cell or point data arrays for any type of dataset. This filer also adds support for computing vorticity or curl, as well as the Q-criterion of the selected 3-component array.

5.8.4   Mesh Quality

The `Mesh Quality` filter creates a new cell array containing a geometric measure of each cell's fitness. Different quality measures can be chosen for different cell shapes.

`Triangle Quality` indicates which quality measure will be used to evaluate triangle quality. The `Radius Ratio` is the size of a circle circumscribed by a triangle's three vertices divided by the size of a circle tangent to a triangle's three edges. The `Edge Ratio` is the ratio of the longest edge length to the shortest edge length.

`Quad Quality` indicates which quality measure will be used to evaluate quad cells.

`Tet Quality` indicates which quality measure will be used to evaluate tetrahedral quality. The `Radius Ratio` is the size of a sphere circumscribed by a tetrahedron's four vertices divided by the size of a circle tangent to a tetrahedron's four faces. The `Edge Ratio` is the ratio of the longest edge length to the shortest edge length. The `Collapse Ratio` is the minimum ratio of height of a vertex above the triangle opposite it, divided by the longest edge of the opposing triangle across all vertex/triangle pairs.

`HexQualityMeasure` indicates which quality measure will be used to evaluate quality of hexahedral cells.

5.9   White-box filters

This includes the `Programmable Filter` and `Programmable Source`. For these filters/sources, you can add Python code to do the data generation or processing. We'll cover writing Python code for these in Chapter 13.

5.10 Best practices

5.10.1 Avoiding data explosion

The pipeline model that ParaView presents is very convenient for exploratory visualization. The loose coupling between components provides a very flexible framework for building unique visualizations, and the pipeline structure allows you to tweak parameters quickly and easily.

The downside of this coupling is that it can have a larger memory footprint. Each stage of this pipeline maintains its own copy of the data. Whenever possible, ParaView performs shallow copies of the data so that different stages of the pipeline point to the same block of data in memory. However, any filter that creates new data or changes the values or topology of the data must allocate new memory for the result. If ParaView is filtering a very large mesh, inappropriate use of filters can quickly deplete all available memory. Therefore, when visualizing large datasets, it is important to understand the memory requirements of filters.

Please keep in mind that the following advice is intended only for when dealing with very large amounts of data and the remaining available memory is low. When you are not in danger of running out of memory, the following advice is not relevant.

When dealing with structured data, it is absolutely important to know what filters will change the data to unstructured. Unstructured data has a much higher memory footprint, per cell, than structured data because the topology must be explicitly written out. There are many filters in ParaView that will change the topology in some way, and these filters will write out the data as an unstructured grid, because that is the only dataset that will handle any type of topology that is generated. The following list of filters will write out a new unstructured topology in its output that is roughly equivalent to the input. These filters should never be used with structured data and should be used with caution on unstructured data.

- *Append Datasets*
- *Append Geometry*
- *Clean*
- *Clean to Grid*
- *Connectivity*
- *D3*
- *Delaunay 2D/3D*
- *Extract Edges*
- *Linear Extrusion*
- *Loop Subdivision*
- *Reflect*
- *Rotational Extrusion*
- *Shrink*
- *Smooth*
- *Subdivide*
- *Tessellate*
- *Tetrahedralize*
- *Triangle Strips*
- *Triangulate*

Technically, the Ribbon and Tube filters should fall into this list. However, as they only work on 1D cells in poly data, the input data is usually small and of little concern.

This similar set of filters also outputs unstructured grids, but also tends to reduce some of this data. Be aware though that this data reduction is often smaller than the overhead of converting to unstructured data. Also note that the reduction is often not well balanced. It is possible (often likely) that a single process may not lose any cells. Thus, these filters should be used with caution on unstructured data and extreme caution on structured data.

- *Clip*
- *Decimate*
- *Extract Cells by Region*
- *Extract Selection*
- *Quadric Clustering*
- *Threshold*

Similar to the items in the preceding list, Extract Subset performs data reduction on a structured dataset, but also outputs a structured dataset. So the warning about creating new data still applies, but you do not have to worry about converting to an unstructured grid.

This next set of filters also outputs unstructured data, but it also performs a reduction on the dimension of the data (for example 3D to 2D), which results in a much smaller output. Thus, these filters are usually safe to use with unstructured data and require only mild caution with structured data.

- *Cell Centers*
- *Contour*
- *Extract CTH Fragments*
- *Extract CTH Parts*
- *Extract Surface*

- *Feature Edges*
- *Mask Points*
- *Outline (curvilinear)*
- *Slice*
- *Stream Tracer*

The filters below do not change the connectivity of the data at all. Instead, they only add field arrays to the data. All the existing data is shallow copied. These filters are usually safe to use on all data.

- *Block Scalars*
- *Calculator*
- *Cell Data to Point Data*
- *Curvature*
- *Elevation*
- *Generate Surface Normals*
- *Gradient*
- *Level Scalars*
- *Median*
- *Mesh Quality*
- *Octree Depth Limit*

- *Octree Depth Scalars*
- *Point Data to Cell Data*
- *Process Id Scalars*
- *Random Vectors*
- *Resample with dataset*
- *Surface Flow*
- *Surface Vectors*
- *Texture Map to...*
- *Transform*
- *Warp (scalar)*
- *Warp (vector)*

This final set of filters either add no data to the output (all data of consequence is shallow copied) or the data they add is generally independent of the size of the input. These are almost always safe to add under any circumstances (although they may take a lot of time).

- *Annotate Time*
- *Append Attributes*
- *Extract Block*
- *Extract Datasets*
- *Extract Level*
- *Glyph*
- *Group Datasets*
- *Histogram*
- *Integrate Variables*
- *Normal Glyphs*

- *Outline*
- *Outline Corners*
- *Plot Global Variables Over Time*
- *Plot Over Line*
- *Plot Selection Over Time*
- *Probe Location*
- *Temporal Shift Scale*
- *Temporal Snap-to-Time-Steps*
- *Temporal Statistics*

There are a few special case filters that do not fit well into any of the previous classes. Some of the filters, currently Temporal Interpolator and Particle Tracer, perform calculations based on how data changes over time. Thus, these filters may need to load data for two or more instances of time, which can double or more the amount of data needed in memory. The Temporal Cache filter will also hold data for multiple instances of time. Keep in mind that some of the temporal filters such as the Temporal Statistics and the filters that plot over time may need to iteratively load all data from disk. Thus, it may take an impractically long amount of time even if does not require any extra memory.

The Programmable Filter is also a special case that is impossible to classify. Since this filter does whatever it is programmed to do, it can fall into any one of these categories.

5.10.2 Culling data

When dealing with large data, it is best to cull out data whenever possible and do so as early as possible. Most large data starts as 3D geometry and the desired geometry is often a surface. As surfaces usually have a much smaller memory footprint than the volumes that they are derived from, it is best to convert to a surface early on. Once you do that, you can apply other filters in relative safety.

A very common visualization operation is to extract isosurfaces from a volume using the Contour filter. The Contour filter usually outputs geometry much smaller than its input. Thus, the Contour filter should be applied early if it is to be used at all. Be careful when setting up the parameters to the Contour filter because it still is possible for it to generate a lot of data. which can happen if you specify many isosurface values. High frequencies such as noise around an isosurface value can also cause a large, irregular surface to form.

Another way to peer inside of a volume is to perform a Slice on it. The Slice filter will intersect a volume with a plane and allow you to see the data in the volume where the plane intersects. If you know the relative location of an interesting feature in your large dataset, slicing is a good way to view it.

If you have little a-priori knowledge of your data and would like to explore the data without the long memory and processing time for the full dataset, you can use the Extract Subset filter to subsample the data. The subsampled data can be dramatically smaller than the original data and should still be well load balanced. Of course, be aware that you may miss small features if the subsampling steps over them and that once you find a feature you should go back and visualize it with the full data set.

There are also several features that can pull out a subset of a volume: Clip, Threshold, Extract Selection, and Extract Subset can all extract cells based on some criterion. Be aware, however, that the extracted cells are almost never well balanced; expect some processes to have no cells removed. All of these filters, with the exception of Extract Subset, will convert structured data types to unstructured grids. Therefore, they should not be used unless the extracted cells are of at least an order of magnitude less than the source data.

When possible, replace the use of a filter that extracts 3D data with one that will extract 2D surfaces. For example, if you are interested in a plane through the data, use the Slice filter rather than the Clip filter. If you are interested in knowing the location of a region of cells containing a particular range of values, consider using the Contour filter to generate surfaces at the ends of the range rather than extract all of the cells with the Threshold filter. Be aware that substituting filters can have an effect on downstream filters. For example, running the Histogram filter after Threshold will have an entirely different effect then running it after the roughly equivalent Contour filter.

SELECTING DATA

A typical visualization process has two components: setting up the visualization scene and performing the analysis of the results to gain insight. It is not uncommon for this process to be iterative. Often, what you are looking for drives from what filters you should use to extract the relevant information from the input datasets and what views will best represent that data. One of the ways of evaluating the results is inspecting the data or probing into it by identifying elements of interest. ParaView data selection mechanisms are designed specifically for such use-cases. In this chapter, we take a closer look at various ways of selecting data in ParaView and making use of these selections for data analysis.

6.1   Understanding selection

Broadly speaking, selection refers to selecting elements (either cells, points, rows (in case of tabular datasets), etc.) from datasets. Since data is ingested into ParaView using readers or sources and transformed using filters, when you create a selection, you are selecting elements from the dataset produced as the output of source, filter, or any such pipeline module.

There are many ways to create selections. Several views provide means to create specific selections. For example, in the `SpreadSheet View`, which shows the data attributes as a spreadsheet, you can simply click on any row to *select* that row. You can, of course, use the ⟨⇧⟩ and ⟨Ctrl⟩ (or ⟨⌘⟩) keys to select multiple rows, as in typical spreadsheet-based applications.

While this seems like an exercise in futility, you are hardly achieving anything by highlighting rows in a spreadsheet. What transforms this into a key tool is the fact that selections are *linked* among views (whenever possible). Linked selection means that you select an element from a dataset in a specific view. All other views that are showing the *same* dataset will also highlight the selected elements.

To make this easier, let's try a quick demo:

Starting with a fresh *paraview* session, create a sample dataset using the ⟨Sources⟩⟩⟨Wavelet⟩ menu, and then hit the `Apply` button. If you are using *paraview* with a default setup, that should result in a dataset outline being shown in the default `Render View`. Next, let's split the view and create `SpreadSheet View`. The `SpreadSheet View` will automatically show the data produced by the `Wavelet` source. Upon closer inspection of the header in the `SpreadSheet View`, we see that the view is showing the `Point Data` or point attributes associated with the dataset. Now we have the same dataset, the data produced by the `Wavelet` source, shown in two views. Now, highlight a few rows in the `SpreadSheet View` by clicking on them. As soon as you start selecting rows, the `Render View` will start highlighting some points in space as tiny magenta specks (Figure 6.1). That's linked selection in action! What is happening is that, as you highlight rows in the `SpreadSheet View`, you are creating a selection for selecting points (since the view is showing `Point Data`) corresponding to the rows. Due to the linking of selections between views, any other view that is showing the dataset (in this case, the `Render View`) will also highlight the selected points.

Of course, if you want to select cells instead of points, switch the `SpreadSheet View` to show cells by flipping the

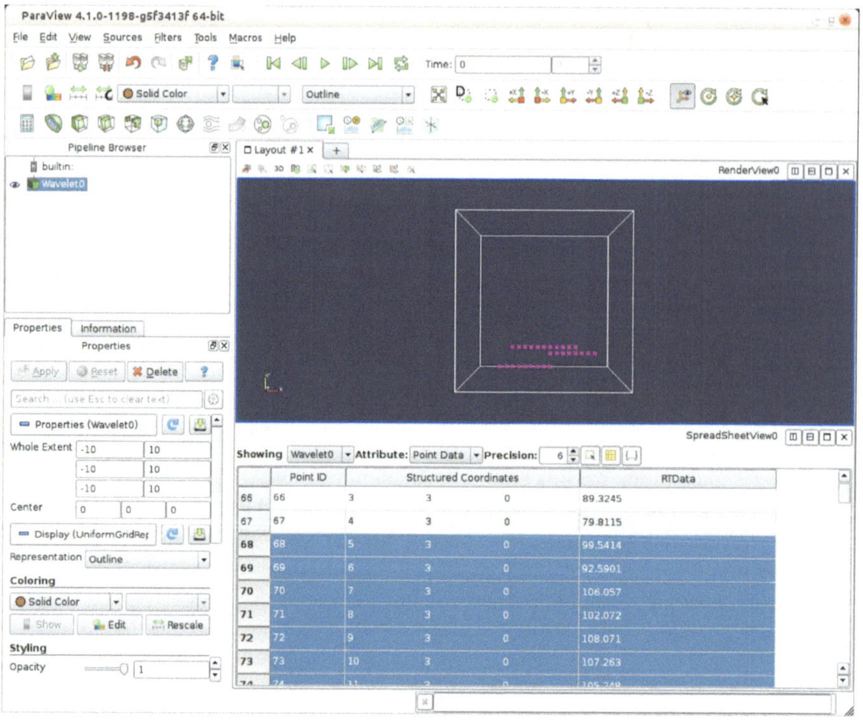

Figure 6.1: Linked selection between views allows you to select elements in a view and view them in all other views showing the selected data. In this demo, as we select rows in the SpreadSheet View, the corresponding points in the 3D View get highlighted.

Attribute combo-box to Cell Data and then highlight rows. The Render View will show the selected cells as a wireframe, rather than points.

Conversely, you could have created the selection in the Render View, and the SpreadSheet View will also highlight the selected elements. We will see how to create such selection later in this chapter.

The first thing to note is that, when you create a new selection, the existing selection is cleared. Thus, there is at most one active selection in the application at any given time. As we shall see, certain views provide ways of expanding on the existing selection.

The second thing to note is that selections are *transient*, i.e., they cannot be undone/redone or saved in state files and loaded back. Nor can you apply filters or other transformation to the selections themselves. There are cases, however, where you may want to subset your dataset using the selection defined interactively and then apply filters and other analysis to that extracted subset. For that, there are filters available, namely Extract Selection and Plot Selection Over Time, that can capture the active selection in as the filter parameters and then produce a new dataset that is comprised of the selected elements.

The third thing to note is that there are different types of selections, e.g., id-based selections, where the selected elements are identified by their indices; frustum-based selections, where the selected elements are those that intersect a frustum defined in 3D space; query-based selections, where the selected elements are those that match the specified query string; and so on.

(i) Did you know?

> *While, technically, selection is possible using a Python-based API, that API is currently cumbersome and requires understanding of some of ParaView internals. There are plans to simplify that API in future releases. As a result, we do not cover Python API for selection in this chapter. Once this new API is available, it will be included in this chapter.*

6.2 Creating selections using views

Views provide a convenient mechanism for creating selections interactively. Views like `Render View` can create multiple types of selection (id- or frustum-based selections for selecting points and cells), while others like the `SpreadSheet View` and `Line Chart View` only support one type (id-based selections for points or cells).

6.2.1 Selecting in Render View

To create a selection in the `Render View`, you use the toolbar at the top of the view frame. You enter *selection mode* by clicking one of the selection buttons. The type of selection you are creating will depend on the button you clicked. Once in selection mode, the cursor will switch to cross-hair and you can click and drag to create a selection region. Once you release the mouse, ParaView will attempt to create a selection for any elements in the selection region and will go back to default interaction mode.

To create an id-based selection for cells visible in the view, use the button. For selecting visible points, use the button instead. Visible cells (and points) are only those cells (or points) that are currently rendered on the screen. Thus, elements that are occluded or are too small to be rendered on the screen will not be selected. If you want to select all data elements that intersect the view frustum formed by the selection rectangle you drew on the screen, use the button (or for points). In this case, all elements, visible or otherwise, that are within the 3D space defined by the selection frustum are selected.

While most selection modes allow you to define the selection region as a rectangle, (and for points) enables you to define the selection region as a closed polygon. However, this is limited to surface elements (i.e., no frustum-based selection).

Several of these buttons have hotkeys too, such as ⌷S⌷ for id-based visible cell selection, ⌷D⌷ for id-based visible points selection, ⌷F⌷ for frustum-based cell selection, and ⌷G⌷ for frustum-based point selection. If you notice, these are keys are right next to each other on the keyboard, starting with ⌷S⌷, and are in the same order as the toolbar buttons themselves.

(i) Did you know?

> *For id-based cell (or point) selection, you can expand the current selection by keeping the ⌷Ctrl⌷ (or ⌷⌘⌷) key pressed when clicking and dragging in selection mode. paraview will then try to expand the current selection by adding the newly selected elements to the existing one. This does not work, however, if the selection type (or the selected data) is different from the current selection. If so, the current selection will be cleared (as is the norm) and then the new selection will be created.*

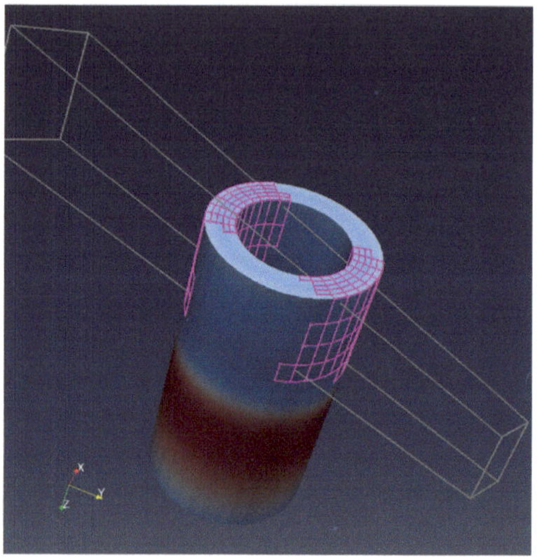

Figure 6.2: Result of a frustum cell selection on disk_out_ref.ex2 dataset showing the frustum used to identify selected cells. All cells that fall in that frustum or that intersect it, irrespective of whether they were visible from the view angle when the selection was made, are selected.

6.2.2 Selecting in SpreadSheet View

To create a selection in the SpreadSheet View, you simply click on the corresponding rows in the spreadsheet. You can use the Ctrl (or ⌘) and ⇧ keys to expand the selection. Based on which data attribute the view is currently showing, i.e., Point Data, Cell Data, or Row Data, the selection will select points, cells, or rows, respectively.

6.2.3 Selecting in Line Chart View

Line Chart View enables you to select the elements corresponding to the plotted data values. The selection interaction is similar to Render View. By default, you are in the interaction mode. You enter selection mode to create a selection by using the buttons in the view toolbar for creating a rectangular selection ⬚ or a polygonal selection ⬚. Once in selection mode, you can click and drag to define the selection region. The selection is created once you release the mouse press.

When a new selection is created, by default, it will clear any existing selection in the view. The selection modifier buttons in the view toolbar can be used to control whether a new selection adds to selected elements ⬚, removes points from the selected elements ⬚, or toggles it ⬚. These modifier buttons are mutually exclusive and modal, i.e., they remain pressed until you click to unpress them or until you press another modifier button.

6.3 Creating selections using the *Find Data* dialog

Views provide mechanisms to create selections interactively. Selections in chart views and SpreadSheet View can be used to select elements with certain data properties, rather than spatial locations (Figure 6.3). For a richer data-based selection for selecting elements matching certain criteria, you can use the Find Data mechanism in *paraview*.

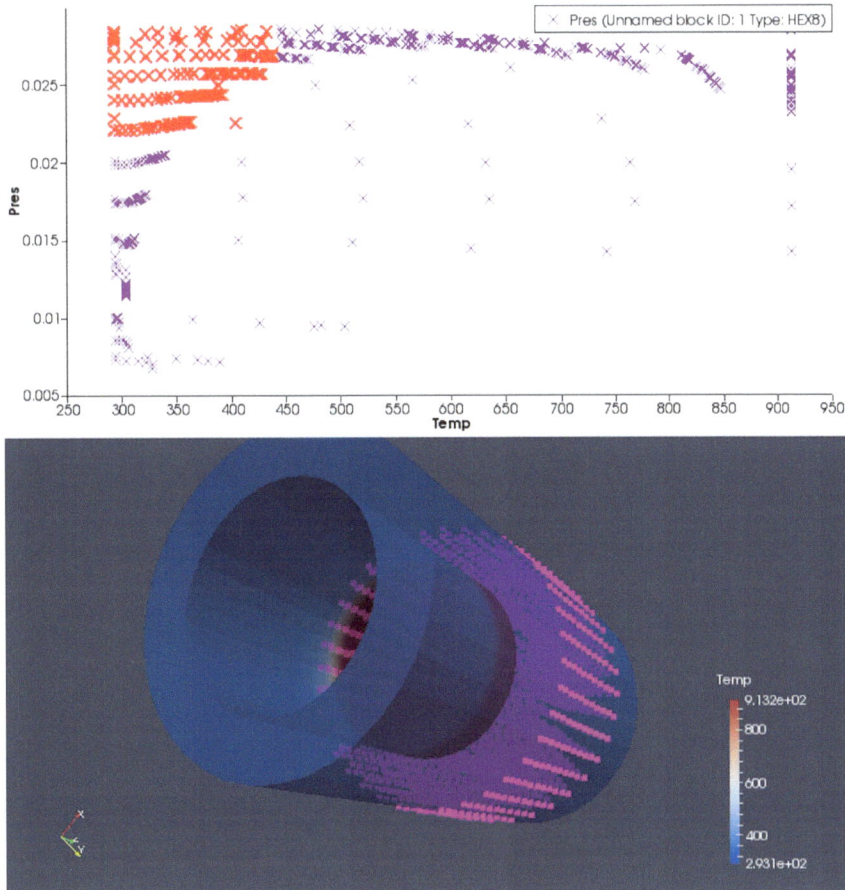

Figure 6.3: Selection in `Line Chart View` can be used to locate elements matching attribute criteria. In this visualization, by generating a scatter plot plotting Pres against Temp in the disk_out_ref.ex2 dataset by selecting the top-left corner of the `Line Chart View`, we can easily locate elements in the high Pres, low Temp regions in the dataset.

The `Find Data` dialog can be accessed from the `Edit` menu or by using the keyboard shortcut `V` or the ⬚ button on the `Main Controls` toolbar.

The `Find Data` dialog can be split into three components, reflecting how you would use this dialog. The `Create Selection` component includes UI elements to help you define the selection criteria or the query for defining the data elements to find. The `Current Selection` component shows the results from the most recent selection results in a spreadsheet. Finally, the `Selection Display Properties` component allows you to control how the selected elements are shown in the active view.

You can create selections or define queries in the `Find Data` dialog using the widgets under the `Create Selection` group. The UI is designed to be read left-to-right. Thus, you start by specifying which data attributes you are interested in selecting: cells, points, or rows. Then select which pipeline module is producing the dataset of interest. Once that's done, the next step is to specify the selection criteria. The left-most combo-box is used to select the array of interest. The available options reflect the data array currently available on the dataset. The next combo-box is used to select the operator. Options include the following:

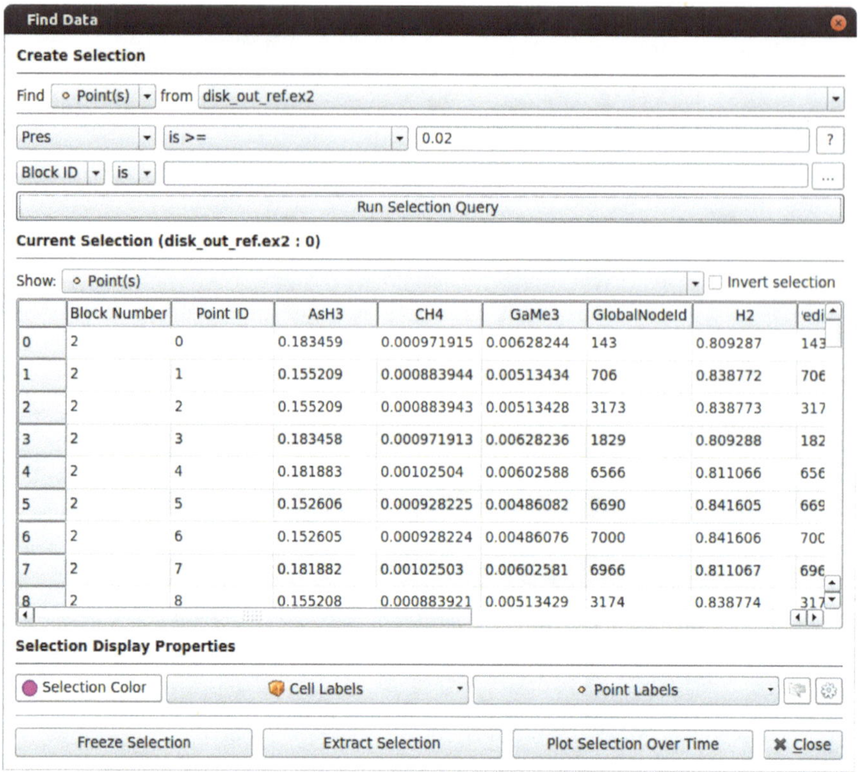

Figure 6.4: The `Find Data` dialog in *paraview* can be used to find data elements matching specific conditions. In this example, we are selecting all *Points* in *disk_out_ref.ex2* dataset where *Pres is* >= 0.02.

- `is` matches a single value
- `is between` matches a range of values specified by min and max
- `is one of` matches a list of comma separated values
- `is` >= matches all values greater than or equal to the specified value
- `is` <= matches all values lesser than or equal to the specified value
- `is min` matches the minimum value for the array for the current time step
- `is max` matches the maximum value for the array for the current time step
- `is` <= `mean` matches values lesser than or equal to the mean
- `is` >= `mean` matches values greater than or equal to the mean
- `is equal to mean with tolerance` matches values equal to the mean within the specified tolerance

Based on your selection of the operator, input widgets will be shown next to this combo-box, where you enter the corresponding values. For example, for `is between`, you enter the min and max values for defining the range in the two text entry widgets.

Once you are satisfied with the selection criteria, hit the `Run Selection Query` button to execute the query. On success, the `Current Selection` spreadsheet will update to show the selected elements. You switch which element attributes your are viewing in the spreadsheet using the `Show` combo-box. Additionally, you can invert the selection by checking `Invert selection`.

Similar to selecting in views, once you create a selection, any view showing the selected data will also highlight the selected elements, if possible. For example, the `Render View` will show a colored wireframe marking the selected elements, `SpreadSheet View` will highlight the rows, etc. The `Selection Display Properties` group allows you to change the selection that is shown in the active view. Currently, it is primarily designed for `Render View`. In the future, however, it could support changing selection attributes for other views as well. The available options allow you select the color to use to show the selected elements, as well as the data attributes to use to label the cells/points. For finer control on the label formatting, color, font, etc., use the ⚙ button. That will pop up the `Advanced Selection Display Properties` dialog (Figure 6.5).

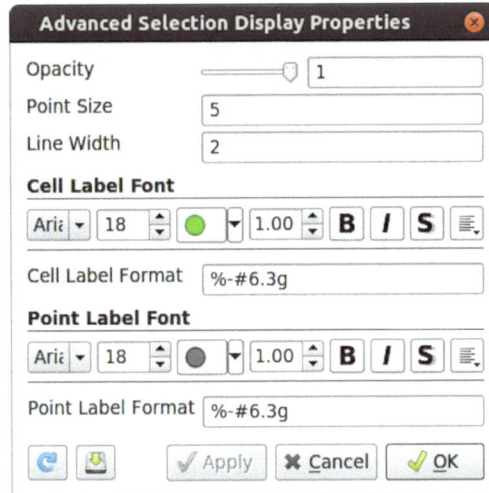

Figure 6.5: `Advanced Selection Display Properties` dialog for controlling selection labelling parameters.

ℹ️ Did you know?

Besides creating new selections, the `Find Data` *dialog can also be used to inspect the current selection made from outside the dialog. For example, if you select elements in the* `Render View` *using the options described in Section 6.2.1, the* `Current Selection` *component in the* `Find Data` *dialog will indeed update to reflect the newly selected elements. Furthermore, you can change its display properties and extract this selection using the extraction buttons (which we will cover in Section 6.5).*

6.4 Displaying selections

The `Find Data` dialog provides easy access to changing the `Selection Display Properties` for the selection in the active view. The same functionality can also be accessed using the `Selection Display Inspector` panel, which is a dockable panel that can be shown/hidden using the `View ⟩ Selection Display Inspector` menu. Currently, selection display properties apply to `Render Views` alone. In the future, this will be expanded to other view types, as appropriate.

The `Current Selection` section in the `Find Data` dialog shows the selected elements in a spreadsheet view. You can also make a regular `SpreadSheet View` do the same by checking the ⬚ button in the view toolbar to show only selected elements.

6.5 Extracting selections

All the types of selections created through mechanisms discussed so far are transient and primarily used for highlighting data. If you want to do further operations on the selected subset, such as extract the selected elements and then save the result out as a new dataset or apply other filters only on the selected elements, then you need to use one of the extract selection filters. The `Extract Selection` and `Plot Selection Over Time` filters fall in this category of filters.

6.5.1 Extract selection

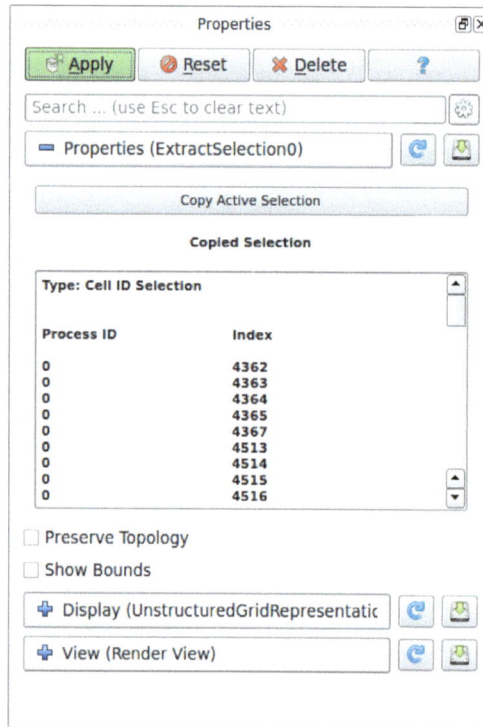

Figure 6.6: `Properties` panel showing the properties for the `Extract Selection` filter.

The `Extract Selection` filter is used to extract the selected elements as a new dataset for further filtering. There are multiple ways of creating this filter. You can use the conventional method for creating filters, i.e., using the Filters menu. When the filter is created, if there is any active selection, the filter will automatically copy that selection for convenience. Another way to extract the active selection is using the `Extract Selection` button in the `Find Data` dialog (Figure 6.4).

The `Properties` panel shows what defines the selection. You can update the selection by making a new active selection using any of the mechanisms described earlier in this Chapter and then clicking on the `Copy Active Selection` button on the `Properties` panel for the `Extract Selection` filter.

By default, the filter is set up to extract the selected elements alone. This filter also supports passing the entire input dataset through by simply marking which elements are selected. For that, check the `Preserve Topology` check box on the `Properties` panel.

6.5.2   Plot selection over time

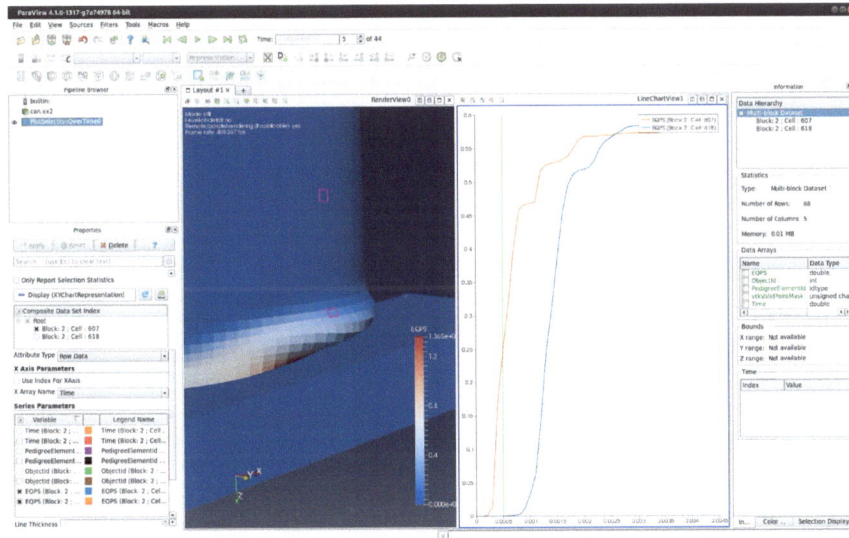

Figure 6.7: `Plot Selection Over Time` in action in *paraview*. The filter provides a convenient way to plot changes in attributes over time for the selected set of cells or for points in a temporal dataset.

`Plot Selection Over Time` is similar to `Extract Selection` in the sense that it too extracts the selected elements from the input dataset. However, instead of simply extracting the result, the goal here is to plot attributes at the selected elements over time.

Figure 6.7 shows an example use of this filter. In this case, we wanted to see how the strain (or *EQPS*) cell attribute changes over time for two specific cells that we selected in the `Render View` using the view-based selection mechanism. The selected cells are the highlighted elements in the left view. After having selected the cells, we create the `Plot Selection Over Time` filter using the `Filters` 〉 `Data Analysis` menu. (You could also use the ⌾▨ from the `Data Analysis` toolbar.) Similar to the `Extract Selection` filter, when this filter is created, it copies the active selection. You can change it afterwards using the `Copy Active Selection` button on the filter's `Properties` panel. On hitting `Apply`, *paraview* will show a visualization similar to the one shown here.

Instead of using the view for defining the selection, you could have used the `Find Data` dialog. In that case, instead of being able to plot each element over time, you will be plotting summaries for the selected subset over time. This is essential since the selected subset can have a varying number of elements over time. The summaries include quantities like min, max, and median of available variables. You can make the filter always produce these statics alone (even when the selection is created by selecting specific elements in a view) by checking the `Only Report Selection Statistics` property on the `Properties` panel for the `Plot Selection Over Time` filter.

6.6   Freezing selections

When extracting selections, you can use views or the `Find Data` dialog to define the selection. Since the extraction filters are indeed like any other filters in ParaView, they are re-executed any time the input dataset changes, properties on the filter change, or the current time changes. Every time the filter re-executes, it performs the *selection* and *extraction* operations. Thus, if you created the selection using `Render View` to create an id-based selection, the filter will identify which of the elements are of the requested ids and then pass those. For frustum-based selection, it will determine what elements fall within the frustum and extract those. Similarly, with query-based selections created using the `Find Data` dialog, the query is re-evaluated. This can result in the selection of different elements with changes in timestep. For example, if you are selecting the cells where the strain is maximum, that cell(s) will potentially be different for each time step. Suppose you want to plot the changes in a cell that has maximum strain at the last time step – how can we do that? The answer is using the `Freeze Selection` button on the `Find Data` dialog. What that does is convert any type of selection (frustum, query-based) to an id-based selection matching the currently selected element ids. Now you can use this frozen, id-based selection for `Extract Selection` or `Plot Selection Over Time`.

ANIMATION

In ParaView, you can create animations by recording a series of keyframes. At each keyframe, you set values for the properties of the readers, sources, and filters that make up the visualization pipeline, as well as the position and orientation of the camera. Once you have chosen the parameters, you can play through the animation. When you play the animation, you can cache the geometric output of the visualization pipeline in memory. When you replay the animation, playback will be much faster because very little computation must be done to generate the images. Also, the results of the animation can be saved to image files (one image per animation frame) or to a movie file. The geometry rendered at each frame can also be saved in ParaView's PVD file format, which can be loaded back into ParaView as a time varying data set.

7.1 Animation View.

`Animation View` is the user interface used to create animations by adding keyframes. It is modeled similar to popular animation and keyframe editing applications with the ability to create tracks for animating multiple parameters. The `Animation View` is accessible from the View menu.

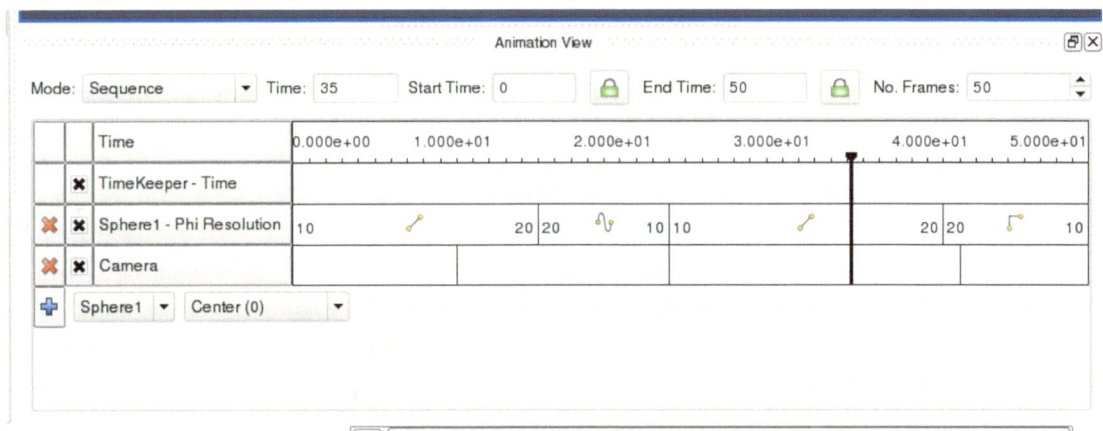

Figure 7.1: Animation View.

As seen in Figure 7.1, this view is presented as a table. Above the table are the controls that administers how time progresses in the animation. These were discussed previously. Within the table, the tracks of the animation appear as rows, and animation time is presented as increasing from left-to-right. The first row in the table, simply labeled `Time`, shows the total span of time that the animation can cover. The current displayed time is indicated both in the Time field at the top and with a thick, vertical, draggable line within the table.

Along the left side of the `Animation View` is an expandable list of the names of the animation tracks (i.e., a particular object and property to animate). You choose a data source and then a particular property of the data source in the bottom row. To create an animation track with keyframes for that property, click the + on the left-hand side; this will create a new track. In the figure, tracks already exist for *SphereSource1*'s `Phi Resolution` property and for the camera's position. To delete a track, press the X button. You can temporarily disable a track by unchecking the check box on the right of the track. To enter values for the property, double-click within the white area to the right of the track name. This will bring up the Animation Keyframes dialog. Double-clicking in the camera entry brings up a dialog like the one in Figure 7.2.

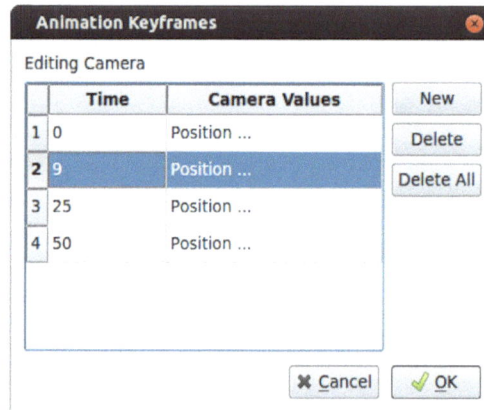

Figure 7.2: Editing the camera track.

From the `Animation Keyframes` dialog, you can press New to create new keyframes. You can also press `Delete` or `Delete All` to delete some or all of the keyframes. Clicking `New` will add a new row to the table. In any row, you can click within the `Time` column to choose a particular time for the keyframe, and you can click in the right-hand column to enter values for the parameter. The exact user interface components that let you set values for the property at the keyframe time vary. When available, you can change the interpolation between two keyframes by double-clicking on the central interpolation column.

Within the tracks of the `Animation View`, the place in time where each keyframe occurs is shown as a vertical line. The values chosen for the property at that time and the interpolation function used between that value and the next are shown as text, when appropriate. In the previous figure, for example, the sphere resolution begins at 10 and then changes to 20, varying by linear interpolation between them. The camera values are too lengthy to show as text so they are not displayed in the track, but we can easily see that there are four keyframes spaced throughout the animation. The vertical lines in the tracks themselves may be dragged, so you can easily adjust the time at which each keyframe occurs.

7.2 Animation View header

The `Animation View` has a header-bar that lets you control some properties of the animation itself, as you can see in Figure 7.3.

`Mode` controls the animation playback mode. ParaView supports three modes for playing animation. In `Sequence` mode, the animation is played as a sequence of images (or frames) generated one after the other and rendered in immediate succession. The number of frames is controlled by the `No. Frames` spinbox at the end of the header. Note that the frames are rendered as fast as possible. Thus, the viewing frame rate depends on the time needed to generate and render each frame.

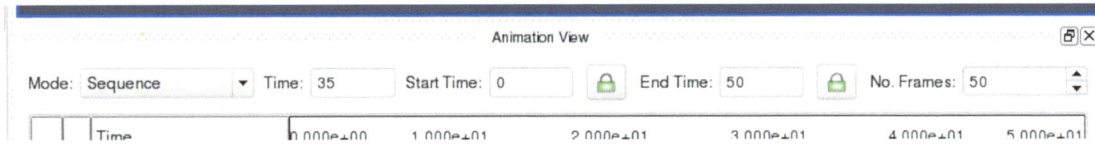

Figure 7.3: Animation View Header.

In `Real Time` mode, the `Duration` spinbox (replacing the `No. Frames` spinbox) indicates the time in seconds over which the entire animation should run. Each frame is rendered using the current wall clock time in seconds, relative to the start time. The animation runs for nearly the number of seconds specified by the `Duration (secs)` spinbox. In turn, the number of frames actually generated (or rendered) depends on the time to generate (or render) each frame.

In `Snap To TimeSteps` mode, the number of frames in the animation is determined by the number of time values in the data set being animated. This is the animation mode used for ParaView's default animations: playing through the time values in a data set one after the other. Default animations are created by ParaView when a data set with time values is loaded; no action is required by the user to create the animation. Note that using this mode when no time-varying data is loaded will result in no animation at all.

In `Sequence` mode, the final item in the header is the `No. Frames` spinbox. This spinbox lets you pick the total number of frames for the animation. Similarly, in `Real Time` mode, the final line lets you choose the duration of the animation. In `Snap To TimeSteps` mode, the total number of frames is dictated by the data set and, therefore, the spinbox is disabled.

The `Time` entry-box shows the current animation time, which is the same as shown by a vertical marker in this view. You can change the current animation time by either entering a value in this box, if available, or by dragging the vertical marker. The `Start Time` and `End Time` entry-boxes display the start and end times for the animation. By default, when you load time varying data sets, the start and end times are automatically adjusted to cover the entire time range present in the data. The lock check-buttons to the right of the `Start Time` and `End Time` widgets will prevent this from happening, so that you can ensure that your animation covers a particular time domain of your choosing.

7.3 Animating time-varying data

When you load time-varying data, ParaView automatically creates a default animation that allows you to play through the temporal domain of the data without manually creating an animation to do so. With the `Animation View`, you can uncouple the data time from the animation time so that you can create keyframes that manipulate the data time during animation as well.

If you double-click in the `TimeKeeper Time` track, the `Animation Keyframes` dialog, an example of which is shown in Figure 7.4, appears. In this dialog, you can make data time progress in three fundamentally different ways. If the `Animation Time` radio-button is selected, the data time will be tied to and scaled with the animation time so that, as the animation progresses, you will see the data evolve naturally. If you want to ignore the time varying nature of the data, you can select `Constant Time` instead. In this case, you choose a particular time value at which the data will be displayed for the duration of the animation. Finally, you can select the `Variable Time` radio-button to have full control over data time and to control it as you do any other animatable property in the visualization pipeline. In the example shown in Figure 7.4, time is made to progress forward for the first 15 frames of the animation, backward for the next 30, and forward for the final 15.

Figure 7.4: Controlling Data Time with keyframes.

7.4 Playing an animation

Once you have designed your animation, you can play through it with the VCR controls toolbar seen in Figure 7.5.

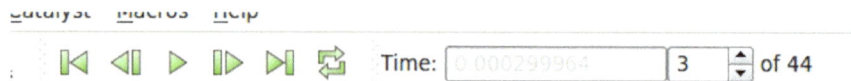

Figure 7.5: VCR Controls and Current Time Controls toolbars in *paraview*.

7.5 Animating the camera

Just like you can change parameters on sources and filters in an animation, you can also change the camera parameters. As seen in Figure 7.6, you can add animation tracks to animate the camera for all the 3D render views in the setup separately. To add a camera animation track for a view, with the view selected, click on the + button after choosing Camera from the first drop-down menu. The second drop-down list allows you to choose how to animate the camera. There are three possible options, each of which provides different mechanisms to specify the keyframes. It's not possible to change the mode after the animation track has been added, but you can simply delete the track and create a new one.

7.5.1 Interpolate camera locations

In this mode, you specify camera position, focal point, view angle, and up direction at each keyframe. The animation player interpolates between these specified locations. As with other parameters, to edit the keyframes, double-click on the track. It is also possible to capture the current location as a keyframe by using the Use Current button.

It can be quite challenging to add keyframes correctly and frequently to ensure that the animation results in a smooth visualization using this mode.

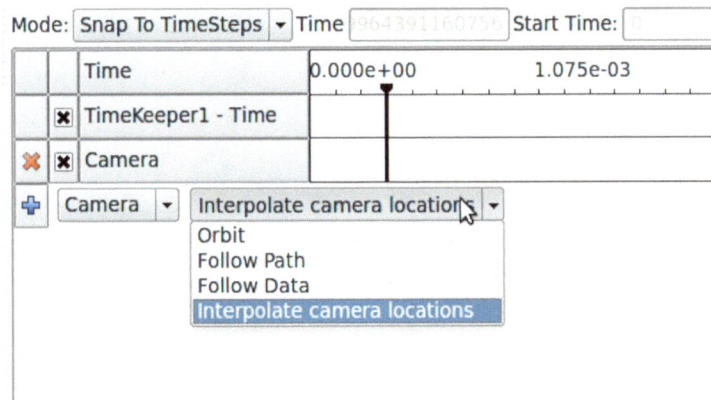

Figure 7.6: Add camera track.

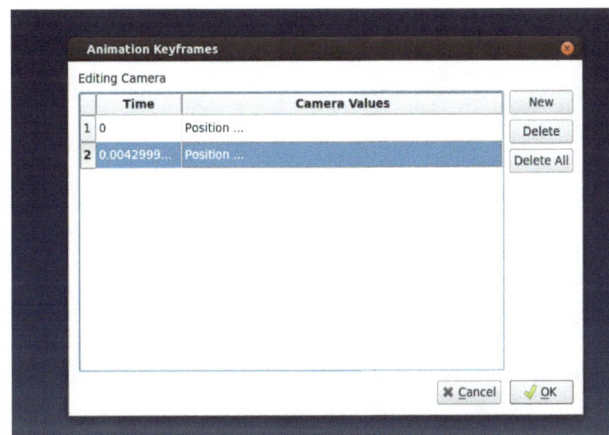

Figure 7.7: Setting animation parameters.

7.5.2 Orbit

This mode makes it possible to quickly create a camera animation in which the camera revolves around objects of interest. Before adding the `Camera` track, select the objects in the pipeline browser that you want to revolve around; then choose `Orbit` from the `Camera` combo-box in the `Animation View`, and hit +. This will pop up a dialog where you can edit the orbit parameters such as the center of revolution, the normal for the plane of revolution, and the origin (i.e., a point on the plane where the revolution begins). By default, the `Center` is the center of the bounds of the selected objects, the `Normal` is the current up direction used by the camera, while the origin is the current camera position.

7.5.3 Follow path

In this mode, you get the opportunity to specify the path taken by the camera position and the camera focal point. By default, the path is set up to orbit around the selected objects. You can then edit the keyframe to change the paths.

Figure 7.9 shows the dialog for editing these paths for a keyframe. When Camera Position or Camera Focus is selected, a widget is shown in the 3D view that can be used to set the path. Use $\boxed{Ctrl}$+$\boxed{Left Click}$ to insert new control points, and $\boxed{⇧}$+

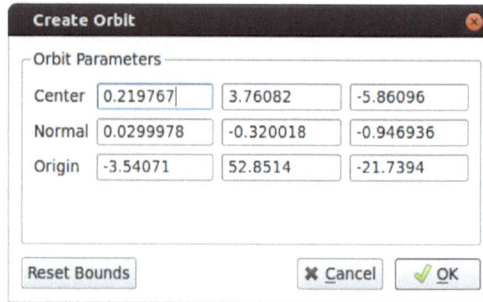

Figure 7.8: Creating a camera orbit.

Left Click to remove control points. You can also toggle when the path should be closed or not.

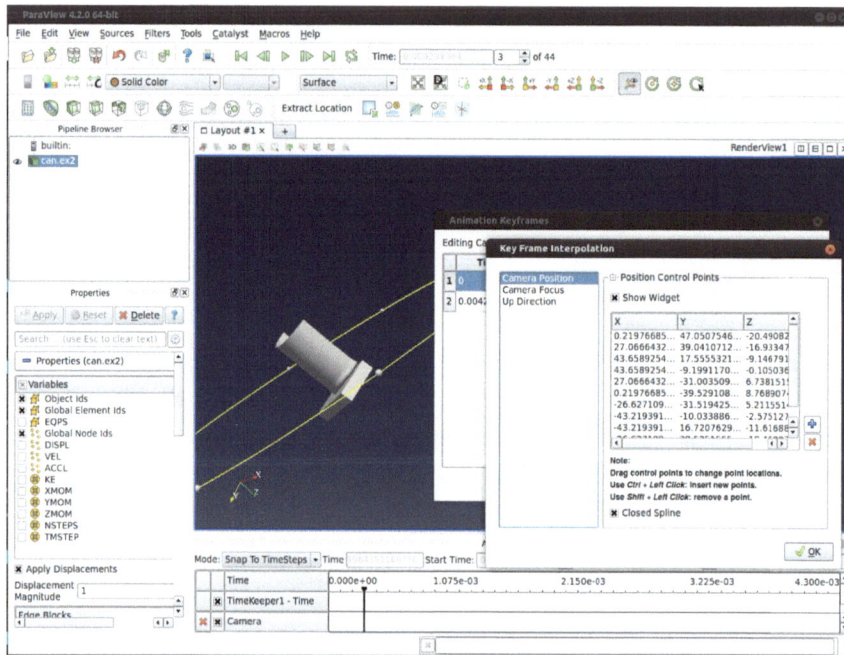

Figure 7.9: Creating a camera path.

SAVING RESULTS

In this chapter, we will introduce various ways of saving visualization results in ParaView. Results generated throughout the visualization process not only include the images and the rendering results, but also include the datasets generated by filters, the scene representations that will be imported into other rendering applications, and the movies generated from animations.

8.1   Saving datasets

You can save the dataset produced by any pipeline module in ParaView, including sources, readers, and filters. To save the dataset in *paraview*, begin by selecting the pipeline module in the `Pipeline` browser to make it the active source. For modules with multiple output ports, select the output port producing the dataset of interest. To save the dataset, use the `File` ⟩ `Save Data` menu or the 📂 button in the `Main Controls` toolbar. You can also use the keyboard shortcut `Ctrl` + `S` (or `⌘` + `S`). The `Save File` dialog (Figure 8.1) will allow you to select the filename and the file format. The available list of file formats depends on the type of the dataset you are trying to save.

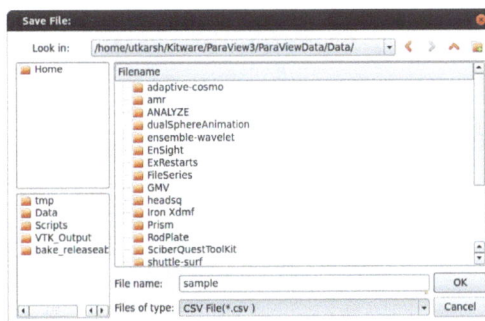

Figure 8.1: `Save File` dialog in *paraview*.

On accepting a filename and file format to use, *paraview* may show the `Configure Writer` dialog (Figure 8.2). This dialog allows you to further customize the writing process. The properties shown in this dialog depend on the selected file format and range from enabling you to `Write All Time Steps`, to selecting the attributes to write in the output file.

In *pvpython* too, you can save the datasets as follows:

```
1
2   # Saving the data using the default properties for
```

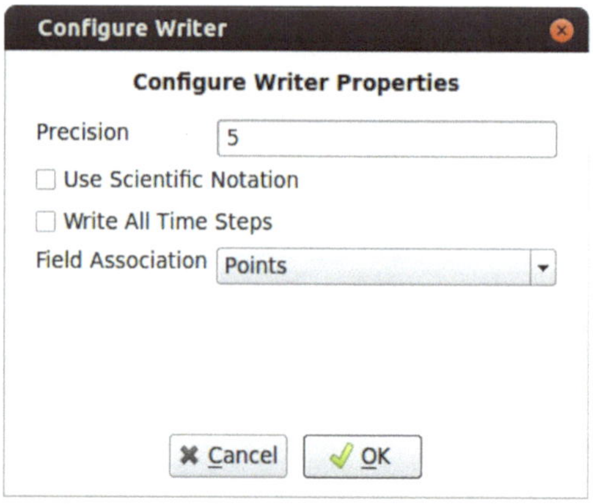

Figure 8.2: `Configure Writer` dialog in *paraview* shown when saving a dataset as a csv file.

```
 3   # the used writer, if any.
 4   >>> SaveData("sample.csv", source)
 5
 6   # the second argument is optional, and refers to the pipeline module
 7   # to write the data from. If none is specified the active source is used.
 8
 9   # To pass parameters to configure the writer
10   >>> SaveData("sample.csv", source,
11               Precision=2,
12               FieldAssociation='Cells')
```

pvpython will pick a writer based on the file extension and the dataset type selected for writing, similar to what it does in *paraview*. Admittedly, it can be tricky to figure out what options are available for the writer. The best way is to use the *Python tracing* capabilities in *paraview* and to use the generated sample script as a reference (Section 1.6.2). Make sure you use a similar type of dataset and the same file format as you want to use in your Python script, when tracing, to avoid runtime issues.

8.2 Saving rendered results

Views that render results (this includes almost all of the views, except `SpreadSheet View`) support saving images (or screenshots) in one of the standard image formats (png, jpeg, tiff, bmp, ppm). Certain views also support exportings the results in several formats such as pdf, x3d, and vrml.

8.2.1 Saving screenshots

To save the render image from a view in *paraview*, use the File ⟩ Save Screenshot menu option. This will pop up the `Save Screenshot Options` dialog (Figure 8.3). This dialog allows you to select various image parameters, such as image resolution and image quality (which depends on the file format chosen). The dialog also provides an option to change the color palette to use to save the image using `Override Color Palette`.

By default, *paraview* will save rendered results from the active view. Optionally, you can save an image comprising of all the views layed out exactly as on the screen by unchecking the `Save only selected view` button.

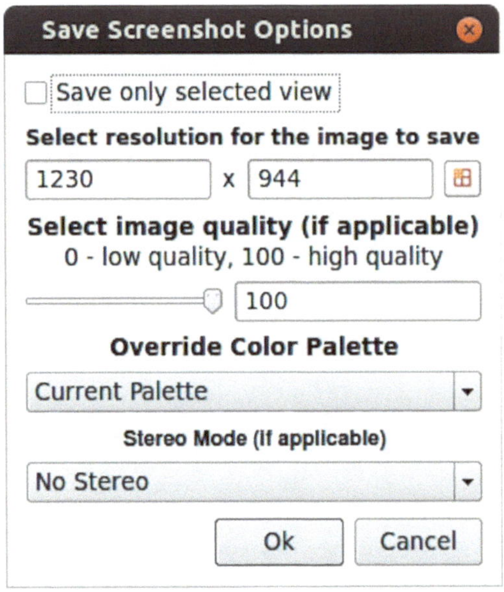

Figure 8.3: The `Save Screenshot Options` dialog, which is used to customize saving screenshots in *paraview*

When saving mutliple views, you can customize the border to use between views, as well as the color to use for that border, from the `General` tab in `Settings` dialog (Edit ⟩ Settings), as shown in the Figure 8.4

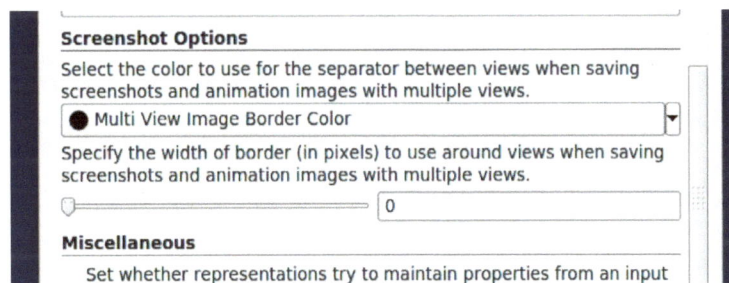

Figure 8.4: `Screenshot Options` in the `Settings` dialog allow you to set the size in pixels and the color for the border to use to separate views with saving multiple views in a screenshot.

ⓘ Did you know?

You can save high-resolution images at a resolution higher than your monitor by specifying a higher resolution in the `Save Screenshot Options` dialog. paraview will use tiling and magnification internally to produce an image of the requested size.

Saving a screenshot is also possible in *paraview*.

```
1  # Save a screenshot from a specific view.
2  >>> myview = GetActiveView()
3  >>> SaveScreenshot("sample.png", view=myview)
```

```
4
5   # To specify magnification and quality, use the following form:
6   >>> SaveScreenshot("sample2X.png", view=myview, magnification=2, quality=100)
7
8   # You can skip the 'view' parameter if you simply want to save the active view.
9   >>> SaveScreenshot("sample.png")
10
11  # To save multiple views, you can use the following form:
12
13  # Get the layout in which a specific view is placed
14  # if 'myview' is not provided, active view will be used.
15  >>> layout = GetLayout(myview)
16
17  >>> SaveScreenshot("multiview.png", layout=layout)
```

As always, you can use *Python tracing* in *paraview* to trace the exact form of the method to use to save a specific screenshot image.

8.2.2   Exporting scenes

When available, you can export a visualization in a view in several of the supported formats using the `File` `Export View` menu option in *paraview*. For a `Render View` (or similar), the available formats include EPS, PDF, PS, SVG, POV, VRML, WebGL, X3D, and X3DB. On selecting a file as which to export, *paraview* may pop up an `Export Options` dialog that allows you to set up parameters for the exporter, similar to saving datasets (Section 8.1).

In addition, from *paraview*, exporting takes the following form (again, just use *Python trace* to figure out the proper form – that's the easiest way).

```
1   >>> myview = GetActiveView()
2   >>> ExportView('/tmp/sample.svg', view=myview,
3                  Plottitle='ParaView GL2PS Export',
4                  Compressoutputfile=1)
5   # the arguments after 'view' depend on the exporter selected.
```

8.3   Saving animation

In *paraview*, you use the `File` `Save Animation` menu option to save the animation results as a movie or as a series of images. This will pop up the `Animation Settings Dialog`. Here, you can pick the `Frame Rate` in frames-per-second for the generated movie (if applicable for the chosen file format) and the total `Number Of Frames` to render. The `Animation Duration (sec)` field tells you how long the movie file would play given the specified settings. Animation always saves out all the views currently visible in *paraview*. Thus, if you maximize a view, the animation will only include the maximized view. When saving multiple views, the `Screenshot Options` in the `Settings` (Figure 8.4) are used to add borders between views. `Frame range` can be used to specify the range of frame over which to animate, thus allowing you to skip parts of the total animation in the saved file(s).

The available file formats include avi and ogg (when available) movie formats, as well as image formats such png, jpg, and tif. If saving as images, ParaView will generate a series of image files sequentially numbered using the frame number as a suffix to the specified filename.

In *paraview*, you can save an animation using `WriteAnimation`.

```
1   >>> WriteAnimation('animation.avi', Magnification=1, FrameRate=15.0, Compression=True
        )
```

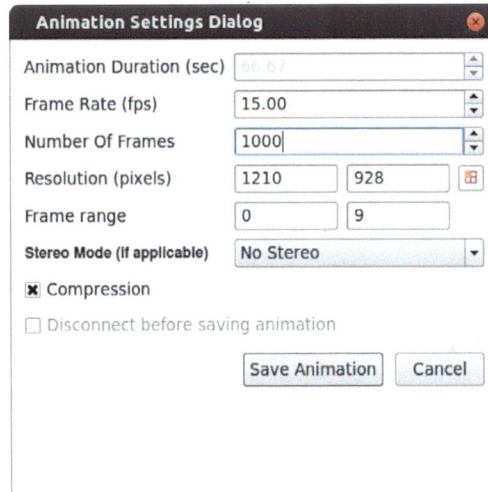

Figure 8.5: The `Animation Settings Dialog` in *paraview*, which is used to customize saving of animation files.

8.4 Saving state

Besides saving the results produced by your visualization setup, you can save the state of the visualization pipeline itself, including all the pipeline modules, views, their layout, and their properties. This is referred to as the application state or, just, state. In *paraview*, you can save the state using the [File ⟩ Save State...] menu option. Conversely, to load a saved state file, you can use [File ⟩ Load State...].

There are two types of state files that you can save in *paraview*: *ParaView state file (*.pvsm)* and *Python state file (*.py)*. The PVSM files are XML-based text files that are human and machine readable, although not necessarily a novice user human friendly. However, if you don't plan to read and make sense of the state files, PVSM is the most robust and reliable way to save the application state. For those who want to save the state and then modify it manually, using Python state files may be better, as using Python trace simply traces the actions that you perform in the UI as a Python script. Python state files, on the other hand, save the entire current state of the application as a Python script that you can use in *paraview* or the `Python Shell`.

To load a PVSM file, you use the [File ⟩ Load State...] menu. Note that loading a state file will affect the current visualization state. To load the Python state file in *paraview*, you will need to use the `Python Shell`, which is accessible from the [Tools] menu.

You can save/load the PVSM state file in *pvpython* as follows:

```
1  >>> from paraview.simple import *
2
3  # Save the PVSM state file. Currently, this doesn't support
4  # saving Python state files.
5  >>> SaveState("sample.pvsm")
6
7  # To load a PVSM state file.
8  >>> LoadState("sample.pvsm")
```

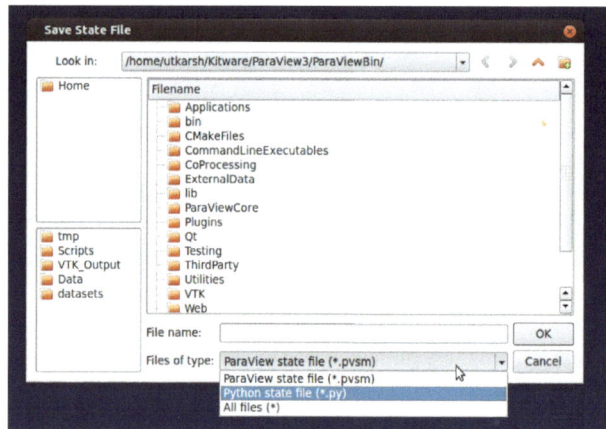

Figure 8.6: The `Save State File` dialog in *paraview*.

Part II

Reference Manual

PROPERTIES PANEL

The Properties panel is perhaps the most often used panel in *paraview*. This is the panel you would use to change properties on modules in the visualization pipeline, including sources and filters, to control how they are displayed in views using the Display properties, and to customize the view itself. In this chapter, we take a closer look at the Properties panel to understand how it works.

9.1 Anatomy of the Properties panel

Before we start dissecting the Properties, remember that the Properties panel works on *active* objects, i.e., it shows the properties for the active source and active view, as well as the display properties, if any, for active source in the active view.

9.1.1 Buttons

Figure 9.1 shows the various parts of the Properties panel. At the top is the group of buttons that let you accept, reject your changes to the panel or Delete the active source.

> **Did you know?**
> *You can delete multiple sources by selecting them using the* `Ctrl` *(or* `⌘` *) key when selecting in the* Pipeline Browser *and then clicking on the* Delete *button. Sometimes, the* Delete *button may be disabled. That happens when the selected source(s) have other filters connected to them. You will need to delete those filters first.*

9.1.2 Search box

The Search box allows you to search for a property by using the name or the label for the property. Simply start typing text in the Search box, and the panel will update to show widgets for the properties matching the text.

The Properties panel has two modes that control the verbosity of the panel: default and advanced. In the default mode, a smaller subset of the available properties is shown. These are generally the frequently used properties for the pipeline modules. In advanced mode, you can see all the available properties. You can toggle between default and advanced modes using the ⚙ button next the Search box.

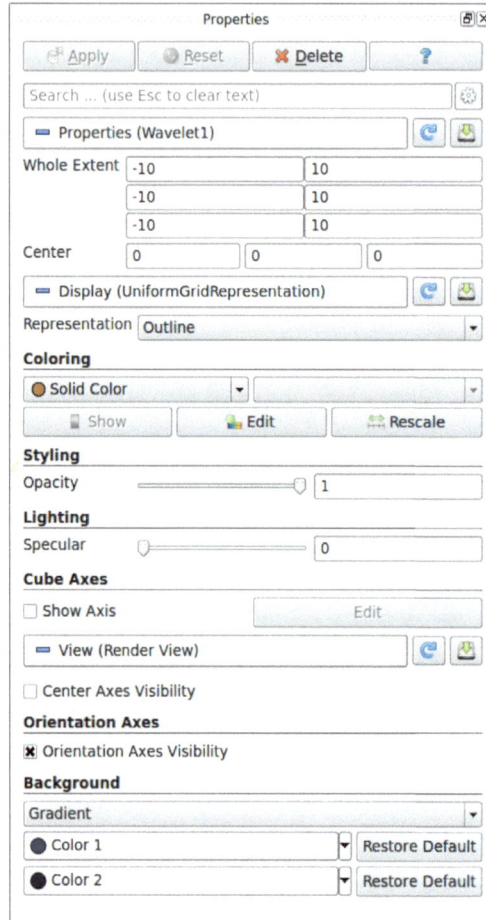

Figure 9.1: `Properties` Panel in *paraview*

When you start searching for a property by typing text in the `Search` box, irrespective of the current mode of the panel (i.e., default or advanced), all properties that match the search text will be shown.

ℹ️ Did you know?

The `Search` box is a recurring widget in paraview. Several other panels and dialog boxes, including the `Settings` dialog and the `Color Map Editor`, show a similar widget. Its behavior is also exactly the same as in the case of the `Properties` panel. Don't forget that the ⚙ button can be used to toggle between default and advanced modes.

9.1.3 Properties

The `Properties`, `Display`, and `View` sections in the panel show widgets for properties on the active source, its display properties in the active view, and the properties for the active view, respectively. You can collapse/expand each of these sections by clicking on the section name. The buttons next to the next header allow you to customize the default values used for those properties. Refer to Chapter 10 to learn more about customizing default property values.

9.2 Customizing the layout

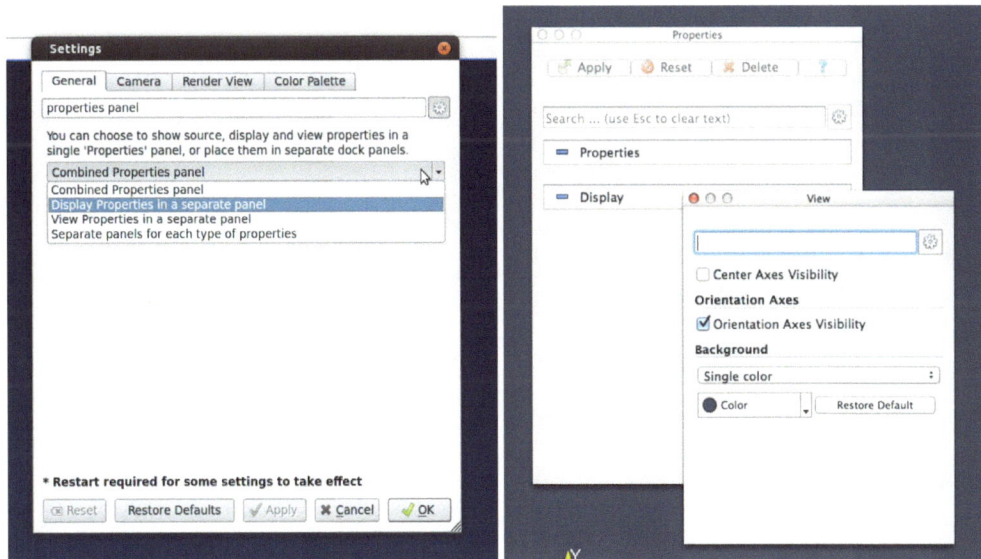

Figure 9.2: Options for customizing the `Properties` panel layout using the `Settings` (left). View properties in a separate dock panel (right).

The `Properties` panel, by default, is set up to show the source, display, and view properties on the same panel. You may, however, prefer to have each of these sections in a separate dockable panel. You can indeed do so using the `Settings` dialog accessible from the Edit ⟩ Settings menu.

On the `General` tab search of the `properties panel` using the `Search` box, you should see the setting that lets you pick whether to combine all the sections in one (default), to separate out either the `Display` or View sections in a panel, or to create separate panels for each of the sections. You will need to restart *paraview* for this change to take effect. Also, since the `Apply` and `Reset` buttons only apply to the `Properties` section, they will only be shown in the dock panel that houses it.

CUSTOMIZING DEFAULTS

The chapter describes how to specify custom default settings for the properties of sources, readers, filters, representations, and views. This can be used to specify, for example, the default background color for new views, whether a gradient background should be used, the resolution of a sphere source, which data arrays to load from a particular file format, and the default setting for almost any other object property.

The same custom defaults are used across all the ParaView executables. This means that custom defaults specified in the *paraview* executable are also used as defaults in *pvpython* and *pvbatch*, which makes it easier to set up a visualization with *paraview* and use *pvpython* or *pvbatch* to generate an animation from time-series data, for example.

10.1   Customizing defaults for properties

The Properties panel in *paraview* has three sections, Properties, Display, and View. Each section has two buttons. These buttons are circled in red in Figure 10.1. The button with the disk icon is used to save the current property values in that section that have been applied with the Apply button. Property values that have been changed but not applied with the Apply button will not be saved as custom default settings.

The button with the circular arrow (or reload icon) is used to restore any custom property settings for the object to ParaView's application defaults. Once you save the current property settings as defaults, those values will be treated as the defaults from then on until you change them to another value or reset them. The saved defaults are written to a configuration file so that they are available when you close and launch ParaView again.

You can undo your changes to the default property values by clicking on the reload button. This will reset the current view property values to *paraview*'s application defaults. To fully restore *paraview*'s default values, you need to click the save button again. If you don't, the restored default values will be applied only to the current object, and new instances of that object will have the custom default values that were saved the last time you clicked the save button.

10.2   Example: specifying a custom background color

Suppose you want to change the default background color in the Render View. To do this, scroll down to the View section of the Properties panel and click on the combo box that shows the current background color. Select a new color, and click OK. Next, scroll up to the View (Render View) section header and click on the disk button to the right of the header. This will save the new background color as the default background color for new views. To see this, click on the + sign next to the tab above the 3D view to create a new layout. Click on the Render View button. A new render view will be created with the custom background color you just saved as default.

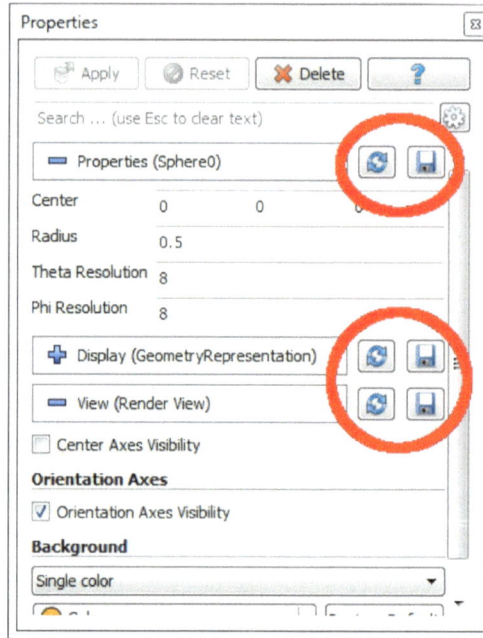

Figure 10.1: Buttons for saving and restoring default property values in the `Properties` panel.

10.3 Configuring default settings with JSON

Custom default settings are stored in a text file in the JavaScript Object Notation (JSON) format. We recommend to use the user interface in *paraview* to set most default values, but it is possible to set them by editing the JSON settings file directly. It is always a good idea to make a backup copy of a settings file prior to manual editing.

The ParaView executables read from and write to a file named `ParaView-UserSettings.json`, which is located in your home directory on your computer. On Windows, this file is located at `%APPDATA%/ParaView/ParaView-UserSettings.json`, where the `APPDATA` environment variable is usually something like `C:/Users/USERNAME/AppData/Roaming`, where `USERNAME` is your login name. On Unix-like systems, it is located under `~/.config/ParaView/ParaView-UserSettings.json`. This file will exist if you have made any default settings changes through the user interface in the *paraview* executable. Once set, these default settings will be available in subsequent versions of ParaView.

A simple example of a file that specifies custom default settings is shown below:

```
 1  {
 2    "sources" : {
 3      "SphereSource" : {
 4        "Radius" : 3.5,
 5        "ThetaResolution" : 32
 6      },
 7      "CylinderSource" : {
 8        "Radius" : 2
 9      }
10    },
11    "views" : {
12      "RenderView" : {
```

```
13        "Background" : [0.0, 0.0, 0.0]
14      }
15    }
16 }
```

Note the hierarchical organization of the file. The first level of the hierarchy specifies the group to which the object whose settings are being specified refers ("sources" in this example). The second level names the object whose settings are being specified. Finally, the third level specifies the custom default settings themselves. Note that default values can be set to literal numbers, strings, or arrays (denoted by comma-separated literals in square brackets).

The names of groups and objects come from the XML proxy definition files in ParaView's source code in the directory ParaView/ParaViewCore/ServerManager/SMApplication/Resources. The group name is defined by the name attribute in a ProxyGroup element. The object name comes from the name attribute in the Proxy element (or elements of vtkSMProxy subclasses). The property names come from the name attribute in the *Property XML elements for the object.

> **ⓘ Did you know?**
>
> *The application-wide settings available in paraview through the* Edit ⟩ Settings *menu are also saved to this user settings file. Hence, if you have changed the application settings, you will see some entries under a group named "settings".*

10.4 Configuring site-wide default settings

In addition to individual custom default settings, ParaView offers a way to specify site-wide custom default settings for a ParaView installation. These site-wide custom defaults must be defined in a JSON file with the same structure as the user settings file. In fact, one way to create a site settings file is to set the custom defaults desired in *paraview*, close the program, and then copy the user settings file to the site settings file. The site settings file must be named ParaView-SiteSettings.json.

The ParaView executables will search for the site settings file in several locations. If you installed ParaView in the directory INSTALL, then the ParaView executables will search for the site settings file in these directories in the specified order:

- INSTALL/share/paraview-X.Y

- INSTALL/lib

- INSTALL

- INSTALL/..

where X is ParaView's major version number and Y is the minor version number. ParaView executables will search these directories in the given order, reading in the first ParaView-SiteSettings.json file it finds. The conventional location for this kind of configuration file is in the share directory (the first directory searched), so we recommend placing the site settings file there.

Custom defaults in the user settings file take precedence over custom defaults in the site settings. If the same default is specified in both the ParaView-SiteSettings.json file and ParaView-UserSettings.json file in a user's directory, the default specified in the ParaView-UserSettings.json file will be used. This is true for both object property settings and application-settings set through the Edit ⟩ Settings menu.

To aid in debugging problems with the site settings file location, you can define an evironment variable named `PV_SETTINGS_DEBUG` to something other than an empty string. This will turn on verbose output showing where the ParaView executables are looking for the site settings file.

COLOR MAPS AND TRANSFER FUNCTIONS

One of the first things that any visualization tool user does when opening a new dataset and looking at the mesh is to color the mesh with some scalar data. Color mapping is a common visualization technique that maps data to colo, and displays the colors in the rendered image. Of course, to map the data array to colors, we use a transfer function. A transfer function can also be used to map the data array to opacity for rendering translucent surfaces or for volume rendering. This chapter desribes the basics of mapping data arrays to color and opacity.

11.1   The basics

Color mapping (which often also includes opacity mapping) goes by various names including scalar mapping and pseudo-coloring. The basic principle entails mapping data arrays to colors when rendering surface meshes or volumes. Since data arrays can have arbitrary values and types, you may want to create a mapping to define to which color a particular data value maps. This mapping is defined using what are called *color maps* or *transfer functions*. Since such mapping from data values to rendering primitives can be defined for not just colors, but opacity values as well, we will use the more generic term *transfer functions*.

Of course, there are cases when your data arrays indeed specify the red-green-blue color values to use when rendering (i.e., not using a transfer function at all). This can controlled using the `Map Scalars` display property. Refer to Chapter 4.4.2 for details. This chapter relates to cases when `Map Scalars` is enabled, i.e., when the transfer function is being used to map arrays to colors and/or opacity.

In ParaView, you can set up a transfer function for each data array for both color and opacity separately. ParaView associates a transfer function with the data array identified by its name. The same transfer function is used when coloring with the same array in different 3D views or results from different stages in the pipeline.

For arrays with more than one component, such as vectors or tensors, you can specify whether to use the magnitude or a specific component for the color/opacity mapping. Similar to the transfer functions themselves, this selection of how to map a multi-component array to colors is also associated with the array name. Thus, two pipeline modules being colored with the arrays that have the same name will not only be using the same transfer functions for opacity and color, but also the component/magnitude selection.

> ### ⚫ Common Errors
>
> *Beginners find it easy to forget that the transfer function is associated with an array name and, hence, are surprised when changing the transfer function for a dataset being shown in one view affects other views as well. Using different transfer functions for the same variable is discouraged by design in ParaView, since it can lead to the misinterpretation of values. If you want to use different transfer functions, despite this caveat, you can use a filter like the* `Calculator` *or* `Programmable Filter` *to rename the array and then use a different transfer function for it.*

There are separate transfer functions for color and opacity. The opacity transfer function is optional when doing surface renderings (You can turn it on/off by using the `Color Map Editor` as explained later), but it gets used for volume rendering.

11.1.1 Color mapping in `paraview`

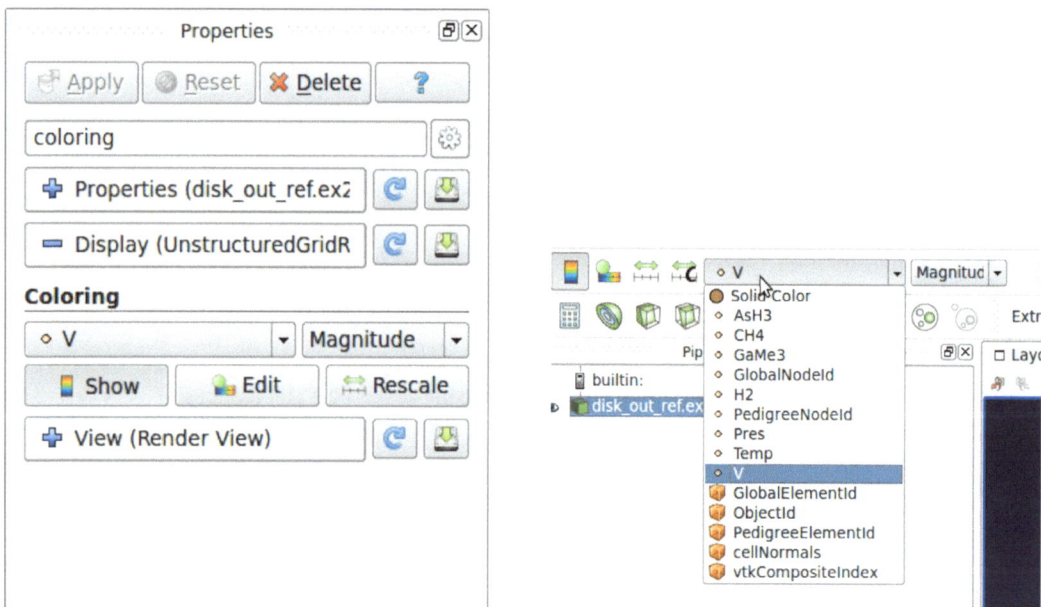

Figure 11.1: The controls used for selecting the array to color within the `Properties` panel (left) and the `Active Variables Controls` toolbar (right).

You can pick an array to use for color mapping, using either the `Properties` panel or the `Active Variables Controls` toolbar. You first select the array with which to color and then select the component or magnitude for multi-component arrays. ParaView will either use an existing transfer function or create a new one for the selected array.

11.1.2 Color mapping in `pvpython`

Here's a sample script for coloring using a data array from the `disk_out_ref.ex2` dataset.

```
1  from paraview.simple import *
```

```
2
3  # create a new 'ExodusIIReader'
4  reader = ExodusIIReader(FileName=['disk_out_ref.ex2'])
5  reader.PointVariables = ['V']
6  reader.ElementBlocks = ['Unnamed block ID: 1 Type: HEX8']
7
8  # show data in view
9  display = Show(reader)
10
11 # set scalar coloring
12 ColorBy(display, ('POINTS', 'V'))
13
14 # rescale color and/or opacity maps used to include current data range
15 display.RescaleTransferFunctionToDataRange(True)
```

The `ColorBy` function provided by the `simple` module ensures that the color and opacity transfer functions are setup correctly for the selected array, which is using an existing one already associated with the array name or is creating a new one. Passing `None` as the second argument to `ColorBy` will display scalar coloring.

11.2   Editing the transfer functions in `paraview`

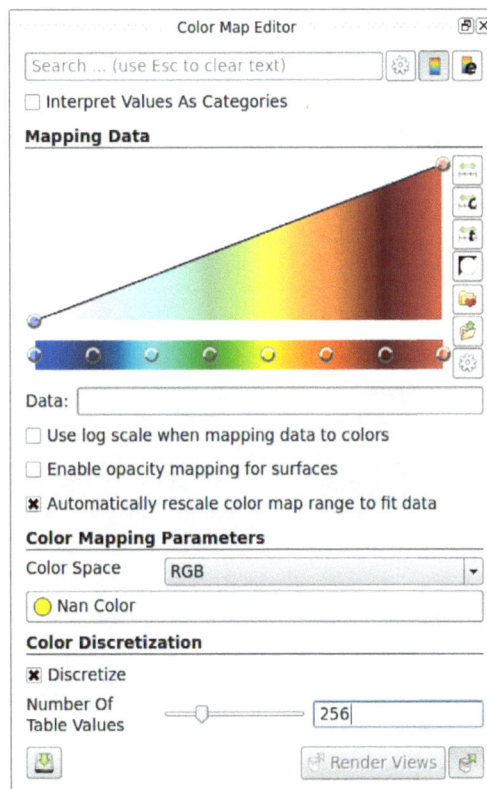

Figure 11.2: `Color Map Editor` panel in `paraview` showing the major components of the panel .

In `paraview`, you use the `Color Map Editor` to customize the color and opacity transfer functions. You can toggle the `Color Map Editor` visibility using the |View⟩⟩Color Map Editor| menu option.

As shown in Figure 11.2, the panel follows a layout similar to the `Properties` panel. The panel shows the properties for the transfer function, if any, used for coloring the active data source (or filter) in the active view. If the active source if not visible in the active view, or is not employing scalar coloring, then the panel will be empty.

Similar to the Properties panel, by default, the commonly used properties are shown. You can toggle the visibility of advanced properties by using the ⚙ button. Additionally, you can search for a particular property by typing its name in the `Search` box.

Whenever the transfer function is changed, we need to re-render, which may be time consuming. By default, the panel requests renders on every change. To avoid this, you can toggle the 🗁 button. When unchecked, you will need to manually update the panel using the `Render Views` button.

11.2.1 Mapping data

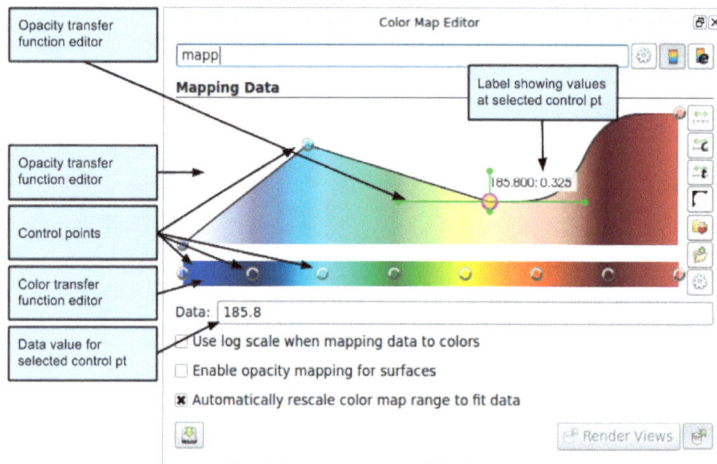

Figure 11.3: Transfer function editor and related properties

The `Mapping Data` group of properties controls how the data is mapped to colors or opacity. The transfer function editor widgets are used to control the transfer function for color and opacity. The panel always shows both the transfer functions. Whether the opacity transfer function gets used depends on several things:

- When doing surface mesh rendering, it will be used only if `Enable opacity mapping for surfaces` is checked
- When doing volume rendering, the opacity mapping will always be used.

To map the data to color using a log scale, rather than a linear scale, check the `Use log scale when mapping data to colors`. It is assumed that the data is in the non-zero, positive range. ParaView will report errors and try to automatically fix the range if it's ever invalid for log mapping.

Based on the user preference set in the `Settings` dialog, ParaView can automatically rescale the transfer function every time when the user hits the `Apply` button on the `Properties` panel or when the time step changes. This behavior can be disabled by unchecking the `Automatically rescale transfer functions to fit data` checkbox. When unchecked, whatever scalar range you specify for the transfer function will remain unchanged.

11.2.2 Transfer function editor

Using the transfer function editors is pretty straight forward. Control points in the opacity editor widget and the color editor widget are independent of each other. To select a control point, click on it. When selected, the control point is highlighted with a red circle and data value associated with the control point is shown in the Data input box under the widget. Clicking in an empty area will add a control point at that location. To move a control point, click on the control point and drag it. You can fine tune the data value associated with the selected control point using the `Data` input box. To delete a control point, select the control point and then hit the `Del.` key. Note that the mouse pointer should be within the transfer function widget for Qt to send the event to the editor widget correctly. While the end control points cannot be moved or deleted, you can rescale the entire transfer function to move the control points, as is explained later.

In the opacity transfer function widget, you can move the control points vertically to control the opacity value associated with that control point. In the color transfer function widget, you can double click on the control point to pop up a color chooser widget to set the color associated with that control point.

The opacity transfer function widget also offers some control over the interpolation between the control points. Double click on a control point to show the interpolation control widget, which allows for changing the sharpness and midpoint that affect the interpolation. Click and drag the control points to see the change in interpolation.

The several control buttons on the right side of the transfer function widgets support the following actions:

- : Rescales the color and opacity transfer functions using the data range from the data source selected in the Pipeline browser, i.e., the active source. This rescales the entire transfer function. Thus, all control points including the intermediate ones are proportionally adjusted to fit the new range.

- : Rescales the color and opacity transfer functions using a range provided by the user. A dialog will be popped up for the user to enter the custom range.

- : Inverts the color transfer function by moving the control points, e.g,. a red-to-green transfer function will be inverted to a green-to-red one. This only affects the color transfer function and leaves the opacity transfer function untouched.

- : Loads the color transfer function from a preset. Color present manager dialog pops up to allow the user to load presets from file, if needed. Currently, this only supports the color transfer function. In the future, however, it will be extended to support the opacity transfer function as well.

- : Saves the current color transfer function to presets. Color present manager dialog pops up to allow the user to export the transfer function to a file, if needed. Currently, this only supports the color transfer function. In the future, however, it will be extended to support the opacity transfer function as well.

- : This toggles the detailed view for the transfer function control points. This is useful to manually enter values for the control points rather than using the UI.

11.2.3 Color mapping parameters

The `Color Mapping Parameters` group of properties provides additional control over the color transfer function, including control over the color interpolation space: RGB, HSV, Lab, or diverging. When color mapping floating point arrays with NaNs, you can select the color to use for NaN values. You can also affect whether the color transfer function uses smooth interpolation or a discretization of the same into a fixed number of bins.

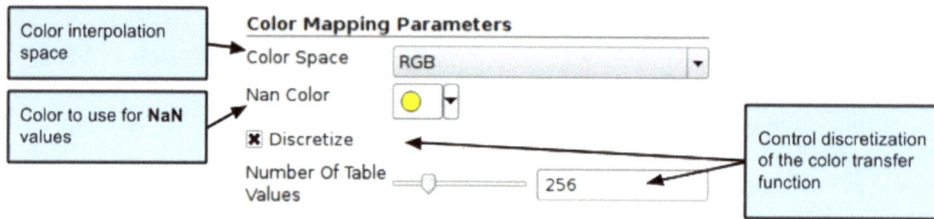

Figure 11.4: Color Mapping Parameters (showing advanced properties as well)

11.3 Editing the transfer functions in `pvpython`

In *pvpython*, you control the transfer functions by getting access to the transfer function objects and then changing properties on those. The following script shows how you can access transfer functions objects.

```
from paraview.simple import *

# You can access the color and opacity transfer functions
# for a particular array as follows. These functions will
# create new transfer functions if none exist.
# The argument is the array name used to locate the transfer
# functions.
>>> colorMap = GetColorTransferFunction('Temp')
>>> opacityMap = GetOpacityTransferFunction('Temp')
```

Once you have access to the color and opacity transfer functions, you can change properties on these similar to other sources, views, etc. Using the Python tracing capabilities to discover this API is highly recommended.

```
# Rescale transfer functions to a specific range
>>> colorMap.RescaleTransferFunction(1.0, 19.9495)
>>> opacityMap.RescaleTransferFunction(1.0, 19.9495)

# Invert the color map.
>>> colorMap.InvertTransferFunction()

# Map color map to log-scale preserving relative positions for
# control points
>>> colorMap.MapControlPointsToLogSpace()
>>> colorMap.UseLogScale = 1

# Return back to linear space.
>>> colorMap.MapControlPointsToLinearSpace()
>>> colorMap.UseLogScale = 0

# Change using of opacity mapping for surfaces
>>> colorMap.EnableOpacityMapping = 1

# Explicitly specify color map control points
# The value is a flattened list of tuples
# (data-value, red, green, blue). The color components
# must be in the range [0.0, 1.0]
>>> colorMap.RGBPoints = [1.0, 0.705, 0.015, 0.149,
```

```
25                              5.0, 0.865, 0.865, 0.865,
26                             10.0, 0.627, 0.749, 1.0,
27                             19.9495, 0.231373, 0.298039, 0.752941]
28
29  # Similarly, for opacity map. The value here is
30  # a flattened list of (data-value, opacity, mid-point, sharpness)
31  >>> opacity.Points = [1.0, 0.0, 0.5, 0.0,
32                        9.0, 0.404, 0.5, 0.0,
33                       19.9495, 1.0, 0.5, 0.0]
34
35  # Note, in both these cases the controls points are assumed to be sorted
36  # based on  the data values. Also, not setting the first and last
37  # control point to have same data value can have unexpected artifacts
38  # in the 'Color Map Editor' panel.
```

Oftentimes, you want to rescale the color and opacity maps to fit the current data ranges. You can do this as follows:

```
1   >>> source = GetActiveSource()
2
3   # Update the pipeline, if hasn't been updated already.
4   >>> source.UpdatePipeline()
5
6   # First, locate the display properties for the source of interest.
7   >>> display = GetDisplayProperties()
8
9   # Reset the color and opacity maps currently used by 'display' to
10  # using the range for the array 'display' is set to color with.
11  # This requires that the 'display' has been set to use scalar coloring
12  # using an array that is available in the data generated. If not, you will
13  # get errors.
14  >>> display.RescaleTransferFunctionToDataRange()
```

11.4   Color legend

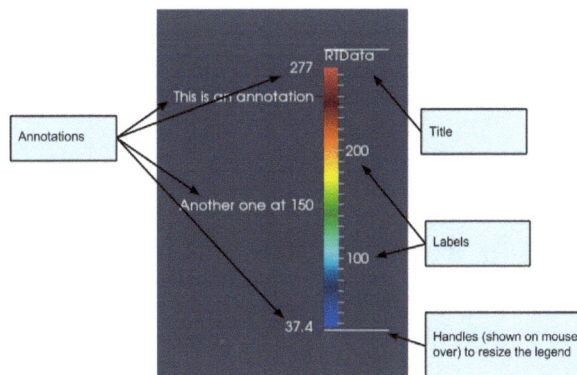

Figure 11.5: Color legend in ParaView.

The color legend, also known as scalar bar or color bar, is designed to provide the user information about which color corresponds to what data value in the rendered view. You can toggle the visibility of the color legend corresponding to the transfer function being shown/edit in the `Color Map Editor` by using the ▪ button near the top of the panel. This button affects the visibility of the legend in the active view.

Figure 11.4 shows the various components of the color legend. By default, the title is typically the name of the array (and component number or magnitude for non-scalar data arrays) being mapped. On one side are the automatically generated labels, while on the other side are the annotations, including the start and end annotations, which correspond to the data range being mapped.

You can control the characteristics of the color legend using the 🔵 button. The color legend is interactive. You can click and drag the legend to place it interactively at any position in the view. Additionally, you can change the length of the legend by dragging the end-markers shown when you hover the mouse pointer over the legend.

11.4.1 Color legend parameters

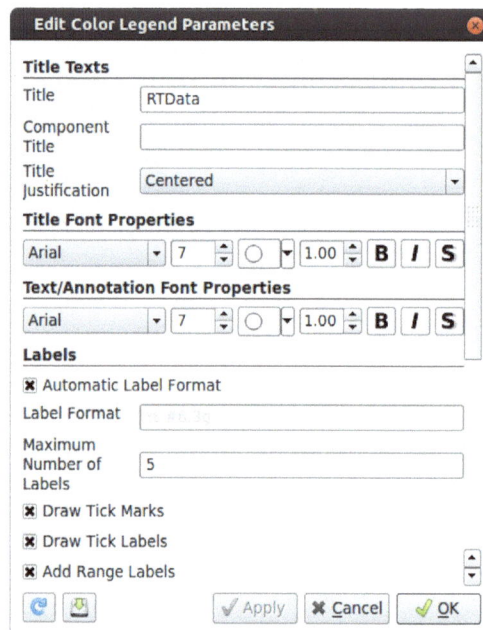

Figure 11.6: `Edit Color Legend Parameters` dialog in *paraview*.

You can edit the color legend parameters by clicking on the 🔵 button on the `Color Map Editor` panel. This will pop up a dialog that shows the available parameters. Any changes made only affect the particular color legend in the active view.

Besides the obvious changing of title text and font properties for the title, labels, and annotations, some of the other parameters that the user can change are as follows: `Draw Annotations` controls whether the annotations (including the start and end annotations) are to be drawn at all.

When checked, `Draw NaN Annotations` results in the color legend showing the NaN color setup in the `Color Map Editor` panel in a separate box right beside the color legend. The annotation text shown for that box can be modified by changing the `NaN Annotation` text.

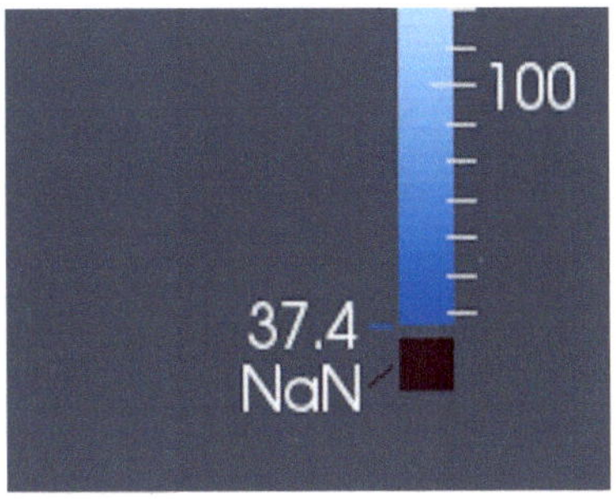

Figure 11.7: Color legend showing NaN annotation

If `Automatic Label Format` is checked, ParaView will try to pick an optimal representation for numerical values based on the value and available screen space. By unchecking it, you can explicitly specify the `printf`-style format to use for numeric values. Number of Labels is a suggestion for maximum number of labels to show on the legend. Note that this is a suggestion and may not exactly match the number of labels shown. To explicitly label values of interest, use the annotations discussed later in this post. `Aspect Ratio` is used to control the thickness of the legend: The greater the number, the thinner the legend.

11.4.2 Color legend in `pvpython`

To show the color legend or scalar bar for the transfer function used for scalar mapping a source in a view, you can use API on its display properties:

```
1  >>> source = ...
2  >>> display = GetDisplayProperties(source, view)
3
4  # to show the color legend
5  >>> display.SetScalarBarVisibility(view, True)
6
7  # to hide the same
8  >>> display.SetScalarBarVisibility(view, False)
```

To change the color legend properties as in Section 11.4.1, you need to first get access to the color legend object for the color transfer function in a particular view. These are analogous to display properties for a source in a view.

```
1  >>> colorMap = GetColorTransferFunction('Temp')
2
3  # get the scalar bar in a view (akin to GetDisplayProperties)
4  >>> scalarBar = GetScalarBar(colorMap, view)
5
6  # Now, you can change properties on the scalar bar object.
7  >>> scalarBar.TitleFontSize = 8
8  >>> scalarBar.DrawNanAnnotation = 1
```

11.5 Annotations

Simply put, annotations allow users to put custom text at particular data values in the color legend. The min and max data mapped value annotations are automatically added. To add any other custom annotations, you can use the `Color Map`

`Editor.`

Since annotations is an advanced parameter, you have to either toggle the visibility of advanced properties using the ⚙ icon near the top of the panel or simply search for `annotations` in the search box. That will show the `Annotations` widget, which is basically a list widget where users can enter key-value pairs, rather than value-annotation pairs, as shown in Figure 11.5.

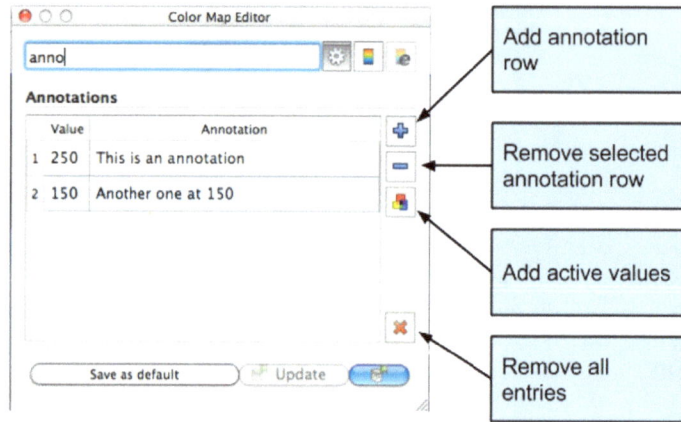

Figure 11.8: Widget to add/edit annotations on the `Color Map Editor` panel

You can use the buttons of the right on the widget to add/remove entries. Enter the data value to annotate under the `Value` column and then enter the text to use under the `Annotation` column.

You can use the ⇥ key to edit the next entry. Hitting ⇥ after editing the last entry in the table will automatically result in adding a new row, thus, making it easier to add bunch of annotations without having to click any buttons.

There are two reasons in which annotation texts may not show up on the legend: First, the value added is outside the mapped range of the color transfer function; second, `Draw Annotations` is unchecked in the `Color Legend Parameters dialog`.

The ⊞ button can be used to fill the annotations widget with unique discrete values from the data array, if possible. Based on the number of distinct values present in the data array, this may not yield any result. (Instead, a warning message will be shown.)

11.5.1 Annotations in `pvpython`

Annotations is a property on the color map object. You simply get access to the color map of interest and then change the `Annotations` property.

```
1  >>> colorMap = GetColorTransferFunction('Temp')
2
3  # Annotations are specified as a flattened list of tuples
4  # (data-value, annotation-text)
5  >>> colorMap.Annotations = ['1', 'Slow',
6                              '10', 'Fast']
```

11.6   Categorical colors

A picture is worth a thousand words, they say, so let's just let the picture do the talking. Categorical color maps allow you to render visualizations as shown in Figure 11.6.

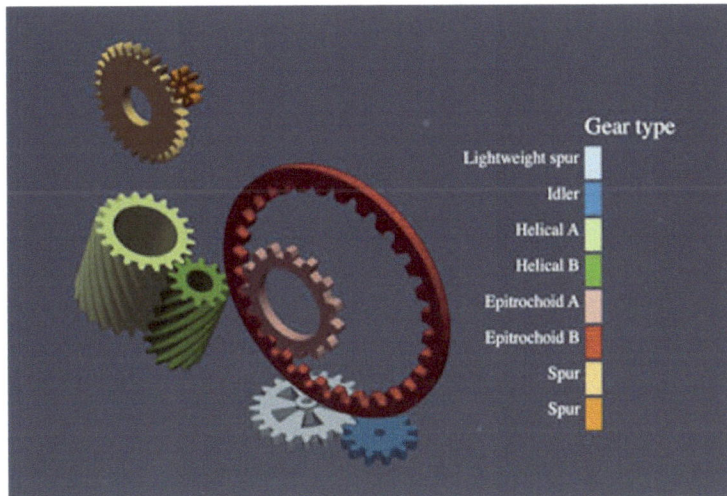

Figure 11.9: Visualization using a categorical color map for discrete coloring

When one thinks of scalar coloring, one is typically talking of mapping numerical values to colors. However, in some cases, the numerical values are not really numbers, but enumerations such as elements types and gear types (as in Figure 11.6) or generally, speaking, categories. The traditional approach of using an interpolated color map specifying the range of values with which to color doesn't really work here. While users could always play tricks with the number of discrete steps, multiple control points, and annotations, it is tedious and cumbersome.

Categorical color maps provide an elegant solution for such cases. Instead of a continuous color transfer function, the user specifies a set of discrete values and colors to use for those values. For any element where the data value matches the values in the lookup table exactly, ParaView renders the specified color; otherwise, the NaN color is used.

The color legend or scalar bar also switches to a new mode where it renders swatches with annotations, rather than a single bar. You can add custom annotations for each value in the lookup table.

Categorical Color: User Interface

To tell ParaView that the data array is to be treated as categories for coloring, check the `Interpret Values As Categories` checkbox in the `Color Map Editor` panel. As soon as that's checked, the panel switches to categorical mode: The `Mapping Data` group is hidden, and the `Annotations` group becomes a non-advanced group, i.e., the annotations widget is visible even if the panel is not showing advanced properties, as is shown in Figure 11.6.

The annotations widget will still show any annotations that may have been added earlier, or it may be empty if none were added. You can add annotations for data values as was the case before using the buttons on the side of the widget. This time, however, each annotation entry also has a column for color. If color has not been specified, a question mark icon will show up; otherwise, a color swatch will be shown. You can double click the color swatch or the question mark icon to specify the color to use for that entry. Alternatively, you can choose from a preset collection of categorical color maps by clicking the button.

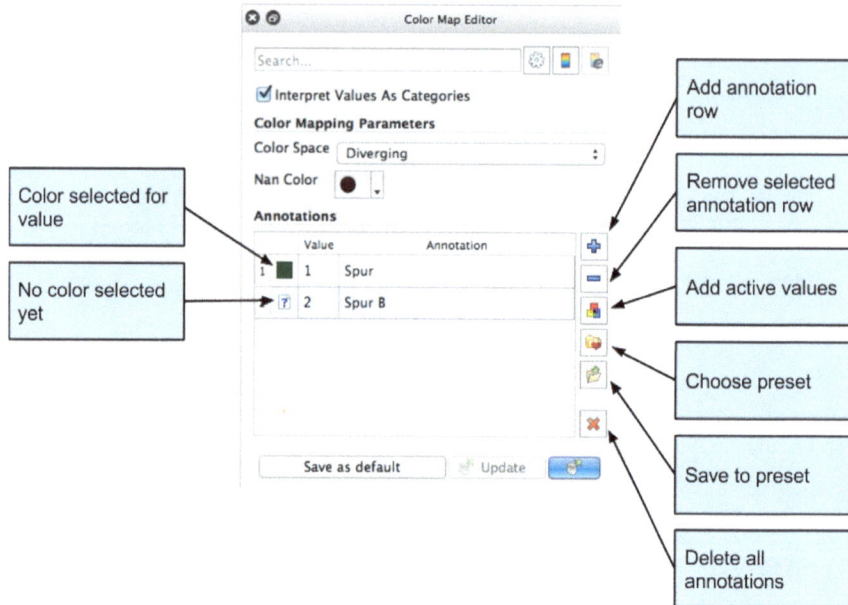

Figure 11.10: Default Color Map Editor when Interpret Values As Categories is checked

As before, you can use ⟨⇤⟩ key to edit and add multiple values. Hence, you can first add all the values of interest in one pass and then pick a preset color map to set colors for the values added. If the preset has fewer colors than the annotated values, then the user may have to manually set the colors for those extra annotations.

Also ▦ plays the same role as described in the previous post: Fill the annotations widget with unique discrete values from the data array, is possible. Based on the number of distinct values present in the data array, this may not yield any result. (Instead, a warning message will be shown.)

Common Errors

Categorical color maps are designed for data arrays with enumerations, which are typically integer arrays. However, they can be used for arrays with floating point numbers as well. With floating point numbers, the value specified for annotation may not match the value in the dataset exactly, even when the user expects it to match. In that case, the NaN color will be used. In the future, we may add a mechanism to specify a delta to use to when comparing data values to annotated values.

Categorical colors in `pvpython`

```
1 >>> categoricalColorMap = GetColorTransferFunction('Modes')
2 >>> categoricalColorMap.InterpretValuesAsCategories = 1
3
4 # specify the labels for the categories. This is similar to how
5 # other annotations are specified.
6 >>> categoricalColorMap.Annotations = ['0', 'Alpha', '1', 'Beta']
7
```

```
 8  # now, set the colors for each category. These are an ordered list
 9  # of flattened tuples (red, green, blue). The first color gets used for
10  # the first annotation, second for second, and so on
11  >>> categoricalColorMap.IndexedColors = [0.0, 0.0, 0.0,
12                                           0.89, 0.10, 0.10]
```

COMPARATIVE VISUALIZATION

Comparative visualization in ParaView refers to the ability to create side-by-side visualizations for comparing with one another. In its most basic form, you can indeed use ParaView's ability to show multiple views side by side to set up simultaneous visualizations. But, that can get cumbersome too quickly. Let's take a look at a simple example: Let's say you want to do a parameter study where you want to compare isosurfaces generated by a set of isovalues in a dataset. To set such a visualization up, you'll need to first create as many `Render Views` as isovalues. Then, create just as many `Contour` filters, setting each one up with a right isovalue for the contour to generate and display the result in one of the views. As the number of isovalues increases, you can see how this can get tedious. It is highly error prone, as you need to keep track of which view shows which isovalue. Now, imagine after having set up the entire visualization that you need to change the `Representation` type for all the of the isosurfaces to `Wireframe`!

`Comparative Views` were designed to handle such use-cases. Instead of creating separate views, you create a single view `Render View (Comparative)`. The view itself comprises of a configurable $m \times n$ `Render Views`. Any data that you show in this view gets shown in all the internal views simultaneously. Any display property changes, such as scalar coloring and representation type are also maintained consistently between these internal views. The interactions in the internal views are linked, so when you interact with one, all other views update as well. While this is all nice and well, where the real power of `Comparative Views` becomes apparent is when you set up a parameter to vary across the views. This parameter can be any of the properties on the pipeline modules such as filter properties and opacity, or it could be the data time. Each of these internal views will now render the result obtained by setting the parameter as per your selection. Going back to our original example, we will create a single `Contour` filter that we show in `Render View (Comparative)` with as many internal views as the isovalue to compare. Next, we will set up a parameter study for varying the `Isosurfaces` property on the `Contour` filter, and, viola! The view will generate the comparative visualization for us!

In this chapter, we look at how to configure this view and how to set these parameters to compare. We limit our discussion to `Render View (Comparative)`. However, the same principles are applicable to other comparative views, including `Bar Chart View (Comparative)` and `Line Chart View (Comparative)`.

12.1 Setting up a comparative view

To create `Render View (Comparative)` in *paraview*, split or close the active view and select `Render View (Comparative)` from the new view creation widget. *paraview* will immediately show four `Render Views` laid out in a 2×2 grid. While you cannot resize these internal views, notice that you can still split the view frame and create other views if needed.

The `Properties` panel will show properties similar to those available on the `Render View` under the `View` properties section. If you change any of these properties, they will affect all these internal views, e.g., setting the `Background` color to `Gradient` will make all the views show a gradient background.

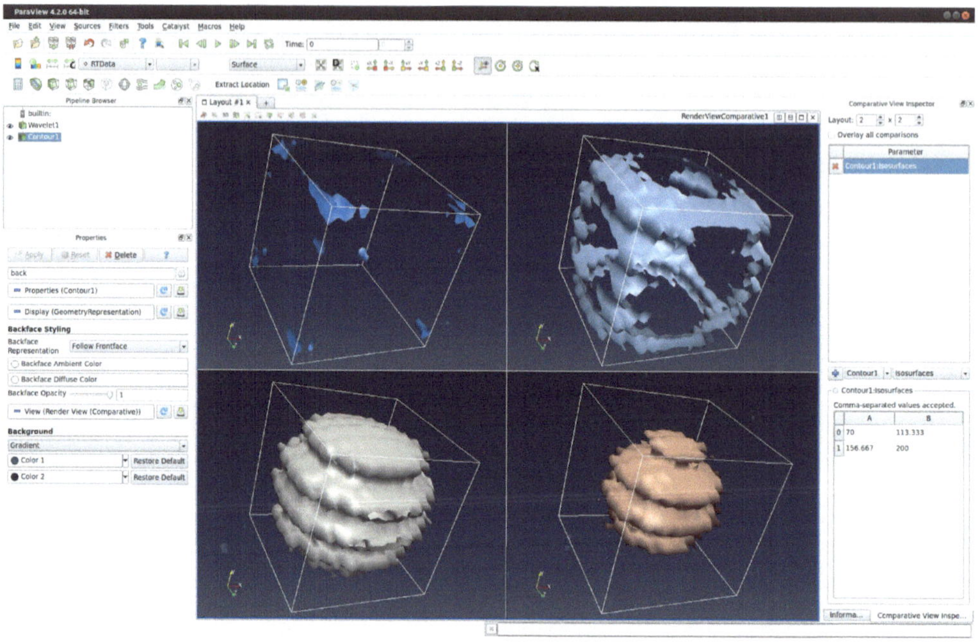

Figure 12.1: `Render View (Comparative)` in *paraview* showing a parameter study. In this case, we are comparing the visualization generated using different isovalues for the `Contour` filter. The `Comparative View Inspector` dockpanel (on the right) is used to configure the parameter study.

To configure the comparative view itself, you must to use the `Comparative View Inspector` (Figure 12.2) accessible from the View menu. The `Comparative View Inspector` is a dockable panel that becomes enabled when the active view is a comparative view.

To change how many internal views are used in the active comparative view and how they are laid out, use the `Layout`. The first value is the number of views in the horizontal direction and the second is the count in the vertical direction.

Besides doing a parameter study in side-by-side views, you can also show all the results in a single view. For that, simply check the `Overlay all comparisons` checkbox. When checked, instead of getting a grid of $m \times n$ views, you will only see one view with all visible data displayed $m \times n$ times.

To show data in this view is the same as any other view: Make this view active and use the `Pipeline Browser` to toggle the eyeball icons to show data produced by the selected pipeline module(s). Showing any dataset in this view will result in the data being shown in all the internal views simultaneously. As is true with `View` properties, with `Display` properties, changing `Coloring`, `Styling`, or any other properties will reflect in all internal views.

Since the cameras among the internal views are automatically linked, if you interact with one of the views, all views will also update simultaneously when you release the mouse button.

12.2 Setting up a parameter study

To understand how to setup a parameter study, let's go back to our original example. Our visualization pipeline is simply `Wavelet`→`Contour` (assuming default property values), and we are showing the result from the `Contour` filter in the 2×2 `Render View (Comparative)` with `Overlay all comparisons` unchecked.

Now, we want to vary the `Isosurfaces` property value for the visualization in each of the internal views. That's our

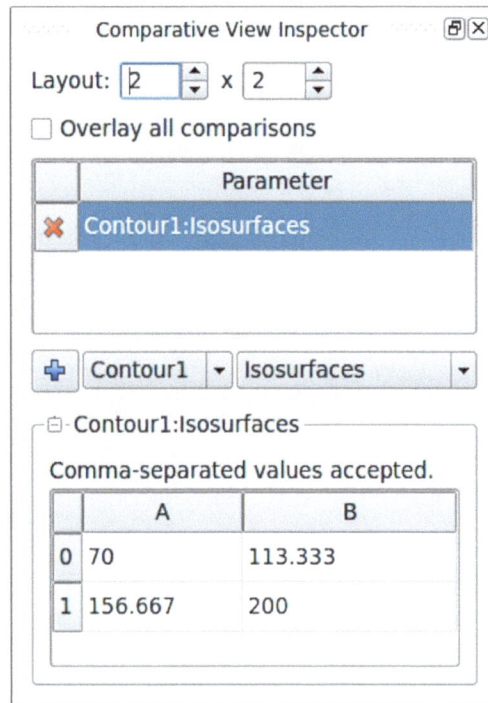

Figure 12.2: `Comparative View Inspector` in *paraview* used to configure the active comparative view.

parameter to study. Since that's a property on the `Contour` filter, we select the `Contour` filter instance. Then, its property `Isosurfaces` is in the parameter selection combo-boxes. To add the parameter to the study, you must hit the ✚ button. The parameter `Contour1:Isosurfaces` will then show up in the `Parameter` list above the combo-boxes. You can delete this parameter by using the ✖ button next to the parameter name.

ⓘ Did you know?
Notice how this mechanism for setting up a parameter study is similar to how animations are set up. In fact, under the cover, the two mechanisms are not that different, and they share a lot of implementation code.

Simultaneously, the table widget below the combo-boxes is populated with a default set of values for the `Isosurfaces`. This is where you specify the parameter values for each of the views. The location of the views matches the location in the table. Hence, $0 - A$ is the top-left view, $0 - B$ is the second view from the left in the topmost row, and so on. The parameter value at a specific location in the table is the value used to generate the visualization in the corresponding view.

To change the parameter (in our case `Isosurfaces`) value, you can double click on the cell in the table and change it one at a time. Also, to make it easier to fill the cells with a range of values, you can click and drag over multiple cells. When you release the mouse, a dialog will prompt you to enter the data value range (Figure 12.4). In case you selected a combination of rows and columns, the dialog will also let you select in which direction must the parameter be varied using the range specified. You can choose to vary the parameter horizontally first, vertically first, or only along one of the directions while keeping the other constant. This is useful when doing a study with multiple parameters.

As soon as you change the parameter values, the view will update to reflect the change.

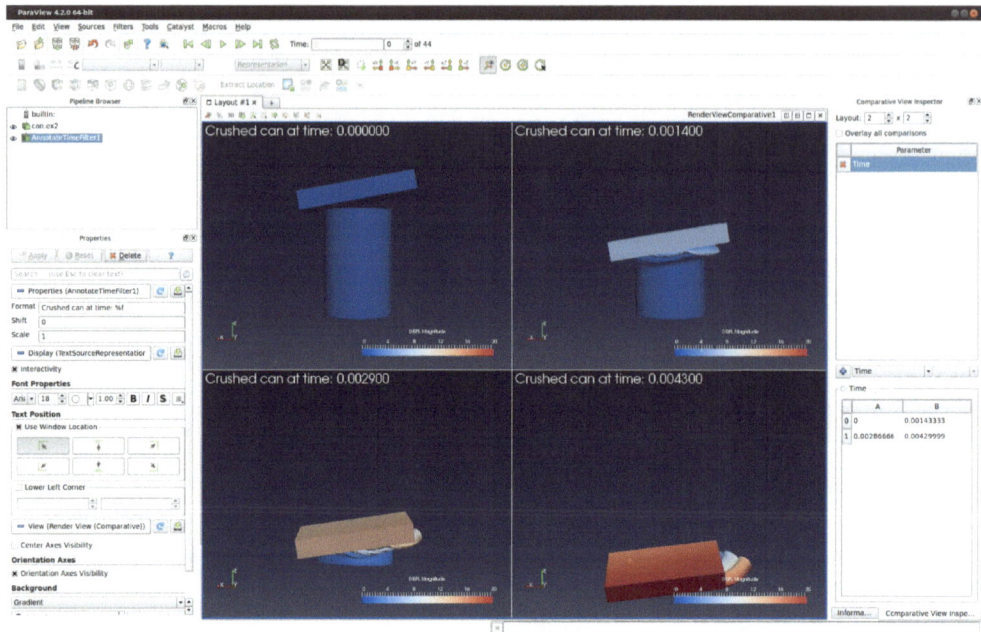

Figure 12.3: `Render View (Comparative)` with `Annotate Time` filter showing the time for each of the views. In this case, the parameter study is varying `Time` across the views.

12.3   Adding annotations

You add annotations like scalar bar (or color legends), text, and cube-axes exactly as you would with a regular `Render View`. As with other properties, when added, these will show up in all of the internal views.

> **Did you know?**
> *You can use the* `Annotate Time` *source or filter to show the data time or the view time in each of the internal views. If* `Time` *is one of the parameters in your study, the text will reflect the time values for each of the individual views, as expected (Figure 12.3)!*

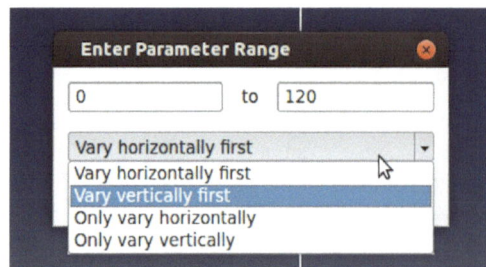

Figure 12.4: Dialog used to select a range of parameter values and control how to vary them in *paraview*.

PROGRAMMABLE FILTER

Any of the pipeline modules in ParaView are doing one of two things: They are either generating data or processing input data. The generation of data can happen either using mathematical models (any of the sources created from the Sources menu) or by reading files on disks or other media. ParaView includes several types of readers and filters, many (if not all) of which are written using C++ by the ParaView and VTK developers and then compiled into the executables and runtime libraries.

One of the primary focuses of ParaView since its early development is customizability. We wanted to enable developers and users to plug in their own code to read custom file formats or to execute special algorithms for data processing. Thus, an extensive plugin infrastructure was born, enabling developers to write C++ code that be compiled into plugins that can be imported into the ParaView executables at runtime. While such plugins are immensely flexible, the process can be tedious and overwhelming, since developers would need to familiarize themselves with the large C++ APIs provided by VTK and ParaView. Hence, easier mechanisms were needed to enable ParaView end users to create such custom sources and filters more easily. Thus, the programmable modules, which includes the `Programmable Source` and `Programmable Filter`, were born.

With these programmable modules, you can write Python scripts that get executed by ParaView to generate and process data, just like the other C++ modules. Since the programming environment is Python, it means that you have access to a plethora of Python packages including NumPy and SciPy By using such packages, along with the data processing API provided by the ParaView, you can quickly put together readers, and filters to extend and customize ParaView.

In this chapter, we will look at writing `Programmable Sources` and `Programmable Filters` using ParaView's Python-based data processing API through a collection of recipes and examples. A thorough discussion on the data processing API itself is covered in Chapter 14.

Common Errors

In this guide so far, we have been looking at examples of Python scripts for pvpython. These scripts are used to script the actions you would perform using the paraview UI. The scripts you would write for `Programmable Source` and `Programmable Filter` are entirely different. The data processing API executes within the data processing pipeline and, thus, has access to the data being processed. In client-server mode, this means that such scripts are indeed executed on the server side, potentially in parallel, across several MPI ranks. Therefore, attempting to import the `paraview.simple` Python module in the `Programmable Source` script, for example, is not supported and will have unexpected consequences.

13.1 Understanding the programmable modules

With programmable modules, you are writing custom code for filters and sources. You are expected to understand the basics of a VTK (and ParaView) data processing pipeline, including the various stages of the pipeline execution as well as the data model. Refer to Section 3.1 for an overview of the VTK data model. While a detailed discussion of the VTK pipeline execution model is beyond the scope of this book, the fundamentals covered in this section, along with the examples in the rest of this chapter, should give you enough to get started and write useful scripts.

To create the programmable source or filter in *paraview*, you use the `Sources` ⟩ `Programmable Source` or `Filters` ⟩ ⟩ `Programmable Filter` menus, respectively. Since the `Programmable Filter` is a filter, like other filters, it gets connected to the currently active source(s), i.e., the currently active source(s) become the input to this new filter. `Programmable Source`, on the other hand, does not have any inputs.

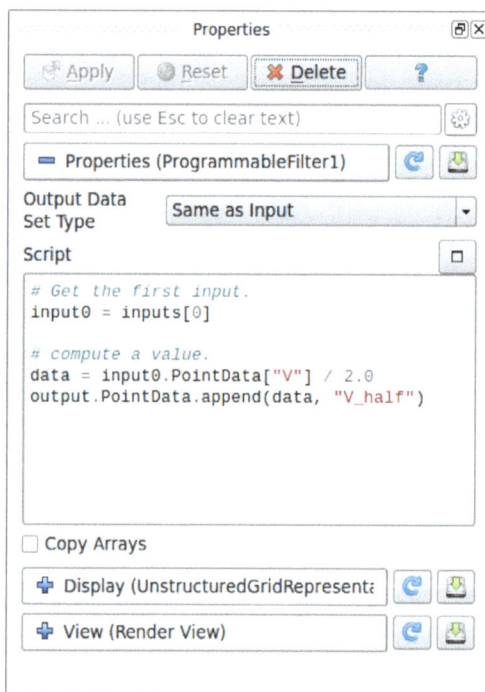

Figure 13.1: `Properties` panel for `Programmable Filter` in *paraview*

One of the first things that you specify after creating any of these programmable modules is the `Output Data Set Type`. This option lets you select the type of dataset this module will produce. The options provided include several of the data types discussed in Section 3.1. Additionally, for the `Programmable Filter`, you can select `Same as Input` to indicate that the filter preserves the input dataset type.

Next is the primary part: the `Script`. This is where you enter the Python script to generate or process from the inputs the dataset that the module will produce. As with any Python script, you can import other Python packages and modules in this script. Just be aware that when running in client-server mode, this script is going to be executed on the server side. Accordingly, any modules or packages you import must be available on the server side to avoid errors.

This script gets executed in what's called the *RequestData* pass of the pipeline execution. This is the pipeline pass in which an algorithm is expected to produce the output dataset.

There are several other passes in a pipeline's execution. The ones for which you can specify a Python script to execute with these programmable modules are:

- *RequestInformation*: In this pass, the algorithm is expected to provide the pipeline with any meta-data available about the data that will be produced by it. This includes things like number of timesteps in the dataset and their time values for temporal datasets or extents for structured datasets. This gets called before *RequestData* pass. In the *RequestData* pass, the pipeline could potentially qualify the request based on the meta-data provided in this pass. (E.g., if an algorithm announces that the temporal dataset has multiple timesteps, in `RequestData`, the pipeline could request the algorithm in a specific timestep to produce.)

- *RequestUpdateExtent*: In this pass, a filter gets the opportunity to qualify requests for execution passed on to the upstream pipeline. (E.g., if an upstream reader announced in its *RequestInformation* that it can produce several timesteps, in *RequestUpdateExtent*, this filter can make a request to the upstream reader for a specific timestep.) This pass gets called after *RequestInformation*, but before `RequestData`. It's not very common to provide a script for this pass.

You can specify the script for *RequestInformation* pass in `RequestInformation Script` and for *RequestUpdateExtent* pass in `RequestUpdateExtent Script`. Since *RequestUpdateExtent* pass does not make much sense for an algorithm that does not have any inputs, `RequestUpdateExtent Script` is not available on `Programmable Source`.

13.2 Recipes for Programmable Source

In this section, we look at several recipes for `Programmable Source`. A common use of `Programmable Source` is to prototype readers. If your reader library already provides a Python API, then you can easily import the appropriate Python package to read your dataset using `Programmable Source`.

> 🛈 Did you know?
>
> *Most of the examples in this chapter use a NumPy-centric API for accessing and creating data arrays. Additionally, you can use VTK's Python wrapped API for creating and accessing arrays. Given the omnipresence of NumPy, there is rarely any need for using this API directly, however.*

13.2.1 Reading a CSV file

For this example, we will read in a CSV file to produce a Table (Section 3.1.9) using `Programmable Source`. We will use NumPy to do the parsing of the CSV files and pass the arrays read in directly to the pipeline.

`Output DataSet Type` **must be set to** `vtkTable`.

```
1  # Code for 'Script'
2
3  # We will use NumPy to read the csv file.
4  # Refer to NumPy documentation for genfromtxt() for details on
5  # customizing the CSV file parsing.
6
7  import numpy as np
8  # assuming data.csv is a CSV file with the 1st row being the names names for
9  # the columns
10 data = np.genfromtxt("data.csv", dtype=None, names=True, delimiter=',', autostrip=True
       )
```

```
11  for name in data.dtype.names:
12      array = data[name]
13
14      # You can directly pass a NumPy array to the pipeline.
15      # Since ParaView expects all arrays to be named, you
16      # need to assign it a name in the 'append' call.
17      output.RowData.append(array, name)
```

13.2.2 Reading a CSV file series

Building on the example from Section 13.2.1, let's say we have a series of files that we want to read in as a temporal series. Recall from Section 13.1 that meta-data about data to be produced, including timestep information, is announced in *RequestInformation* pass. Hence, for this example, we will need to specify the RequestInformation Script as well.

As was true earlier, Output DataSet Type must be set to vtkTable. Now, to announce the timesteps, we use the following as the RequestInformation Script.

```
1   # Code for 'RequestInformation Script'.
2   def setOutputTimesteps(algorithm, timesteps):
3       "helper routine to set timestep information"
4       executive = algorithm.GetExecutive()
5       outInfo = executive.GetOutputInformation(0)
6
7       outInfo.Remove(executive.TIME_STEPS())
8       for timestep in timesteps:
9           outInfo.Append(executive.TIME_STEPS(), timestep)
10
11      outInfo.Remove(executive.TIME_RANGE())
12      outInfo.Append(executive.TIME_RANGE(), timesteps[0])
13      outInfo.Append(executive.TIME_RANGE(), timesteps[-1])
14
15  # As an example, let's say we have 4 files in the file series that we
16  # want to say are producing time 0, 10, 20, and 30.
17  setOutputTimesteps(self, (0, 10, 20, 30))
```

The Script is similar to earlier, except that based on which timestep was requested, we will read a specific CSV file.

```
1   # Code for 'Script'
2   def GetUpdateTimestep(algorithm):
3       """Returns the requested time value, or None if not present"""
4       executive = algorithm.GetExecutive()
5       outInfo = executive.GetOutputInformation(0)
6       return outInfo.Get(executive.UPDATE_TIME_STEP()) \
7               if outInfo.Has(executive.UPDATE_TIME_STEP()) else None
8
9   # This is the requested time-step. This may not be exactly equal to the
10  # timesteps published in RequestInformation(). Your code must handle that
11  # correctly
12  req_time = GetUpdateTimestep(self)
13
14  # Now, use req_time to determine which CSV file to read and read it as before.
15  # Remember req_time need not match the time values put out in
16  # 'RequestInformation Script'. Your code need to pick an appropriate file to
17  # read, irrespective.
18
```

```
19  ...
20  # TODO: Generate the data as you want.
21
22  # Now mark the timestep produced.
23  output.GetInformation().Set(output.DATA_TIME_STEP(), req_time)
```

13.2.3   Reading a CSV file with particles

This is similar to Section 13.2.1. Now, however, let's say the CSV has three columns named "X", "Y" and "Z" that we want to treat as point coordinates and produce a vtkPolyData with points instead of a vtkTable. For that, we first ensure that `Output DataSet Type` is set to `vtkPolyData`. Next, we use the following `Script`:

```
1   # Code for 'Script'
2
3   from vtk.numpy_interface import algorithms as algs
4   from vtk.numpy_interface import dataset_adapter as dsa
5   import numpy as np
6
7   # assuming data.csv is a CSV file with the 1st row being the names names for
8   # the columns
9   data = np.genfromtxt("/tmp/points.csv", dtype=None, names=True, delimiter=',',
        autostrip=True)
10
11  # convert the 3 arrays into a single 3 component array for
12  # use as the coordinates for the points.
13  coordinates = algs.make_vector(data["X"], data["Y"], data["Z"])
14
15  # create a vtkPoints container to store all the
16  # point coordinates.
17  pts = vtk.vtkPoints()
18
19  # numpyTovtkDataArray is needed to called directly to convert the NumPy
20  # to a vtkDataArray which vtkPoints::SetData() expects.
21  pts.SetData(dsa.numpyTovtkDataArray(coordinates, "Points"))
22
23  # set the pts on the output.
24  output.SetPoints(pts)
25
26  # next, we define the cells i.e. the connectivity for this mesh.
27  # here, we are creating merely a point could, so we'll add
28  # that as a single poly vextex cell.
29  numPts = pts.GetNumberOfPoints()
30  # ptIds is the list of point ids in this cell
31  # (which is all the points)
32  ptIds = vtk.vtkIdList()
33  ptIds.SetNumberOfIds(numPts)
34  for a in xrange(numPts):
35      ptIds.SetId(a, a)
36
37  # Allocate space for 1 cell.
38  output.Allocate(1)
39  output.InsertNextCell(vtk.VTK_POLY_VERTEX, ptIds)
40
41  # We can also pass all the array read from the CSV
```

```
42  # as point data arrays.
43  for name in data.dtype.names:
44      array = data[name]
45      output.PointData.append(array, name)
```

The thing to note is that this time, we need to define the geometry and topology for the output dataset. Each data type has different requirements on how these are specified. For example, for unstructured datasets like vtkUnstructuredGrid and vtkPolyData, we need to explicitly specify the geometry and all the connectivity information. For vtkImageData, the geometry is defined using origin, spacing, and extents, and connectivity is implicit.

13.2.4 Reading binary 2D image

This recipe shows how to read raw binary data representing a 3D volume. Since raw binary files don't encode information about the volume extents and data type, we will assume that the extents and data type are known and fixed.

For producing image volumes, you need to provide the information about the structured extents in *RequestInformation*. Ensure that the `Output Data Set Type` is set to `vtkImageData`.

```
1  # Code for 'RequestInformation Script'.
2  executive = self.GetExecutive()
3  outInfo = executive.GetOutputInformation(0)
4  # we assume the dimensions are (48, 62, 42).
5  outInfo.Set(executive.WHOLE_EXTENT(), 0, 47, 0, 61, 0, 41)
6  outInfo.Set(vtk.vtkDataObject.SPACING(), 1, 1, 1)
```

The `Script` to read the data can be written as follows.

```
1   # Code for 'Script'
2   import numpy as np
3
4   # read raw binary data.
5   # ensure 'dtype' is set properly.
6   data = np.fromfile("HeadMRVolume.raw", dtype=np.uint8)
7
8   dims = [48, 62, 42]
9   assert data.shape[0] == dims[0]*dims[1]*dims[2], \
10          "dimension mismatch"
11
12  output.SetExtent(0, dims[0]-1, 0, dims[1]-1, 0, dims[2]-1)
13  output.PointData.append(data, "scalars")
14  output.PointData.SetActiveScalars("scalars")
```

13.2.5 Helix source

Here is another polydata source example. This time, we generate the data programmatically.

```
1   # Code for 'Script'
2
3   #This script generates a helix curve.
4   #This is intended as the script of a 'Programmable Source'
5   import math
6   import numpy as np
7   from vtk.numpy_interface import algorithms as algs
8   from vtk.numpy_interface import dataset_adapter as dsa
```

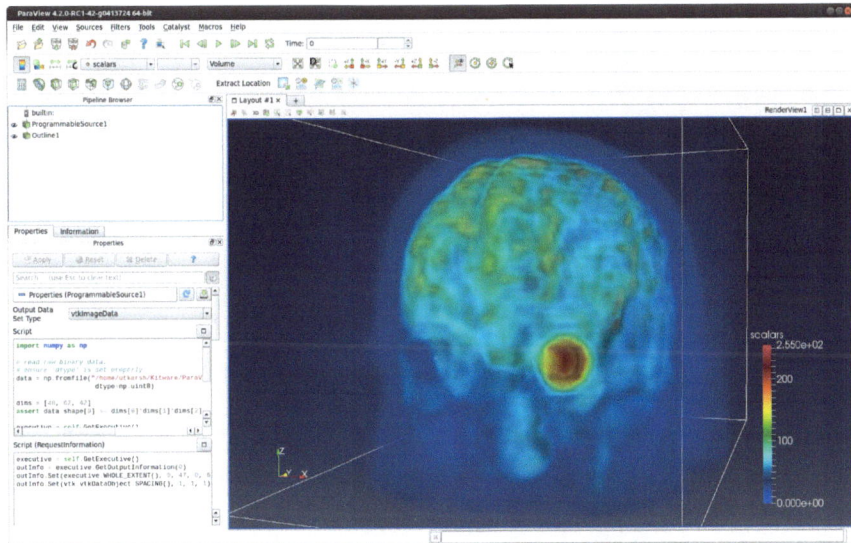

Figure 13.2: `Programmable Source` used to read *HeadMRVolume.raw* file available in the VTK data repository.

```
 9
10   numPts = 80   # Points along Helix
11   length = 8.0  # Length of Helix
12   rounds = 3.0  # Number of times around
13
14   # Compute the point coorindates for the helix.
15   index = np.arange(0, numPts, dtype=np.int32)
16   scalars = index * rounds * 2 * math.pi / numPts
17   x = index * length / numPts;
18   y = np.sin(scalars)
19   z = np.cos(scalars)
20
21   # Create a (x,y,z) coorindates array and associate that with
22   # points to pass to the output dataset.
23   coordinates = algs.make_vector(x, y, z)
24   pts = vtk.vtkPoints()
25   pts.SetData(dsa.numpyTovtkDataArray(coordinates, 'Points'))
26   output.SetPoints(pts)
27
28   # Add scalars to the output point data.
29   output.PointData.append(index, 'Index')
30   output.PointData.append(scalars, 'Scalars')
31
32   # Next, we need to define the topology i.e.
33   # cell information. This helix will be a single
34   # polyline connecting all the  points in order.
35   ptIds = vtk.vtkIdList()
36   ptIds.SetNumberOfIds(numPts)
37   for i in xrange(numPts):
38       #Add the points to the line. The first value indicates
39       #the order of the point on the line. The second value
```

```
40     #is a reference to a point in a vtkPoints object. Depends
41     #on the order that Points were added to vtkPoints object.
42     #Note that this will not be associated with actual points
43     #until it is added to a vtkPolyData object which holds a
44     #vtkPoints object.
45     ptIds.SetId(i, i)
46
47  # Allocate the number of 'cells' that will be added. We are just
48  # adding one vtkPolyLine 'cell' to the vtkPolyData object.
49  output.Allocate(1, 1)
50
51  # Add the poly line 'cell' to the vtkPolyData object.
52  output.InsertNextCell(vtk.VTK_POLY_LINE, ptIds)
```

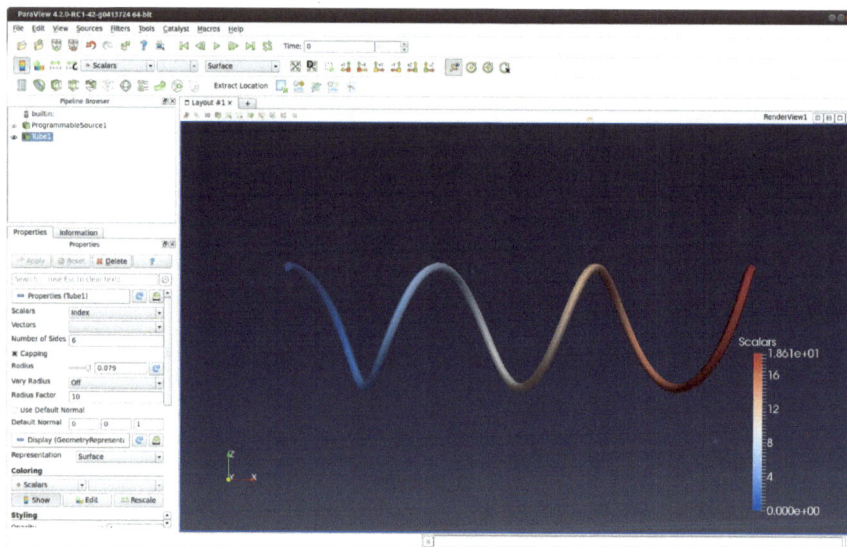

Figure 13.3: `Programmable Source` output generated using the script in Section 13.2.5. This visualization uses `Tube` filter to make the output polyline more prominent.

13.3   Recipes for Programmable Filter

One of the differences between the `Programmable Source` and the `Programmable Filter` is that the latter expects at least 1 input. Of course, the code in the `Programmable Filter` is free to disregard the input entirely and work exactly as `Programmable Source`. `Programmable Filter` is designed to customize data transformations. (E.g., when you want to compute derived quantities using expressions not directly possible with `Python Calculator` and `Calculator` or when you want to use other Python packages or even VTK filters not exposed in ParaView for processing the inputs.)

In this section we look at various recipes for `Programmable Filter`s.

13.3.1 Adding a new point/cell data array based on an input array

`Python Calculator` provides an easy mechanism of computing derived variables. You can also use the `Programmable Filter`. Typically, for such cases, ensure that the `Output DataSet Type` is set to `Same as Input`.

```
1  # Code for 'Script'
2
3  # 'inputs' is set to an array with data objects produced by inputs to
4  # this filter.
5
6  # Get the first input.
7  input0 = inputs[0]
8
9  # compute a value.
10 dataArray = input0.PointData["V"] / 2.0
11
12 # To access cell data, you can use input0.CellData.
13
14 # 'output' is a variable set to the output dataset.
15 output.PointData.append(dataArray, "V_half")
```

The thing to note about this code is that it will work as expected even when the input dataset is a composite dataset such as a Multiblock dataset (Section 3.1.10). Refer to Chapter 14 for details on how this works. There are cases, however, when you may want to explicitly iterate over blocks in an input multiblock dataset. For that, you can use the following snippet.

```
1  input0 = inputs[0]
2  if input0.IsA("vtkCompositeDataSet"):
3      # iterate over all non-empty blocks in the input
4      # composite dataset, including multiblock and AMR datasets.
5      for block in input0:
6          processBlock(block)
7  else:
8      processBlock(input0)
```

13.3.2 Computing tetrahedra volume

This recipe computes the volume for each tetrahedral cell in the input dataset. You can always simply use the `Python Calculator` to compute cell volume using the expression `volume(inputs[0])`. This recipe is provided to illustrate the API.

Ensure that the output type is set to `Same as Input`, and this filter assumes the input is an unstructured grid (Section 3.1.7).

```
1  # Code for 'Script'.
2
3  import numpy as np
4
5  # This filter computes the volume of the tetrahedra in an unstructured mesh.
6  # Note, this is just an illustration and not  the most efficient way for
7  # computing cell volume. You should use 'Python Calculator' instead.
8  input0 = inputs[0]
9
10 numTets = input0.GetNumberOfCells()
11
12 volumeArray = np.empty(numTets, dtype=np.float64)
```

```
13   for i in xrange(numTets):
14          cell = input0.GetCell(i)
15          p1 = input0.GetPoint(cell.GetPointId(0))
16          p2 = input0.GetPoint(cell.GetPointId(1))
17          p3 = input0.GetPoint(cell.GetPointId(2))
18          p4 = input0.GetPoint(cell.GetPointId(3))
19          volumeArray[i] = vtk.vtkTetra.ComputeVolume(p1,p2,p3,p4)
20
21   output.CellData.append(volumeArray, "Volume")
```

13.3.3   Labeling common points between two datasets

In this example, the programmable filter to takes two input datasets: A and B. It outputs dataset B with a new scalar array that labels the points in B that are also in A. You should select two datasets in the pipeline browser and then apply the programmable filter.

```
1   # Code for 'Script'
2
3   # Get the two inputs
4   A = inputs[0]
5   B = inputs[1]
6   # use len(inputs) to determine now many inputs are connected
7   # to this filter.
8
9   # We use numpy.in1d to test all which point coordinate components
10  # in  B are present in A as well.
11  maskX = np.in1d(B.Points[:,0], A.Points[:,0])
12  maskY = np.in1d(B.Points[:,1], A.Points[:,1])
13  maskZ = np.in1d(B.Points[:,2], A.Points[:,2])
14
15  # Combining each component mask, we get the mask for point
16  # itself.
17  mask = maskX & maskY & maskZ
18
19  # Now convert it to uint8, since bool arrays
20  # cannot be passed back to the VTK pipeline.
21  mask = np.asarray(mask, dtype=np.uint8)
22
23  # Initialize the output and add the labels array
24
25  # This ShallowCopy is needed since by default the output is
26  # initialized to be a shallow copy of the first input (inputs[0]),
27  # but we want it to be a description of the second input.
28  output.ShallowCopy(B.VTKObject)
29  output.PointData.append(mask, "labels")
```

13.3.4   Coloring points

Let's consider a case where you have three scalar colors ("R", "G", and "B") available on the point data. Let's say each of these has values in the range [0, 1], and we want to use these for coloring the points directly without using a color map.

Remember, to not use a color map, you uncheck Map Scalars in the Display properties section on the Properties panel. However, the array being color with needs to be an unsigned-char array with values in the range [0, 255] for each component. So, we'll need to convert the three scalar arrays into a single vector and then scale it too. This can be done as follows:

```
1   # Code for 'Script'
2
3   from vtk.numpy_interface import algorithms as algs
4   import numpy as np
5
6   r = inputs[0].PointData["R"]
7   g = inputs[0].PointData["G"]
8   b = inputs[0].PointData["B"]
9
10  # combine components into a single array.
11  rgb = algs.make_vector(r, g, b)
12
13  # now scale and convert the type to uint8 ==> unsigned char
14  rgb = np.asarray(rgb * 255.0, dtype=np.uint8)
15
16  # Add the array
17  output.PointData.append(rgb, "RGBColors")
```

As before, this will work just fine for composite datasets too, without having to iterate over the blocks in the composite dataset explicitly.

USING NUMPY FOR PROCESSING DATA

In chapter 13, we looked at several recipes for writing Python script for data processing that relied heavily on using NumPy for accessing arrays and performing operations on them. In this chapter, we take a closer look at the VTK-NumPy integration layer that makes it possible to use VTK and NumPy together, despite significant differences in the data representations between the two systems.

14.1 Teaser

Let's start with a teaser by creating a simple pipeline with `Sphere` connected to an `Elevation` filter, followed by the `Programmable Filter`. Let's see how we would access the input data object in the `Script` for the `Programmable Filter`.

```
1  from vtk.numpy_interface import dataset_adapter as dsa
2  from vtk.numpy_interface import algorithms as algs
3
4  data = inputs[0]
5  print data.PointData.keys()
6  print data.PointData['Elevation']
```

This example prints out the following in the output window.

```
1  ['Normals', 'Elevation']
2  [ 0.67235619  0.32764378  0.72819519  0.7388373   0.70217478  0.62546903
3    0.52391261  0.41762003  0.75839448  0.79325461  0.77003199  0.69332629
4    0.57832992  0.44781935  0.72819519  0.7388373   0.70217478  0.62546903
5    0.52391261  0.41762003  0.65528756  0.60746235  0.53835285  0.46164712
6    0.39253765  0.34471244  0.58238     0.47608739  0.37453097  0.29782525
7    0.2611627   0.27180481  0.55218065  0.42167011  0.30667371  0.22996798
8    0.20674542  0.24160551  0.58238     0.47608739  0.37453097  0.29782525
9    0.2611627   0.27180481  0.65528756  0.60746235  0.53835285  0.46164712
10   0.39253765  0.34471244]
```

The importance lies in the last three lines. In particular, note how we used a different API to access the `PointData` and the `Elevation` array in the last two lines. Also note that, when we printed the Elevation array, the output didn't look like one from a vtkDataArray. In fact:

```
1  elevation = data.PointData['Elevation']
2  print type(elevation)
3
4  import numpy
```

```
5 print isinstance(elevation, numpy.ndarray)
```

This will produce the following:

```
1 <class 'vtk.numpy_interface.dataset_adapter.VTKArray'>
2 True
```

So, a VTK array is a NumPy array? What kind of trickery is this, you say? What kind of magic makes the following possible?

```
1 data.PointData.append(elevation + 1, 'e plus one')
2 print algs.max(elevation)
3 print algs.max(data.PointData['e plus one'])
4 print data.VTKObject
```

The output here is:

```
1  0.5
2  1.5
3  vtkPolyData (0x7fa20d011c60)
4    ...
5    Point Data:
6      ...
7      Number Of Arrays: 3
8      Array 0 name = Normals
9      Array 1 name = Elevation
10     Array 2 name = e plus one
```

It is all in the numpy_interface module. It ties VTK datasets and data arrays to NumPy arrays and introduces a number of algorithms that can work on these objects. There is quite a bit to this module, and we will introduce it piece by piece in the rest of this chapter.

Let's wrap up this section with one final teaser.

```
1 print algs.gradient(data.PointData['Elevation'])
```

Output:

```
1 [[ 0.32640398   0.32640398   0.01982867]
2  [ 0.32640402   0.32640402   0.01982871]
3  ...
4  [ 0.41252578   0.20134845   0.2212007 ]
5  [ 0.41105482   0.21514832   0.0782456 ]]
```

Please note that this example is not very easily replicated by using pure NumPy. The gradient function returns the gradient of an unstructured grid – a concept that does not exist in NumPy. However, the ease-of-use of NumPy is there.

14.2   Understanding the `dataset_adapter` module

In this section, let's take a closer look at the `dataset_adapter` module. This module was designed to simplify accessing VTK datasets and arrays from Python and to provide a NumPy-style interface.

Let's continue with the example from the previous section. Remember, this script is being put in the `Programmable Filter`'s `Script`, connected to the `Sphere`, followed by the `Elevation` filter pipeline.

```
1 from vtk.numpy_interface import dataset_adapter as dsa
2 ...
3 print data
4 print isinstance(data, dsa.VTKObjectWrapper)
```

This will print:

```
1 <vtk.numpy_interface.dataset_adapter.PolyData object at 0x1101fbb50>
2 True
```

We can access the underlying VTK object using the VTKObject member:

```
1 >>> print type(data.VTKObject)
2 <type 'vtkobject'>
```

What we get as the *inputs* in the `Programmable Filter` is actually a Python object that wraps the VTK data object itself. The `Programmable Filter` does this by manually calling the `WrapDataObject` function from the `vtk.numpy_interface.dataset_adapter` module on the VTK data object. Note that the `WrapDataObject` function will return an appropriate wrapper class for all vtkDataSet subclasses, vtkTable, and all vtkCompositeData subclasses. Other vtkDataObject subclasses are not currently supported.

`VTKObjectWrapper` forwards VTK methods to its VTKObject so the VTK API can be accessed directy as follows:

```
1 >> print data.GetNumberOfCells()
2 96L
```

However, `VTKObjectWrappers` cannot be directly passed to VTK methods as an argument.

```
1 >>> s = vtk.vtkShrinkPolyData()
2 >>> s.SetInputData(data)
3 TypeError: SetInputData argument 1: method requires a VTK object
4 >>> s.SetInputData(data.VTKObject)
```

14.2.1 Dataset attributes

So far, we have a wrapper for VTK data objects that partially behaves like a VTK data object. This gets a little bit more interesting when we start looking at how to access the fields (arrays) contained within this dataset.

For simplicity, we will embed the output generated by the script in the code itself and use the >>> prefix to differentiate the code from the output.

```
1  >>> data.PointData
2  <vtk.numpy_interface.dataset_adapter.DataSetAttributes at 0x110f5b750>
3
4  >>> data.PointData.keys()
5  ['Normals', 'Elevation']
6
7  >>> data.CellData.keys()
8  []
9
10 >>> data.PointData['Elevation']
11 VTKArray([ 0.5       ,  0.        ,  0.45048442,  0.3117449 ,  0.11126047,
12        0.        ,  0.        ,  0.        ,  0.45048442,  0.3117449 ,
13        0.11126047,  0.        ,  0.        ,  0.        ,  0.45048442,
14        ...,
15        0.11126047,  0.        ,  0.        ,  0.        ,  0.45048442,
```

```
16              0.3117449 ,  0.11126047,  0.         ,  0.         ,  0.          ], dtype=float32
                )

17
18  >>> elevation = data.PointData['Elevation']
19
20  >>> elevation[:5]
21  VTKArray([0.5, 0., 0.45048442, 0.3117449, 0.11126047], dtype=float32)
22  Note that this works with composite datasets as well:
23
24  >>> mb = vtk.vtkMultiBlockDataSet()
25  >>> mb.SetNumberOfBlocks(2)
26  >>> mb.SetBlock(0, data.VTKObject)
27  >>> mb.SetBlock(1, data.VTKObject)
28  >>> mbw = dsa.WrapDataObject(mb)
29  >>> mbw.PointData
30  <vtk.numpy_interface.dataset_adapter.CompositeDataSetAttributes instance at 0
         x11109f758>

31
32  >>> mbw.PointData.keys()
33  ['Normals', 'Elevation']
34
35  >>> mbw.PointData['Elevation']
36  <vtk.numpy_interface.dataset_adapter.VTKCompositeDataArray at 0x1110a32d0>
```

It is possible to access `PointData`, `CellData`, `FieldData`, `Points` (subclasses of vtkPointSet only), and `Polygons` (vtkPolyData only) this way. We will continue to add accessors to more types of arrays through this API.

14.3   Working with arrays

For this section, let's change our test pipeline to consist of the `Wavelet` source connected to the `Programmable Filter`.

In the `Script`, we access the `RTData` point data array as follows:

```
1   # Code for 'Script'
2   image = output
3   rtdata = image.PointData['RTData']
4
5   # Let's transform this data as well, using another VTK filter.
6
7   tets = vtk.vtkDataSetTriangleFilter()
8   tets.SetInputDataObject(image.VTKObject)
9   tets.Update()
10
11  # Here, now we need to explicitly warp the output dataset to get a
12  # VTKObjectWrapper instance.
13  ugrid = dsa.WrapDataObject(tets.GetOutput())
14  rtdata2 = ugrid.PointData['RTData']
```

Here, we created two datasets: an image data (vtkImageData) and an unstructured grid (vtkUnstructuredGrid). They essentially represent the same data but the unstructured grid is created by tetrahedralizing the image data. So, we expect the unstructured grid to have the same points but more cells (tetrahedra).

14.3.1 The array API

`numpy_interface` array objects behave very similar to NumPy arrays. In fact, arrays from vtkDataSet subclasses are instances of VTKArray, which is a subclass of `numpy.ndarray`. Arrays from vtkCompositeDataSet and subclasses are not NumPy arrays, but they behave very similarly. We will outline the differences in a separate section. Let's start with the basics. All of the following work as expected.

As before, for simplicity, we will embed the output generated by the script in the code itself and use the >>> prefix to differentiate the code from the output.

```
>>> print rtdata[0]
60.763466

>>> print rtdata[-1]
57.113735

>>> print `rtdata[0:10:3]`
VTKArray([  60.76346588,   95.53707886,   94.97672272,  108.49817657], dtype=float32)

>>> print `rtdata + 1`
VTKArray([ 61.
76346588,   86.87795258,   73.80931091, ...,   68.51051331,
        44.34006882,   58.1137352 ], dtype=float32)

>>> print rtdata < 70
VTKArray([ True , False, False, ...,  True,  True,  True], dtype=bool)

# We will cover algorithms later. This is to generate a vector field.
>>> avector = algs.gradient(rtdata)

# To demonstrate that avector is really a vector
>>> print algs.shape(rtdata)
(9261,)

>>> print algs.shape(avector)
(9261, 3)

>>> print `avector[:, 0]`
VTKArray([ 25.69367027,    6.59600449,    5.38400745, ...,   -6.58120966,
          -5.77147198,   13.19447994])
```

A few things to note in this example:

- Single component arrays always have the following shape: (ntuples,) and not (ntuples, 1)
- Multiple component arrays have the following shape: (ntuples, ncomponents)
- Tensor arrays have the following shape: (ntuples, 3, 3)
- The above holds even for images and other structured data. All arrays have one dimension (1 component arrays), two dimensions (multi-component arrays), or three dimensions (tensor arrays).

One more cool thing: It is possible to use boolean arrays to index arrays. Thus, the following works very nicely:

```
>>> print `rtdata[rtdata < 70]`
VTKArray([ 60.76346588,  66.75043488,  69.19681549,  50.62128448,
        64.8801651 ,  57.72655106,  49.75050354,  65.05570221,
        57.38450241,  69.51113129,  64.24596405,  67.54656982,
        ...,
        61.18143463,  66.61872864,  55.39360428,  67.51051331,
```

```
 7          43.34006882,   57.1137352 ], dtype=float32)
 8
 9 >>> print 'avector[avector[:,0] > 10]'
10 VTKArray([[ 25.69367027,    9.01253319,    7.51076698],
11         [ 13.1944809 ,    9.01253128,    7.51076508],
12         [ 25.98717642,   -4.49800825,    7.80427408],
13         ...,
14         [ 12.9009738 ,  -16.86548471,   -7.80427504],
15         [ 25.69366837,   -3.48665428,   -7.51076889],
16         [ 13.19447994,   -3.48665524,   -7.51076794]])
```

14.3.2 Algorithms

You can do a lot simply using the array API. However, things get much more interesting when we start using the `numpy_interface.algorithms` module. We introduced it briefly in the previous examples. We will expand on it a bit more here. For a full list of algorithms, use help(algs). Here are some self-explanatory examples:

```
 1 >> print 'algs.sin(rtdata)'
 2 VTKArray([-0.87873501, -0.86987603, -0.52497   , ..., -0.99943125,
 3         -0.59898132,  0.53547275], dtype=float32)
 4
 5 >>> print 'algs.min(rtdata)'
 6 VTKArray(37.35310363769531)
 7
 8 >>> print 'algs.max(avector)'
 9 VTKArray(34.781060218811035)
10
11 >>> print 'algs.max(avector, axis=0)'
12 VTKArray([ 34.78106022,  29.01940918,  18.34743023])
13
14 >>> print 'algs.max(avector, axis=1)'
15 VTKArray([ 25.69367027,    9.30603981,    9.88350773, ...,   -4.35762835,
16         -3.78016186,  13.19447994])
```

If you haven't used the axis argument before, it is pretty easy. When you don't pass an axis value, the function is applied to all values of an array without any consideration for dimensionality. When $axis = 0$, the function will be applied to each component of the array independently. When $axis = 1$, the function will be applied to each tuple independently. Experiment if this is not clear to you. Functions that work this way include sum, min, max, std, and var.

Another interesting and useful function is where the indices of an array are returned where a particular condition occurs.

```
 1 >>> print 'algs.where(rtdata < 40)'
 2 (array([ 420, 9240]),)
 3 # For vectors, this will also return the component index if an axis is not
 4 # defined.
 5
 6 >>> print 'algs.where(avector < -29.7)'
 7 (VTKArray([4357, 4797, 4798, 4799, 5239]), VTKArray([1, 1, 1, 1, 1]))
```

So far, all of the functions that we discussed are directly provided by numpy. Many of the numpy ufuncs are included in the algorithms module. They all work with single arrays and composite data arrays. Algorithms also provide some functions that behave somewhat differently than their numpy counterparts. These include cross, dot, inverse, determinant, eigenvalue, eigenvector, etc. All of these functions are applied to each tuple rather than to a whole array/matrix. For example:

```
1  >>> amatrix = algs.gradient(avector)
2  >>> print 'algs.determinant(amatrix)'
3  VTKArray([-1221.2732624 ,  -648.48272183,    -3.55133937, ...,    28.2577152 ,
4         -629.28507693, -1205.81370163])
```

Note that everything above only leveraged per-tuple information and did not rely on the mesh. One of VTK's biggest strengths is that its data model supports a large variety of meshes, while its algorithms work generically on all of these mesh types. The algorithms module exposes some of this functionality. Other functions can be easily implemented by leveraging existing VTK filters. We used gradient before to generate a vector and a matrix. Here it is again:

```
1  >>> avector = algs.gradient(rtdata)
2  >>> amatrix = algs.gradient(avector)
```

Functions like this require access to the dataset containing the array and the associated mesh. This is one of the reasons why we use a subclass of ndarray in dataset_adapter:

```
1  >>> print 'rtdata.DataSet'
2  <vtk.numpy_interface.dataset_adapter.DataSet at 0x11b61e9d0>
```

Each array points to the dataset containing it. Functions such as gradient use the mesh and the array together. Numpy provides a gradient function too, you say. What is so exciting about yours? Well, this:

```
1  >>> print 'algs.gradient(rtdata2)'
2  VTKArray([[ 25.46767712,   8.78654003,    7.28477383],
3         [  6.02292252,   8.99845123,    7.49668884],
4         [  5.23528767,   9.80230141,    8.3005352 ],
5         ...,
6         [ -6.43249083,  -4.27642155,   -8.30053616],
7         [ -5.19838905,  -3.47257614,   -7.49668884],
8         [ 13.42047501,  -3.26066017,   -7.28477287]])
9  >>> rtdata2.DataSet.GetClassName()
10 'vtkUnstructuredGrid'
```

Gradient and algorithms that require access to a mesh work whether that mesh is a uniform grid, a curvilinear grid, or an unstructured grid thanks to VTK's data model. Take a look at various functions in the algorithms module to see all the cool things that can be accomplished using it. In the remaining sections, we demonstrate how specific problems can be solved using these modules.

14.4   Handling composite datasets

In this section, we take a closer look at composite datasets. For this example, our pipeline is Sphere source, and Cone source is set as two inputs to the Programmable Filter.

We can create a multiblock dataset in the Programmable Filter's Script as follows:

```
1  # Let's assume inputs[0] is the output from Sphere and
2  # inputs[1] is the output from Cone.
3  mb = vtk.vtkMultiBlockDataSet()
4  mb.SetBlock(0, inputs[0].VTKObject)
5  mb.SetBlock(1, inputs[1].VTKObject)
```

Many of VTK's algorithms work with composite datasets without any change. For example:

```
1  e = vtk.vtkElevationFilter()
2  e.SetInputData(mb)
```

```
3  e.Update()
4
5  mbe = e.GetOutputDataObject(0)
6  print mbe.GetClassName()
```

This will output `vtkMultiBlockDataSet`.

Now that we have a composite dataset with a scalar, we can use numpy_interface. As before, for simplicity, we will embed the output generated by the script in the code itself and use the `>>>` prefix to differentiate the code from the output.

```
1  >>> from vtk.numpy_interface import dataset_adapter as dsa
2  >>> mbw = dsa.WrapDataObject(mbe)
3  >>> print 'mbw.PointData.keys()'
4  ['Normals', 'Elevation']
5  >>> elev = mbw.PointData['Elevation']
6  >>> print 'elev'
7  <vtk.numpy_interface.dataset_adapter.VTKCompositeDataArray at 0x1189ee410>
```

Note that the array type is different than we have previously seen (`VTKArray`). However, it still works the same way.

```
1  >>> from vtk.numpy_interface import algorithms as algs
2  >>> print algs.max(elev)
3  0.5
4  >>> print algs.max(elev + 1)
5  1.5
```

You can individually access the arrays of each block as follows.

```
1  >>> print 'elev.Arrays[0]'
2  VTKArray([ 0.5        ,  0.        ,  0.45048442,  0.3117449 ,  0.11126047,
3             0.        ,  0.        ,  0.        ,  0.45048442,  0.3117449 ,
4             0.11126047,  0.        ,  0.        ,  0.        ,  0.45048442,
5             0.3117449 ,  0.11126047,  0.        ,  0.        ,  0.        ,
6             0.45048442,  0.3117449 ,  0.11126047,  0.        ,  0.        ,
7             0.        ,  0.45048442,  0.3117449 ,  0.11126047,  0.        ,
8             0.        ,  0.        ,  0.45048442,  0.3117449 ,  0.11126047,
9             0.        ,  0.        ,  0.        ,  0.45048442,  0.3117449 ,
10            0.11126047,  0.        ,  0.        ,  0.        ,  0.45048442,
11            0.3117449 ,  0.11126047,  0.        ,  0.        ,  0.        ], dtype=float32
              )
```

Note that indexing is slightly different.

```
1  >>> print elev[0:3]
2  [VTKArray([ 0.5,  0.,  0.45048442], dtype=float32),
3   VTKArray([ 0.,  0.,  0.43301269], dtype=float32)]
```

The return value is a composite array consisting of two VTKArrays. The [] operator simply returned the first four values of each array. In general, all indexing operations apply to each VTKArray in the composite array collection. It is similar for algorithms, where:

```
1  >>> print algs.where(elev < 0.5)
2  [(array([ 1,  2,  3,  4,  5,  6,  7,  8,  9, 10, 11, 12, 13, 14, 15, 16, 17,
3           18, 19, 20, 21, 22, 23, 24, 25, 26, 27, 28, 29, 30, 31, 32, 33, 34,
4           35, 36, 37, 38, 39, 40, 41, 42, 43, 44, 45, 46, 47, 48, 49]),),
5          (array([0, 1, 2, 3, 4, 5, 6]),)]
```

Now, let's look at the other array called Normals.

```
1  >>> normals = mbw.PointData['Normals']
2  >>> print 'normals.Arrays[0]'
3  VTKArray([[  0.00000000e+00,   0.00000000e+00,   1.00000000e+00],
4            [  0.00000000e+00,   0.00000000e+00,  -1.00000000e+00],
5            [  4.33883727e-01,   0.00000000e+00,   9.00968850e-01],
6            [  7.81831503e-01,   0.00000000e+00,   6.23489797e-01],
7            [  9.74927902e-01,   0.00000000e+00,   2.22520933e-01],
8            ...
9            [  6.89378142e-01,  -6.89378142e-01,   2.22520933e-01],
10           [  6.89378142e-01,  -6.89378142e-01,  -2.22520933e-01],
11           [  5.52838326e-01,  -5.52838326e-01,  -6.23489797e-01],
12           [  3.06802124e-01,  -3.06802124e-01,  -9.00968850e-01]], dtype=float32)
13 >>> print 'normals.Arrays[1]'
14 <vtk.numpy_interface.dataset_adapter.VTKNoneArray at 0x1189e7790>
```

Notice how the second array is a VTKNoneArray. This is because vtkConeSource does not produce normals. Where an array does not exist, we use a VTKNoneArray as placeholder. This allows us to maintain a one-to-one mapping between datasets of a composite dataset and the arrays in the VTKCompositeDataArray. It also allows us to keep algorithms working in parallel without a lot of specialized code.

Where many of the algorithms apply independently to each array in a collection, some algorithms are global. Take min and max, for example, as we demonstrated above. It is sometimes useful to get per-block answers. For this, you can use _per_block algorithms.

```
1  >>> print algs.max_per_block(elev)
2  [VTKArray(0.5, dtype=float32), VTKArray(0.4330126941204071, dtype=float32)]
```

These work very nicely together with other operations. For example, here is how we can normalize the elevation values in each block.

```
1  >>> _min = algs.min_per_block(elev)
2  >>> _max = algs.max_per_block(elev)
3  >>> _norm = (elev - _min) / (_max - _min)
4  >>> print algs.min(_norm)
5  0.0
6  >>> print algs.max(_norm)
7  1.0
```

Once you grasp these features, you should be able to use composite arrays very similarly to single arrays.

A final note on composite datasets: The composite data wrapper provided by numpy_interface.dataset_adapter offers a few convenience functions to traverse composite datasets. Here is a simple example:

```
1  >>> for ds in mbw:
2  >>>     print type(ds)
3  <class 'vtk.numpy_interface.dataset_adapter.PolyData'>
4  <class 'vtk.numpy_interface.dataset_adapter.PolyData'>
```

REMOTE AND PARALLEL VISUALIZATION

One of the goals of the ParaView application is enabling data analysis and visualization for large datasets. ParaView was born out of the need for visualizating simulation results from simulations run on supercomputing resources that are often too big for a single desktop machine to handle. To enable interactive visualization of such datasets, ParaView uses remote and/or parallel data processing. The basic concept is that if a dataset cannot fit on a desktop machine due to memory or other limitations, we can split the dataset among a cluster of machines, driven from your desktop. In this chapter, we will look at the basics of remote and parallel data processing using ParaView. For information on setting up clusters, please refer to the ParaView Wiki.[19]

> **ⓘ Did you know?**
>
> *Remote and parallel processing are often used together, but they refer to different concepts, and it is possible to have one without the other.*
>
> *In the case of ParaView, remote processing refers to the concept of having a client, typically paraview or pvpython, connecting to a pvserver, which could be running on a different, remote machine. All the data processing and, potentially, the rendering can happen on the pvserver. The client drives the visualization process by building the visualization pipeline and viewing the generated results.*
>
> *Parallel processing refers to a concept where instead of single core — which we call a* `rank` *— processing the entire dataset, we split the dataset among multiple ranks. Typically, an instance of pvserver runs in parallel on more than one rank. If a client is connected to a server that runs in parallel, we are using both remote and parallel processing.*
>
> *In the case of pvbatch, we have an application that operates in parallel but without a client connection. This is a case of parallel processing without remote processing.*

15.1   Understanding remote processing

Let's consider a simple use-case. Let's say you have two computers, one located at your office and another in your home. The one at the office is a nicer, beefier machine with larger memory and computing capabilities than the one at home. That being the case, you often run your simulations on the office machine, storing the resulting files on the disk attached to your office machine. When you're at work, to visualize those results, you simply launch *paraview* and open the data file(s). Now, what if you need to do the visualization and data analysis from home? You have several options:

- You can copy the data files over to your home machine and then use *paraview* to visualize them. This is tedious, however, as you not only have to constantly keep copying/updating your files manually, but your machine has poorer performance due to the decreased compute capabilities and memory available on it!
- You can use a desktop sharing system like *Remote Desktop* or *VNC*, but those can be flaky depending on your network connection.

Alternatively, you can use ParaView's remote processing capabilities. The concept is fairly simple. You have two separate processes: *pvserver* (which runs on your work machine) and a *paraview* client (which runs on your home machine). They communicate with each other over sockets (over an SHH tunnel, if needed). As far as using *paraview* in this mode, it's no different than how we have been using it so far – you create pipelines and then look at the data produced by those pipelines in views and so on. The pipelines themselves, however, are created remotely on the *pvserver* process. Thus, the pipelines have access to the disks on your work machine. The `Open File` dialog will in fact browse the file system on your work machine, i.e., the machine on which *pvserver* is running. Any filters that you create in your visualization pipeline execute on the *pvserver*.

While all the data processing happens on the *pvserver*, when it comes to rendering, *paraview* can be configured to either do the rendering on the server process and deliver only images to the client (remote rendering) or to deliver the geometries to be rendered to the client and let it do the rendering locally (local rendering). When remote rendering, you'll be using the graphics capabilities on your work machine (the machine running the *pvserver*). Every time a new rendering needs to be obtained (for example, when pipeline parameters are changed or you interact with the camera, etc.), the *pvserver* process will re-render a new image and deliver that to the client. When local rendering, the geometries to be rendered are delivered to the client and the client renders those locally. Thus, not all interactions require server-side processing. Only when the visualization pipeline is updated does the server need to deliver updated geometries to the client.

15.2 Remote visualization in `paraview`

15.2.1 Starting a remote server

To begin using ParaView for remote data processing and visualization, we must first start the server application *pvserver* on the remote system. To do this, connect to your remote system using a shell and run:

```
> pvserver
```

You will see this startup message on the terminal:

```
Waiting for client...
Connection URL: cs://myhost:11111
Accepting connection(s): myhost:11111
```

This means that the server has started and is listening for a connection from a client.

15.2.2 Configuring a server connection

To connect to this server with the *paraview* client, select File ⟩ Connect or click the ⬢ icon in the toolbar to bring up the `Choose Server Configuration` dialog.

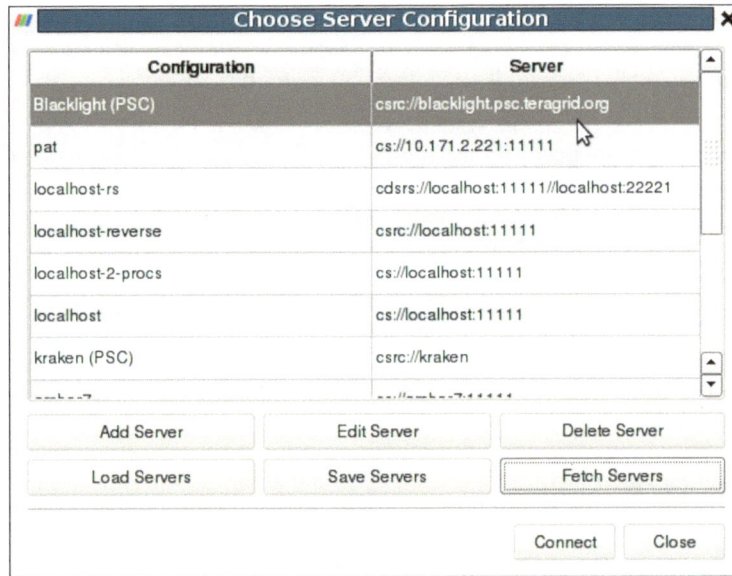

Figure 15.1: The `Choose Server Configuration` dialog is used to connect to a server.

Common Errors

If your server is behind a firewall and you are attempting to connect to it from outside the firewall, the connection may not be established successfully. You may also try reverse connections (Section 15.4) as a workaround for firewalls. Please consult your network manager if you have network connection problems.

Figure 15.1 shows the `Choose Server Configuration` dialog with a number of entries for remote servers. In the figure, a number of servers have already been configured, but when you first open this dialog, this list will be empty. Before you can connect to a remote server, you will need to add an entry to the list by clicking on the `Add Server` button. When you do, you will see the `Edit Server Configuration` dialog as in Figure 15.2.

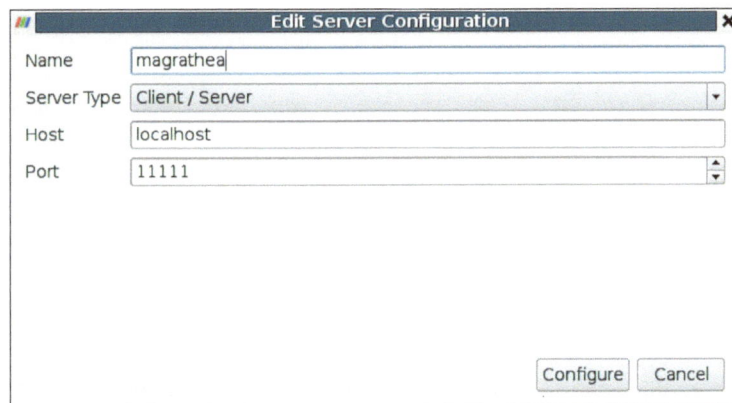

Figure 15.2: The `Edit Server Configuration` dialog is used to configure settings for connecting to remote servers.

You will need to set a name for the connection, the server type, the DNS name of the host on which you just started the server, and the port. The default `Server Type` is set to Client / Server, which means that the server will be listening for an incoming connection from the client. There are several other options for this setting that we will discuss later.

When you are done, click the `Configure` button. Another dialog, as shown in Figure 15.3, will appear where you specify how to start the server. Since we started the server manually, we will leave the `Startup Type` on the default `Manual` setting. You can optionally set the `Startup Type` to `Command` and specify an external shell command to launch a server process.

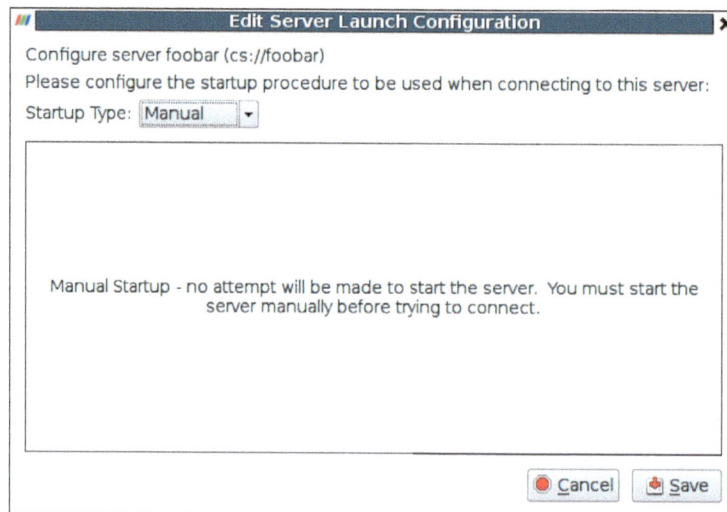

Figure 15.3: Configure the server manually. It must be started outside of ParaView.

When you click the `Save` button, this particular server configuration will be saved for future use. You can go back and edit the server configuration by selecting the entry in the list of servers and clicking the `Edit Server` button in the `Choose Server Configuration` dialog. You can delete it by clicking the `Delete` button.

Server configurations can be imported and exported through the `Choose Server Configuration` dialog. Use the `Load Servers` button to load a server configuration file and the `Save Servers` button to save a server configuration file. Files can be exchanged with others to access the same remote servers.

ⓘ Did you know?

Visualization centers can provide system-wide server configurations on web servers to allow non-experts to simply select an already configured ParaView server. The format of the XML file for saving the server configurations is discussed online on the ParaView Wiki at `http://paraview.org/Wiki/Server_Configuration`. *These site-wide settings can be loaded with the* `Fetch Servers` *button.*

15.2.3 Connect to the remote server

To connect to the server, select the server configuration you just set up from the configuration list and click `Connect`. We are now ready to build the visualization pipelines.

Common Errors

ParaView does not perform any kind of authentication when clients attempt to connect to a server. For that reason, we recommend that you do not run pvserver on a computing resource that is open to the outside world.

ParaView also does not encrypt data sent between the client and server. If your data is sensitive, please ensure that proper network security measures have been taken. The typical approach is to use an SSH tunnel.

15.2.4 Setting up a client/server visualization pipeline

Using *paraview* when connected to a remote server is not any different than when it's being used in the default stand-alone mode. The only difference, as far as the user interface goes, is that the `Pipeline Browser` reflects the name of the server to which you are connected. The address of the server connection next to the 📱 icon changes from `builtin:` to `cs://myhost:11111`.

Since the data processing pipelines are executing on the server side, all file I/O also happens on the server side. Hence, the `Open File` dialog, when opening a new data file, will browse the file system local to the *pvserver* executable and not the *paraview* client.

15.3 Remote visualization in `pvpython`

The *pvpython* executable can be used by itself for visualization of local data, but it can also act as a client that connects to a remote *pvserver*. Before creating a pipeline in *pvpython*, use the `Connect` function:

```
1  # Connect to remote server "myhost" on the default port, 11111
2  >>> Connect("myhost")  # Connect to remote server "myhost" on a
3                         # specified port
4  >>> Connect("myhost", 11111)
```

Now, when new sources are created, the data produced by the sources will reside on the server. In the case of *pvpython*, all data remains on the server and images are generated on the server too. Images are sent to the client for display or for saving to the local filesystem.

15.4 Reverse connections

It is frequently the case that remote computing resources are located behind a network firewall, making it difficult to connect a client outside the firewall to a server behind it. ParaView provides a way to set up a *reverse connection* that reverses the usual client server roles when establishing a connection.

To use a remote connection, two steps must be performed. First, in *paraview*, a new connection must be configured with the connection type set to reverse. To do this, open the `Choose Server Configuration` dialog through the `File` ⟩ ⟩ `Connect` menu item. Add a new connection, setting the `Name` to "myhost (reverse)", and select `Client / Server (reverse connection)` for `Server Type`. Click `Configure`. In the `Edit Server Launch Configuration` dialog that comes up, set the `Startup Type` to `Manual`. Save the configuration. Next, select this configuration and click `Connect`. A message window will appear showing that the client is awaiting a connection from the server.

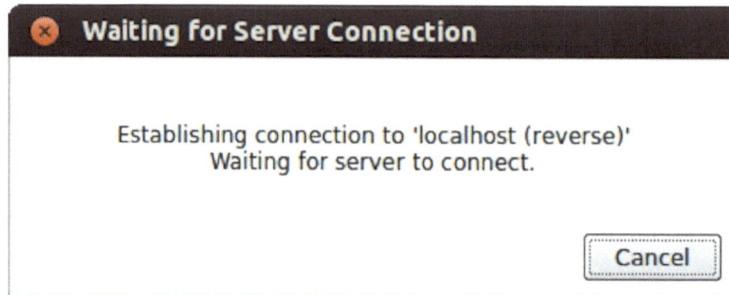

Figure 15.4: Message window showing that the client is awaiting a connection from a server.

Second, *pvserver* must be started with the `--reverse-connection` (`-rc`) flag. To tell *pvserver* the name of the client, set the `--client-host` (`-ch`) command-line argument to the hostname of the machine on which the *paraview* client is running. You can specify a port with the `--server-port` (`-sp`) command-line argument.

```
pvserver -rc --client-host=mylocalhost --server-port=11111
```

When the server starts, it prints a message indicating the success or failure of connecting to the client. When the connection is successful, you will see the following text in the shell:

```
Connecting to client (reverse connection requested)...
Connection URL: csrc://mylocalhost:11111
Client connected.
```

To wait for reverse connections from a *pvserver* in *pvpython*, you use `ReverseConnect` instead of `Connect`.

```
1  # To wait for connects from a 'pvserver' on the default port
2  # viz. 11111
3  >>> ReverseConnect()
4
5  # Optionally, you can specify the port number as the argument.
6  >>> ReverseConnect(11111)
```

15.5   Understanding parallel processing

Parallel processing, put simply, implies processing the data in parallel, simultaneously using multiple workers. Typically, these workers are different processes that could be running on a multicore machine or on several nodes of a cluster. Let's call these ranks. In most data processing and visualization algorithms, work is directly related to the amount of data that needs to be processed, i.e., the number of cells or points in the dataset. Thus, a straight-forward way of distributing the work among ranks is to split an input dataset into multiple chunks and then have each rank operate only an independent set of chunks. Conveniently, for most algorithms, the result obtained by splitting the dataset and processing it separately is same as the result that we'd get if we processed the dataset in a single chunk. There are, of course, exceptions. Let's try to understand this better with an example. For demonstration purposes, consider this very simplified mesh.

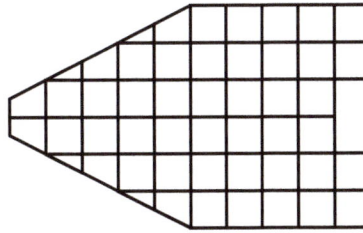

Now, let us say we want to perform visualizations on this mesh using three processes. We can divide the cells of the mesh as shown below with the blue, yellow, and pink regions.

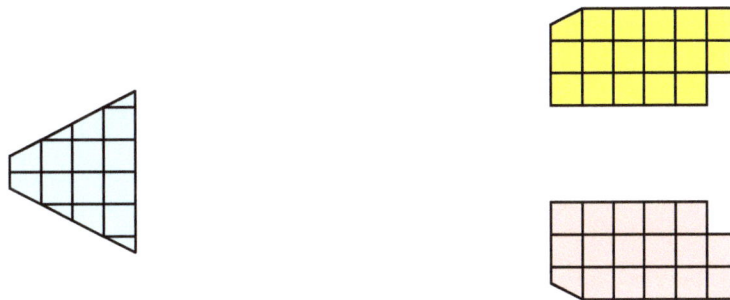

Once partitioned, some visualization algorithms will work by simply allowing each process to independently run the algorithm on its local collection of cells. Take clipping as an example. Let's say that we define a clipping plane and give that same plane to each of the processes.

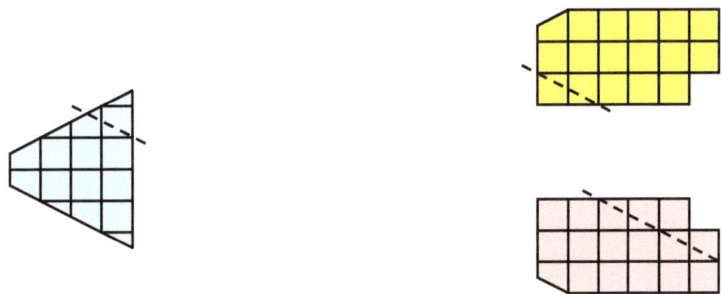

Each process can independently clip its cells with this plane. The end result is the same as if we had done the clipping serially. If we were to bring the cells together (which we would never actually do for large data for obvious reasons), we would see that the clipping operation took place correctly.

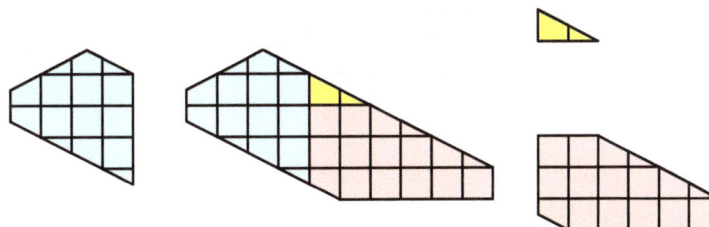

15.5.1 Ghost levels

Unfortunately, blindly running visualization algorithms on partitions of cells does not always result in the correct answer. As a simple example, consider the external faces algorithm. The external faces algorithm finds all cell faces that belong to only one cell, thereby, identifying the boundaries of the mesh.

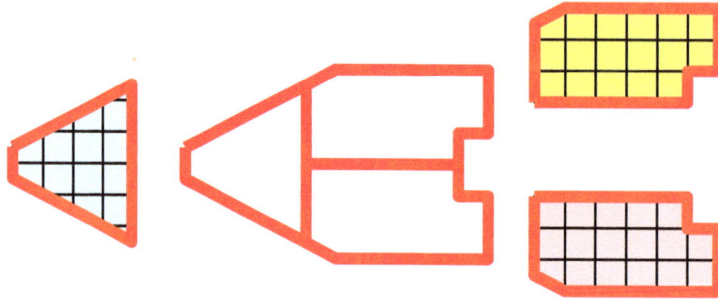

Oops! We see that when all the processes ran the external faces algorithm independently, many internal faces where incorrectly identified as being external. This happens where a cell in one partition has a neighbor in another partition. A process has no access to cells in other partitions, so there is no way of knowing that these neighboring cells exist.

The solution employed by ParaView and other parallel visualization systems is to use ghost cells. Ghost cells are cells that are held in one process but actually belong to another. To use ghost cells, we first have to identify all the neighboring cells in each partition. We then copy these neighboring cells to the partition and mark them as ghost cells, as indicated with the gray colored cells in the following example.

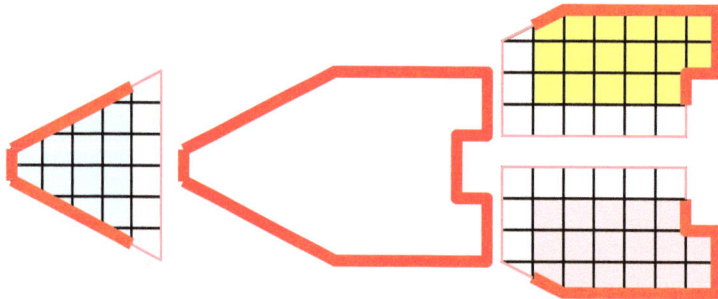

When we run the external faces algorithm with the ghost cells, we see that we are still incorrectly identifying some internal faces as external. However, all of these misclassified faces are on ghost cells, and the faces inherit the ghost status of the cell from which it came. ParaView then strips off the ghost faces, and we are left with the correct answer.

In this example, we have shown one layer of ghost cells: only those cells that are direct neighbors of the partition's cells. ParaView also has the ability to retrieve multiple layers of ghost cells, where each layer contains the neighbors of the previous layer not already contained in a lower ghost layer or in the original data itself. This is useful when we have cascading filters that each require their own layer of ghost cells. They each request an additional layer of ghost cells from upstream, and then remove a layer from the data before sending it downstream.

15.5.2 Data partitioning

Since we are breaking up and distributing our data, it is prudent to address the ramifications of how we partition the data. The data shown in the previous example has a spatially coherent partitioning. That is, all the cells of each partition are located in a compact region of space. There are other ways to partition data. For example, you could have a random partitioning.

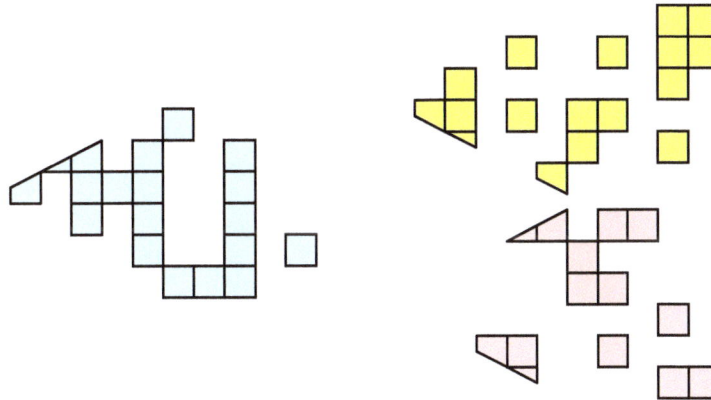

Random partitioning has some nice features. It is easy to create and is friendly to load balancing. However, a serious problem exists with respect to ghost cells.

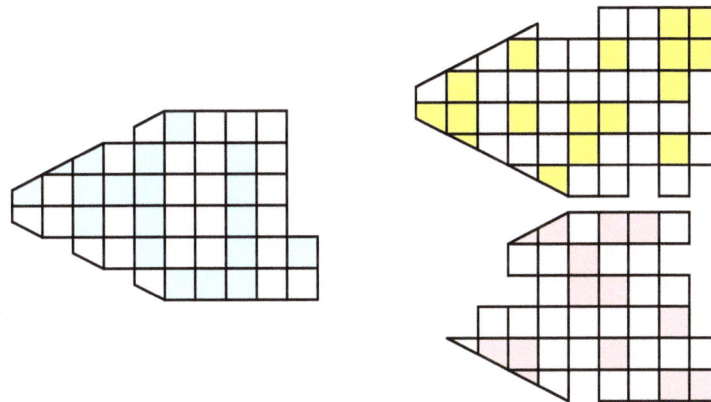

In this example, we see that a single level of ghost cells nearly replicates the entire data set on all processes. We have thus removed any advantage we had with parallel processing. Because ghost cells are used so frequently, random partitioning is not used in ParaView.

15.5.3   D3 Filter

The previous section described the importance of load balancing and ghost levels for parallel visualization. This section describes how to achieve that.

Load balancing and ghost cells are handled automatically by ParaView when you are reading structured data (image data, rectilinear grid, and structured grid). The implicit topology makes it easy to break the data into spatially coherent chunks and identify where neighboring cells are located.

It is an entirely different matter when you are reading in unstructured data (poly data and unstructured grid). There is no implicit topology and no neighborhood information available. ParaView is at the mercy of how the data was written to disk. Thus, when you read in unstructured data, there is no guarantee of how well-load balanced your data will be. It is also unlikely that the data will have ghost cells available, which means that the output of some filters may be incorrect.

Fortunately, ParaView has a filter that will both balance your unstructured data and create ghost cells. This filter is called D3, which is short for distributed data decomposition. Using D3 is easy; simply attach the filter (located in `Filters` ⟩ `Alphabetical` ⟩ `D3`) to whatever data you wish to repartition.

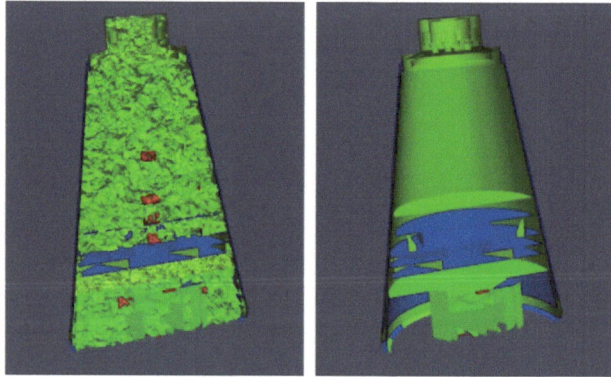

The most common use case for D3 is to attach it directly to your unstructured grid reader. Regardless of how well-load balanced the incoming data might be, it is important to be able to retrieve ghost cell so that subsequent filters will generate the correct data. The example above shows a cutaway of the extract surface filter on an unstructured grid. On the left, we see that there are many faces improperly extracted because we are missing ghost cells. On the right, the problem is fixed by first using the D3 filter.

15.6 ParaView architecture

Before we see how to use ParaView for parallel data processing, let's take a closer look at the ParaView architecture. ParaView is designed as a three-tier client-server architecture. The three logical units of ParaView are as follows.

Data Server The unit responsible for data reading, filtering, and writing. All of the pipeline objects seen in the pipeline browser are contained in the data server. The data server can be parallel.

Render Server The unit responsible for rendering. The render server can also be parallel, in which case built-in parallel rendering is also enabled.

Client The unit responsible for establishing visualization. The client controls the object creation, execution, and destruction in the servers, but does not contain any of the data (thus allowing the servers to scale without bottlenecking on the client). If there is a GUI, that is also in the client. The client is always a serial application.

These logical units need not by physically separated. Logical units are often embedded in the same application, removing the need for any communication between them. There are three modes in which you can run ParaView.

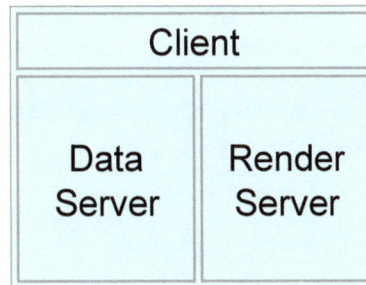

The first mode, with which you are already familiar, is standalone mode. In standalone mode, the client, data server, and render server are all combined into a single serial application. When you run the *paraview* application, you are automatically connected to a builtin server so that you are ready to use the full features of ParaView.

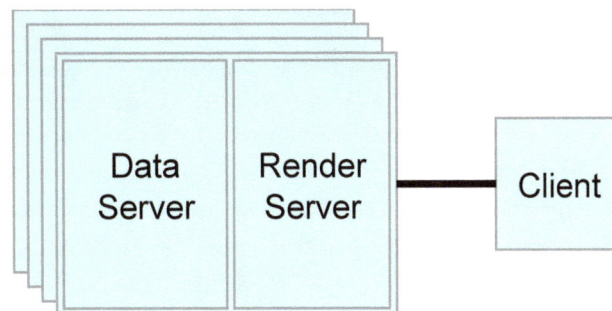

The second mode is client-server mode. In client-server mode, you execute the *pvserver* program on a parallel machine and connect to it with the *paraview* client application (or *pvpython*). The *pvserver* program has both the data server and render server embedded in it, so both data processing and rendering take place there. The client and server are connected via a socket, which is assumed to be a relatively slow mode of communication, so data transfer over this socket is minimized. We saw this mode of operation in Section 15.2.

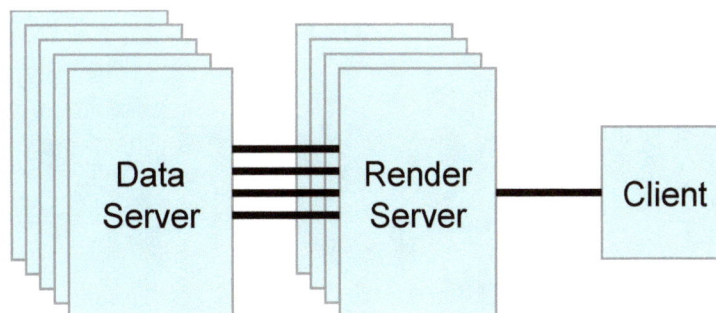

The third mode is client-render server-data server mode. In this mode, all three logical units are running in separate programs. As before, the client is connected to the render server via a single socket connection. The render server and data server are connected by many socket connections, one for each process in the render server. Data transfer over the sockets is minimized.

Although the client-render server-data server mode is supported, we almost never recommend using it. The original intention of this mode is to take advantage of heterogeneous environments where one might have a large, powerful computational platform and a second smaller parallel machine with graphics hardware in it. However, in practice, we find any benefit is almost always outstripped by the time it takes to move geometry from the data server to the render server. If the computational platform is much bigger than the graphics cluster, then use software rendering on the large computational platform. If the two platforms are about the same size, just perform all the computation on the graphics cluster. The executables used for this mode are *paraview* (or *pvpython*) (acting as the client), *pvdataserver* for the data-server, and *pvrenderserver* for the render-server.

15.7 Parallel processing in `paraview` and `pvpython`

To leverage parallel processing capabilities in *paraview* or *pvpython*, one has to use remote visualization, i.e., one has to connect to a *pvserver*. The processing for connecting to this *pvserver* is not different from what we say in Sections 15.2 and 15.3. The only thing that changes is how the *pvserver* is launched.

You can start *pvserver* to run on more than one processing core using *mpirun*.

```
mpirun -np 4 pvserver
```

This will run *pvserver* on four processing cores. It will still listen for an incoming connection from a client on the default port. The big difference when running *pvserver* this way is that when data is loaded from a source, it will be distributed across the four cores if the data source is "parallel aware" and supports distributing the data across the different processing cores.

To see how this data is distributed, run *pvserver* as the command above and connect to it with *paraview*. Next, create another Sphere source using Source ⟩ Sphere. Change the array to color by to vtkProcessId. You will see an image like Figure 15.5.

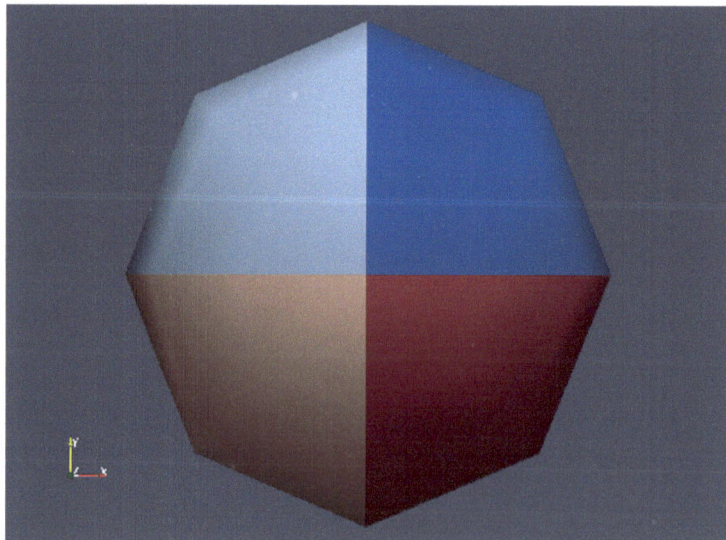

Figure 15.5: Sphere source colored by vtkProcessId array that encodes the processing core on which the sphere data resides. Here, the sphere data is split among the four processing cores invoked by the command mpirun -np 4 pvserver.

If a data reader or source is not "parallel aware", you can still get the benefits of spreading the data among processing cores by using the D3 filter. This filter partitions a dataset into convex regions and transfers each region to a different processing core. To see an example of how D3 partitions a data set, create a Source ⟩ Wavelet while *paraview* is still connected to the *pvserver*. Next, select Filters ⟩ Alphabetical ⟩ D3 and click Apply. The output of D3 will not initially appear different from the original wavelet source. If you color by vtkProcessId, however, you will see the four partitions that have been distributed to the server processing cores.

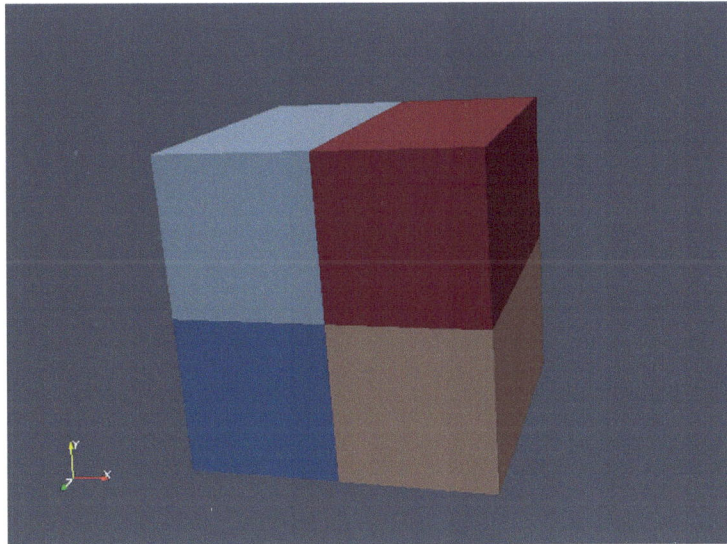

Figure 15.6: Wavelet source processed by the D3 filter and colored by vtkProcessId array. Note how four regions of the image data are split evenly among the four processing cores when *pvserver* is run with mpirun -np 4 pvserver.

15.8 Using pvbatch

In Section 15.7, we said that to use parallel processing capabilities, one has to use remote visualization, i.e., one must use ParaView in a client-server mode with the client (*paraview* or *pvpython*) connecting to a server (*pvserver*) that is being run in parallel using *mpirun*. However, there is one exception: *pvbatch*. *pvpython* and *pvbatch* are quite similar in that both are similar to the *python* executable that can be used to run Python scripts. The extra thing that these executables do when compared with the standard *python* is that they initialize the environment so that any scripts that you run will be able to locate the ParaView Python modules and libraries automatically. *pvpython* is exactly like the *paraview* executable without the GUI. You can think of it as the GUI from *paraview* is replaced by a Python interpreter in *pvpython*. *pvbatch*, on the other hand, can be thought of a *pvserver* where, instead of taking the control command from a remote client (*paraview* or *pvpython*), in *pvbatch*, the commands are taken from a Python script that is executed in the *pvbatch* executable itself. Since *pvbatch* is akin to the *pvserver*, unlike *pvpython*, it can be run in parallel using *mpirun*. In that case, the root rank (or the first rank or the rank with index 0) is the one that acts as the client, interpreting the Python script to execute the commands. Since *pvbatch* is designed to act is its own server, you cannot connect to a remote server in the Python script, i.e., you cannot use simple.Connect. Furthermore, *pvbatch* is designed for batch operation, which means that you can only specify the Python script as a command line argument. Unlike *pvpython*, you cannot run this executable to get an interactive shell to enter Python commands.

```
# process the sample.py script in single process mode.
> pvbatch sample.py

# process the sample.py script in parallel.
> mpirun -np 4 sample.py
```

In general, you should use *pvpython* if you will be using the interpreter interactively and *pvbatch* if you are running in parallel.

15.9 Rendering

Rendering is the process of synthesizing the images that you see based on your data. The ability to effectively interact with your data depends highly on the speed of the rendering. Thanks to advances in 3D hardware acceleration, fueled by the computer gaming market, we have the ability to render 3D quickly even on moderately-priced computers. But, of course, the speed of rendering is proportional to the amount of data being rendered. As data gets bigger, the rendering process naturally gets slower.

To ensure that your visualization session remains interactive, ParaView supports two modes of rendering that are automatically flipped as necessary. In the first mode, still render, the data is rendered at the highest level of detail. This rendering mode ensures that all of the data is represented accurately. In the second mode, interactive render, speed takes precedence over accuracy. This rendering mode endeavors to provide a quick rendering rate regardless of data size.

While you are interacting with a 3D view (for example, rotating, panning, or zooming with the mouse), ParaView uses an interactive render. This is because, during the interaction, a high frame rate is necessary to make these features usable and because each frame is immediately replaced with a new rendering while the interaction is occurring so that fine details are less important during this mode. At any time when interaction of the 3D view is not taking place, ParaView uses a still render so that the full detail of the data is available as you study it. As you drag your mouse in a 3D view to move the data, you may see an approximate rendering. The full detail will be presented as soon as you release the mouse button.

The interactive render is a compromise between speed and accuracy. As such, many of the rendering parameters concern when and how lower levels of detail are used.

15.9.1 Basic Rendering Settings

Some of the most important rendering options are the LOD parameters. During interactive rendering, the geometry may be replaced with a lower level of detail (LOD), an approximate geometry with fewer polygons.

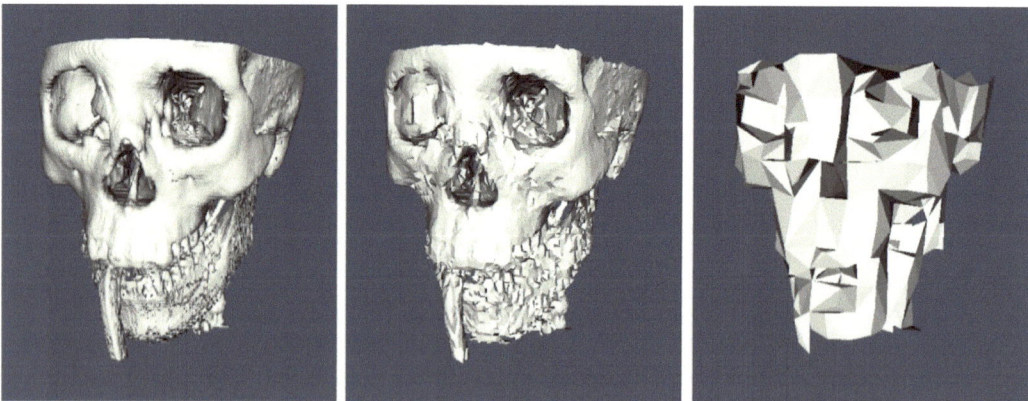

The resolution of the geometric approximation can be controlled. In the proceeding images, the left image is the full resolution, the middle image is the default decimation for interactive rendering, and the right image is ParaView's maximum decimation setting.

The 3D rendering parameters are located in the settings dialog box, which is accessed in the menu from Edit ⟩ Settings (ParaView ⟩ Preferences on the Mac). The rendering options in the dialog are in the Render View tab.

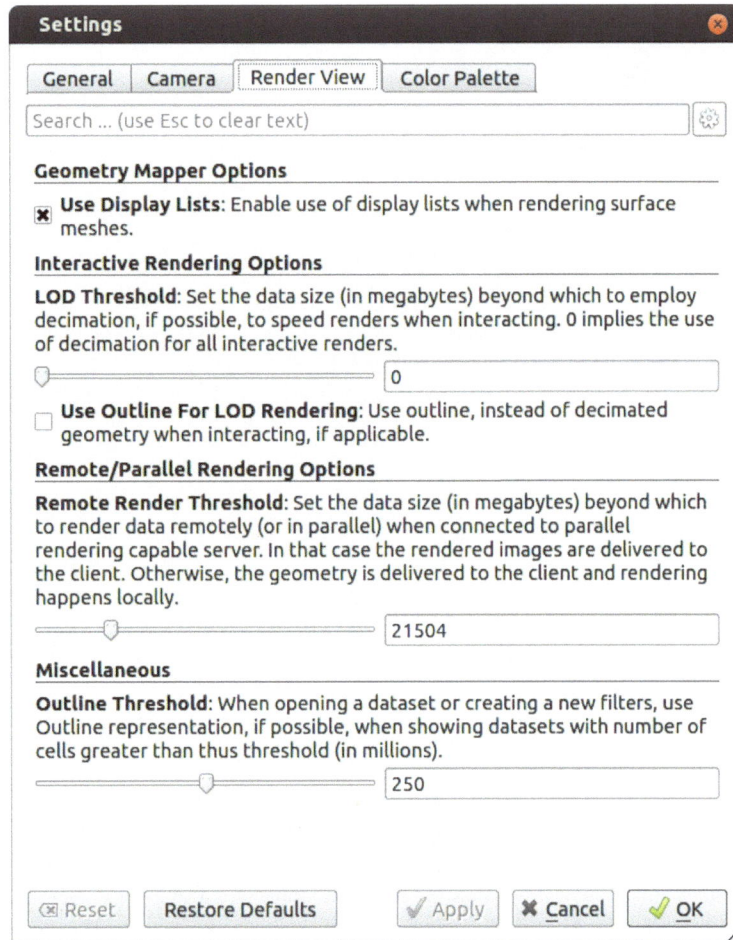

The options pertaining to the geometric decimation for interactive rendering are located in a section labeled `Interactive Rendering Options`. Some of these options are considered advanced, so to access them, you have to either toggle on the advanced options with the ⚙ button or search for the option using the edit box at the top of the dialog. The interactive rendering options include the following.

- `LOD Threshold`: Set the data size at which to use a decimated geometry in interactive rendering. If the geometry size is under this threshold, ParaView always renders the full geometry. Increase this value if you have a decent graphics card that can handle larger data. Try decreasing this value if your interactive renders are too slow.

- `LOD Resolution`: Set the factor that controls how large the decimated geometry should be. This control is set to a value between 0 and 1. 0 produces a very small number of triangles but, possibly, with a lot of distortion. 1 produces more detailed surfaces but with larger geometry. ⚙

- `Non Interactive Render Delay`: Add a delay between an interactive render and a still render. ParaView usually performs a still render immediately after an interactive motion is finished (for example, releasing the mouse button after a rotation). This option can add a delay that can give you time to start a second interaction before the still render starts, which is helpful if the still render takes a long time to complete. ⚙

- Use Outline For LOD Rendering: Use an outline in place of decimated geometry. The outline is an alternative for when the geometry decimation takes too long or still produces too much geometry. However, it is more difficult to interact with just an outline.

ParaView contains many more rendering settings. Here is a summary of some other settings that can effect the rendering performance regardless of whether ParaView is run in client-server mode or not. These options are spread among several categories, and several are considered advanced.

Geometry Mapper Options

- Use Display Lists: Enable or disable the use of display lists. Display lists are internal structures built by graphics systems. They can potentially speed up rendering but can also take up memory.

Translucent Rendering Options

- Depth Peeling: Enable or disable depth peeling. Depth peeling is a technique ParaView uses to properly render translucent surfaces. With it, the top surface is rendered and then "peeled away" so that the next lower surface can be rendered and so on. If you find that making surfaces transparent really slows things down or renders completely incorrectly, then your graphics hardware may not be implementing the depth peeling extensions well; try shutting off depth peeling.

- Maximum Number Of Peels: Set the maximum number of peels to use with depth peeling. Using more peels allows more depth complexity, but allowing less peels runs faster. You can try adjusting this parameter if translucent geometry renders too slow or translucent images do not look correct.

Miscellaneous

- Outline Threshold: When creating very large datasets, default to the outline representation. Surface representations usually require ParaView to extract geometry of the surface, which takes time and memory. For data with sizes above this threshold, use the outline representation, which has very little overhead, by default instead.

- Show Annotation: Show or hide annotation providing rendering performance information. This information is handy when diagnosing performance problems.

Note that this is not a complete list of ParaView rendering settings. We have left out settings that do not significantly effect rendering performance. We have also left out settings that are only valid for parallel client-server rendering, which are discussed in Section 15.9.4.

15.9.2 Basic Parallel Rendering

When performing parallel visualization, we are careful to ensure that the data remains partitioned among all of the processes up to and including the rendering processes. ParaView uses a parallel rendering library called IceT. IceT uses a sort-last algorithm for parallel rendering. This parallel rendering algorithm has each process independently render its partition of the geometry and then composites the partial images together to form the final image.

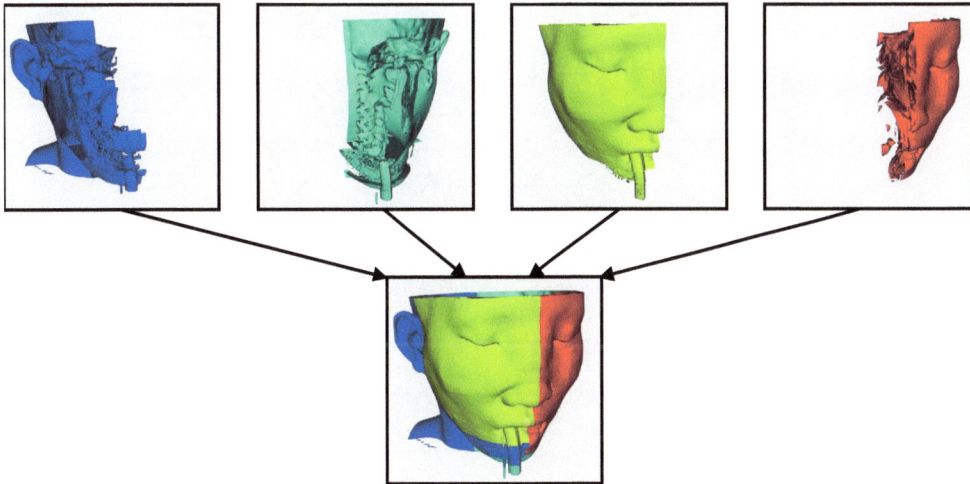

The preceding diagram is an oversimplification. IceT contains multiple parallel image compositing algorithms such as binary tree, binary swap, and radix-k that efficiently divide work among processes using multiple phases.

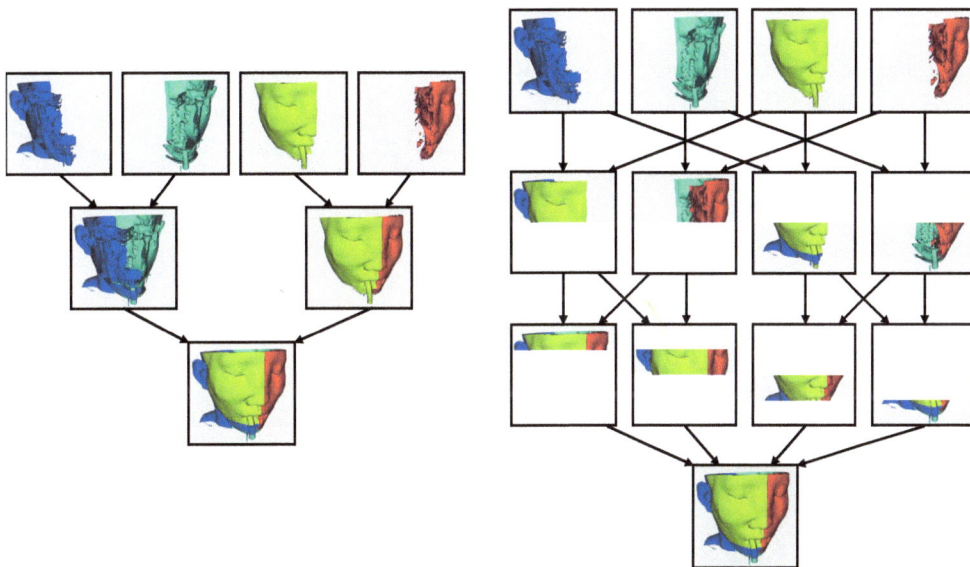

The wonderful thing about sort-last parallel rendering is that its efficiency is completely insensitive to the amount of data being rendered. This makes it a very scalable algorithm and well suited to large data. However, the parallel rendering overhead does increase linearly with the number of pixels in the image. Consequently, some of the rendering parameters deal with the image size.

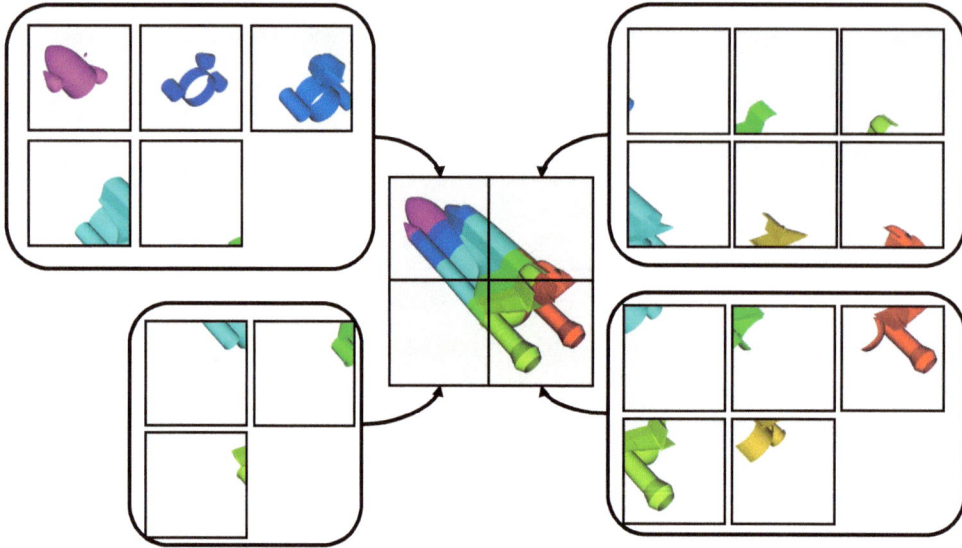

IceT also has the ability to drive tiled displays, which are large, high-resolution displays comprising an array of monitors or projectors. Using a sort-last algorithm on a tiled display is a bit counterintuitive because the number of pixels to composite is so large. However, IceT is designed to take advantage of spatial locality in the data on each process to drastically reduce the amount of compositing necessary. This spatial locality can be enforced by applying the Filters > Alphabetical > D3 filter to your data.

Because there is an overhead associated with parallel rendering, ParaView has the ability to turn off parallel rendering at any time. When parallel rendering is turned off, the geometry is shipped to the location where display occurs. Obviously, this should only happen when the data being rendered is small.

15.9.3   Image Level of Detail

The overhead incurred by the parallel rendering algorithms is proportional to the size of the images being generated. Also, images generated on a server must be transfered to the client, a cost that is also proportional to the image size. To help increase the frame rate during interaction, ParaView introduces a new LOD parameter that controls the size of the images.

During interaction while parallel rendering, ParaView can optionally subsample the image. That is, ParaView will reduce the resolution of the image in each dimension by a factor during interaction. Reduced images will be rendered, composited, and transfered. On the client, the image is inflated to the size of the available space in the GUI.

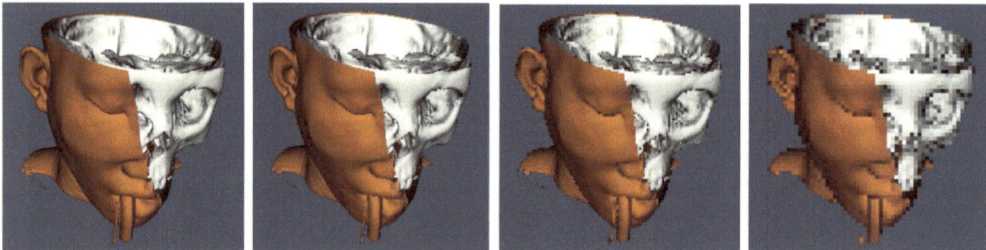

The resolution of the reduced images is controlled by the factor with which the dimensions are divided. In the proceeding images, the left image has the full resolution. The following images were rendered with the resolution reduced by a factor of 2, 4, and 8, respectively.

ParaView also has the ability to compress images before transferring them from server to client. Compression, of course, reduces the amount of data transferred and, therefore, makes the most of the available bandwidth. However, the time it takes to compress and decompress the images adds to the latency.

ParaView contains two different image compression algorithms for client-server rendering. The first is a custom algorithm called Squirt, which stands for Sequential Unified Image Run Transfer. Squirt is a run-length encoding compression that reduces color depth to increase run lengths. The second algorithm uses the Zlib compression library, which implements a variation of the Lempel-Ziv algorithm. Zlib typically provides better compression than Squirt, but it takes longer to perform and, hence, adds to the latency.

15.9.4 Parallel Render Parameters

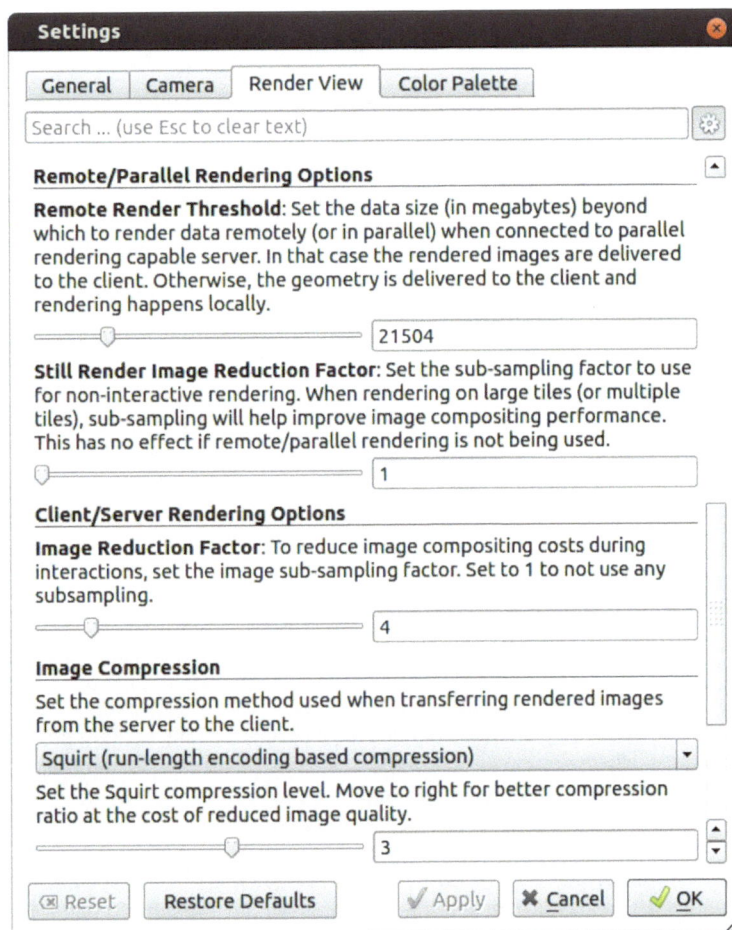

Like the other 3D rendering parameters, the parallel rendering parameters are located in the `Settings` dialog. The parallel rendering options in the dialog are in the `Render View` tab (intermixed with several other rendering options such as those described in Section 15.9.1). The parallel and client-server options are divided among several categories, and several are considered advanced.

`Remote/Parallel Rendering Options`

- `Remote Render Threshold`: Set the data size at which to render remotely in parallel or to render locally. If the geometry is over this threshold (and ParaView is connected to a remote server), the data is rendered in parallel remotely, and images are sent back to the client. If the geometry is under this threshold, the geometry is sent back to the client, and images are rendered locally on the client.

- `Still Render Image Reduction Factor`: Set the sub-sampling factor for still (non-interactive) rendering. Some large displays have more resolution than is really necessary, so this sub-sampling reduces the resolution of all images displayed. ⚙

Client/Server Rendering Options

- `Image Reduction Factor`: Set the interactive subsampling factor. The overhead of parallel rendering is proportional to the size of the images generated. Thus, you can speed up interactive rendering by specifying an image subsampling rate. When this box is checked, interactive renders will create smaller images, which are then magnified when displayed. This parameter is only used during interactive renders. ⚙

Image Compression

- Before images are shipped from server to client, they optionally can be compressed using one of two compression algorithms: Squirt or Zlib. To make the compression more effective, either algorithm can reduce the color resolution of the image before compression. The sliders determine the amount of color bits saved. Full color resolution is always used during a still render. ⚙

- Suggested image compression presets are provided for several common network types. When attempting to select the best image compression options, try starting with the presets that best match your connection. ⚙

15.9.5 Parameters for Large Data

The default rendering parameters are suitable for most users. However, when dealing with very large data, it can help to tweak the rendering parameters. While the optimal parameters depend on your data and the hardware on which ParaView is running, here are several pieces of advice that you should follow.

- Try turning off display lists. Turning this option off will prevent the graphics system from building special rendering structures. If you have graphics hardware, these rendering structures are important for feeding the GPUs fast enough. However, if you do not have GPUs, these rendering structures do not help much.

- If there is a long pause before the first interactive render of a particular data set, it might be the creation of the decimated geometry. Try using an outline instead of decimated geometry for interaction. You could also try lowering the factor of the decimation to 0 to create smaller geometry.

- Avoid shipping large geometry back to the client. The remote rendering will use the power of the entire server to render and ship images to the client. If remote rendering is off, geometry is shipped back to the client. When you have large data, it is always faster to ship images than to ship data. (Although, if your network has a high latency, this could become problematic for interactive frame rates.)

- Adjust the interactive image sub-sampling for client-server rendering as needed. If image compositing is slow, if the connection between client and server has low bandwidth, or if you are rendering very large images, then a higher subsample rate can greatly improve your interactive rendering performance.

- Make sure `Image Compression` is on. It has a tremendous effect on desktop delivery performance, and the artifacts it introduces, which are only there during interactive rendering, are minimal. Lower bandwidth connections can try using Zlib instead of Squirt compression. Zlib will create smaller images at the cost of longer compression/decompression times.

- If the network connection has a high latency, adjust the parameters to avoid remote rendering during interaction. In this case, you can try turning up the remote rendering threshold a bit, and this is a place where using the outline for interactive rendering is effective.

- If the still (non-interactive) render is slow, try turning on the delay between interactive and still rendering to avoid unnecessary renders.

MEMORY INSPECTOR

The ParaView `Memory Inspector` panel provides users with a convenient way to monitor ParaView's memory usage during interactive visualization. It also provides developers with a point-and-click interface for attaching a debugger to local or remote client and server processes. As explained earlier, both the `Information` panel and the `Statistics Inspector` are prone to over and under estimate the total memory used for the current pipeline. The `Memory Inspector` addresses those issues through direct queries to the operating system. A number of diagnostic statistics are gathered and reported, including the total memory used by all processes on a per-host basis, the total cumulative memory use by ParaView on a per-host basis, and the individual per-rank use by each ParaView process. When memory consumption reaches a critical level, either cumulatively on the host or in an individual rank, the corresponding GUI element will turn red, alerting you that you are in danger of potentially being shut down. This gives you a chance to save state and restart the job with more nodes to aviod losing your work. On the flip side, knowing when you're not close to using the full capacity of available memory can be useful to conserve computational resources by running smaller jobs. Of course, the memory foot print is only one factor in determining the optimal run size.

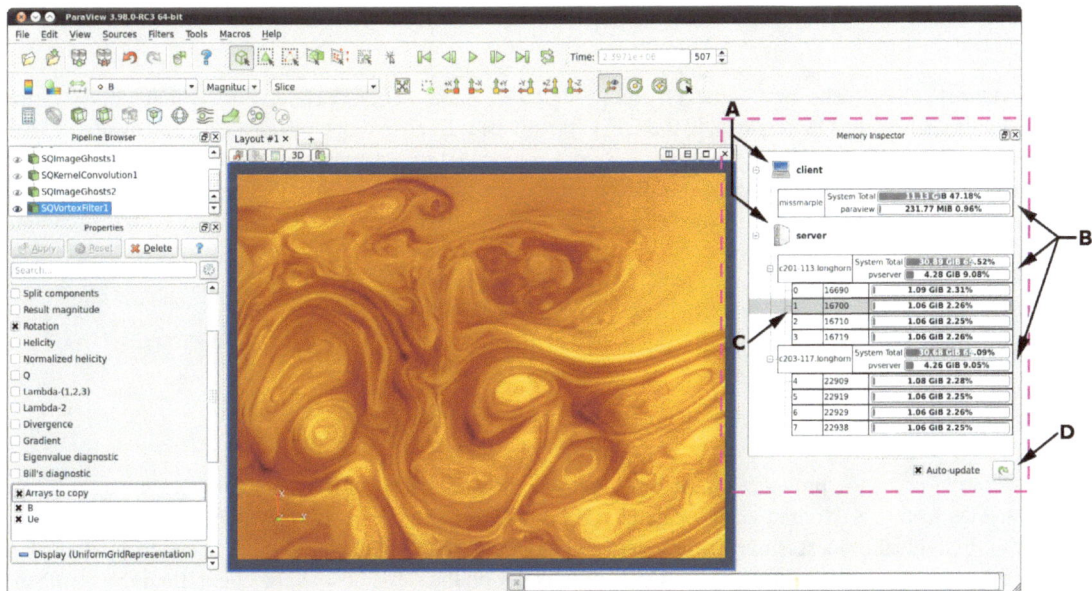

Figure 16.1: The main UI elements of the `Memory Inspector` panel. A: Process Groups, B: Per-Host statistics, C: Per-Rank statistics, and D: Update controls.

16.1   User interface and layout

The Memory Inspector panel displays information about the current memory usage on the client and server hosts. Figure 16.1 shows the main UI elements labeled A-D. A number of additional features are provided via specialized context menus accessible from the Client and Server group, Host, and Rank's UI elements. The main UI elements are:

A *Process Groups*

* *Client* : There is always a client group that reports statistics about the ParaView client.

* *Server* : When running in client-server mode, a server group reports statistics about the hosts where *pvserver* processes are running.

* *Data Sever* : When running in client-data-render server mode, a data server group reports statistics about the hosts where *pvdataserver* processes are running.

* Render Sever : When running in client-data-render server mode, a render server group reports statistics about the hosts where *pvrenderserver* processes are running.

B *Per-Host Statistics* : Per-host statics are reported for each host where a ParaView process is running. Hosts are organized by host name, which is shown in the first column. Two statics are reported: 1) total memory used by all processes on the host and 2) ParaView's cumulative usage on this host. The absolute value is printed in a bar that shows the percentage of the total available memory used. On systems where job-wide resource limits are enforced, ParaView is made aware of the limits via the *PV_HOST_MEMORY_LIMIT* environment variable, in which case, ParaView's cumulative percent used is computed using the smaller of the host total and the resource limit.

C *Update Controls* : By default, when the panel is visible, memory use statistics are updated automatically as pipeline objects are created, modified, or destroyed and after the scene is rendered. Updates may be triggered manually by using the refresh button. Automatic updates may be disabled by un-checking the *Auto-update* check box. Queries to remote systems have proven to be very fast even for fairly large jobs. Hence, the auto-update feature is enabled by default.

D *Host Properties Dialog* : The ‖Host‖ context menu provides the Host Properties dialog, which reports various system details such as the OS version and the CPU version, as well as the memory installed and available to the host context and process context. While the Memory Inspector panel reports memory use as a percent of the available in the given context, the Host Properties dialog reports the total memory installed and available in each context. Comparing the installed and available memory can be used to determine if you are impacted by resource limits.

16.2   Advanced debugging features

16.2.1   Remote commands

The Memory Inspector Panel provides a remote (or local) command feature, allowing you to execute a shell command on a given host. This feature is exposed via a specialized Rank item context menu. Because we have information such as a rank's process id, individual processes may be targeted. For example, this allows you to quickly attach a debugger to a server process running on a remote cluster. If the target rank is not on the same host as the client, then the command is considered remote. Otherwise, it is considered local. Therefore, remote commands are executed via ssh, while local commands are not. A list of command templates is maintained. In addition to a number of pre-defined command templates, you may add templates or edit existing ones. The default templates allow you to:

1. Attach gdb to the selected process
2. Run top on the host of the selected process

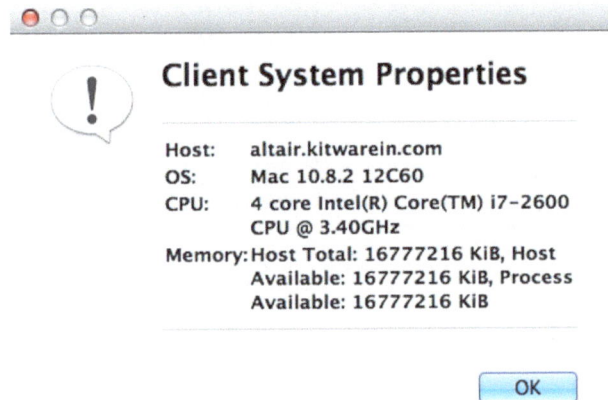

Figure 16.2: Host properties dialog.

3. Send a signal to the selected process

Prior to execution, the selected template is parsed, and a list of special tokens are replaced with runtime-determined or user-provide values. User-provided values can be set and modified in the dialog's parameter group. The command, with tokens replaced, is shown for verification in the dialog's preview pane.

The following tokens are available and may be used in command templates as needed:

1. *$TERM_EXEC$* : The terminal program that will be used to execute commands. On Unix systems, xterm is typically used. On Windows systems, cmd.exe is typically used. If the program is not in the default path, then the full path must be specified.

2. *$TERM_OPTS$* : Command line arguments for the terminal program. On Unix, these may be used to set the terminals window title, size, colors, and so on.

3. *SSH_EXEC* : The program to use to execute remote commands. On Unix, this is typically ssh. On Windows, one option is plink.exe. If the program is not in the default path, then the full path must be specified.

4. *FE_URL* : Ssh URL to use when the remote processes are on compute nodes that are not visible to the outside world. This token is used to construct command templates where two ssh hops are made to execute the command.

5. *PV_HOST* : The hostname where the selected process is running.

6. *PV_PID* : The process-id of the selected process.

Note: On Windows, the debugging tools found in Microsoft's SDK need to be installed in addition to Visual Studio (e.g., windbg.exe). The ssh program plink.exe for Windows doesn't parse ANSI escape codes that are used by Unix shell programs. In general, the Windows-specific templates need some polishing.

16.2.2 Stack trace signal handler

The Process Group's context menu provides a back trace signal handler option. When enabled, a signal handler is installed that will catch signals such as SEGV, TERM, INT, and ABORT and that will print a stack trace before the process exits. Once the signal handler is enabled, you may trigger a stack trace by explicitly sending a signal. The stack

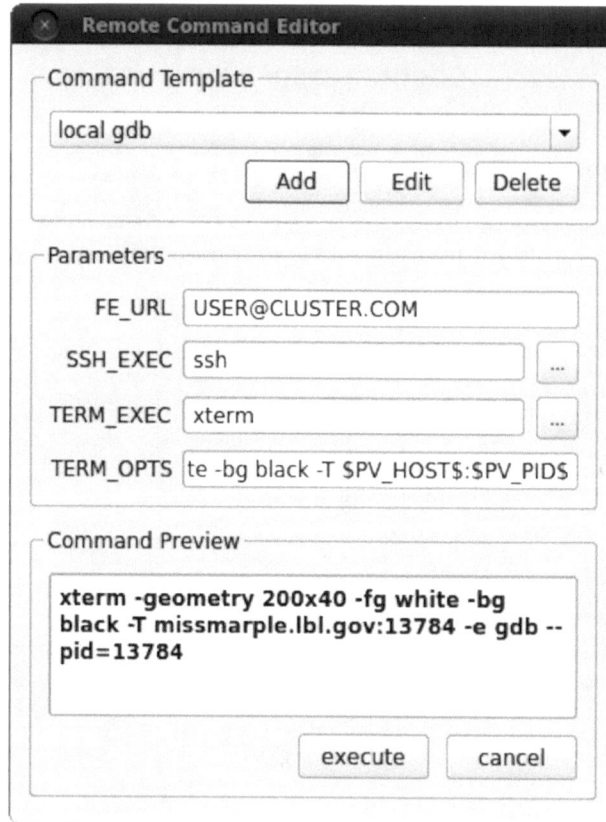

Figure 16.3: The remote command dialog.

trace signal handler can be used to collect information about crashes or to trigger a stack trace during deadlocks when it's not possible to ssh into compute nodes. Sites that restrict users' ssh access to compute nodes often provide a way to signal running processes from the login node. Note that this feature is only available on systems that provide support for POSIX signals, and we currently only have implemented stack trace for GNU-compatible compilers.

16.3 Compilation and installation considerations

If the system on which ParaView will run has special resource limits enforced, such as job-wide memory use limits, or non-standard per-process memory limits, then the system administrators need to provide this information to the running instances of ParaView via the following environment variables. For example, those could be set in the batch system launch scripts.

1. *PV_HOST_MEMORY_LIMIT* : For reporting host-wide resource limits.

2. *PV_PROC_MEMORY_LIMIT* : For reporting per-process memory limits. that are not enforced via standard Unix resource limits.

A few of the debugging features (such as printing a stack trace) require debug symbols. These features will work best when ParaView is built with CMAKE_BUILD_TYPE=Debug or, for release builds,

CMAKE_BUILD_TYPE=RelWithDebugSymbols.

SETTINGS

As with any large application, *paraview* provides mechanisms to customize some of its application behavior. These are referred to as application settings or, just, settings. Such settings can be changed using the Settings dialog, which is accessed from the Edit ⟩ Settings (ParaView ⟩ Preferences on the Mac) menu. We have seen parts of this dialog earlier, e.g., in Sections 9.2, 15.9.1, and 15.9.4. In this chapter, we will take a closer look at some of the other options available in this dialog.

The Settings dialog is split into several tabs. The General tab consolidates most of the miscellaneous settings. The Camera tab enables you to change the mouse interaction mappings for the Render View and similar views. The Render View tab, which we saw earlier in Sections 15.9.1 and 15.9.4, provides options in regards to rendering in Render View and similar views. The Color Palette tab is used to change the active color palette.

Using this dialog is not much different than the Properties panel. You have the Search box at the top, which allows you to search properties matching the input text (Section 9.1.2). The ⚙ button can be used to toggle between default and advanced modes.

To apply the changes made to any of the settings, use the Apply or OK buttons. OK will apply the changes and close the dialog, while Cancel will reject any changes made and close the dialog. Any changes made to the options in this dialog are persistent across sessions. (I.e., the next time you launch *paraview*, you'll still be using the same settings chosen earlier.) To revert to the default, use the Restore Defaults button. You can also manually edit the setting file as in Section 10.3. Furthermore, site maintainers can provide site-wide defaults for these, as is explained in Section 10.4.

Next, we will see some of the important options available. Those that are only available in the advanced mode are indicated as such using the ⚙ icon. You will either need to toggle on the advanced options with the ⚙ button or search for the option using the Search box.

17.1   General settings

General Options

- Show Splash Screen: Uncheck this to not show the splash screen at application startup. You will need to restart *paraview* to see the effect. ⚙

- Crash Recovery: When this is checked, *paraview* will intermittently save a backup state file as you make changes in the visualization pipeline. If *paraview* crashes for some reason, then when you relaunch *paraview*, it will provide you with a choice to load the backup state saved before the crash occurred. This is not 100% reliable, but some users may find it useful to avoid loosing their visualization state due to a crash. ⚙

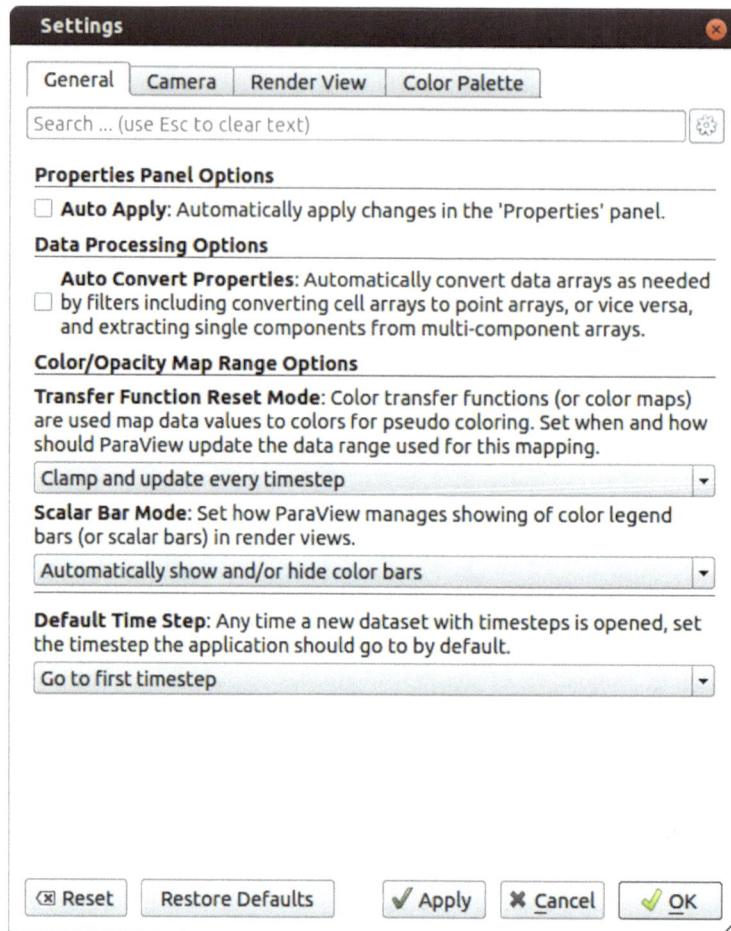

Figure 17.1: Settings dialog in *paraview* showing the General settings tab.

Default View

- Default View Type: When *paraview* starts up, it creates Render View by default. You can use this option to change the type of the view that is created by default, instead of the Render View. You can even pick None if you don't want to create any view by default. ⚙

Properties Panel Options

- Auto Apply: When checked, the Properties panel will automatically apply any changes you make to the properties without requiring you to click the Apply button. The same setting can also be toggled using the ⬚ button in the Main Controls toolbar.

- Auto Apply Active Only: This limits the auto-applying to the properties on the active source alone. ⚙

- Properties Panel Mode: This allows you to split the Properties panel into separate panels as described in Section 9.2. ⚙

Data Processing Options

- `Auto Convert Properties`: Several filters only work on one type of array, e.g., point data arrays or cell data arrays. Before using such filters, you are expected to apply the `Point Data To Cell Data` or `Cell Data To Point Data` filters. To avoid having to add these filters explicitly, you can check this checkbox. When checked, ParaView will automatically convert data arrays as needed by filters, including converting cell array to point arrays and vice-versa, as well as extracting a single component from a multi-component array.

Color/Opacity Map Range Options

- `Transfer Function Reset Mode`: This setting controls when ParaView will reset the ranges for color and opacity maps (or transfer functions). This only affects those color/opacity maps that have the `Automatically rescale transfer functions to fit data` setting enabled (Section 11.2.1). When `Grow and update on 'Apply'` is selected, ParaView will grow the color/opacity map range to include the current data range every time you hit `Apply` on the `Properties` panel. Thus, when the data range changes, if the timestep is changed, the color/opacity map range won't be affected. To grow the range on change in timestep as well, use the `Grow and update every timestep` option. Now the range will be updated on `Apply` as well as when the timestep changes. *Grow* indicates that the color/opacity map range will only be increased, never shrunk, to include the current data range. If you want the range to match the current data range exactly, then you should use the `Clamp and update every timestep` option. Now the range will be clamped to the exact data range each time you hit `Apply` on the `Properties` panel or when the timestep changes.

- `Scalar Bar Mode`: This settings controls how *paraview* manages showing the color legend (or scalar bar) in `Render View` and similar views.

Default Time Step

Whenever a dataset with timesteps is opened, this setting controls how *paraview* will update the current time shown by the application. You can choose between `Leave current time unchanged, if possible`, `Go to first timestep`, and `Go to last timestep`.

Animation

- `Cache Geometry For Animation`: This enables caching of geometry when playing animations to attempt to speed up animation playback in a loop. When caching is enabled, data ranges reported by the `Information` panel and others can be incorrect, since the pipeline may not have updated. ⚙

- `Animation Geometry Cache Limit`: When animation caching is enabled, this setting controls how much geometry (in kilobytes) can be cached by any rank. As soon as a rank's cache size reaches this limit, ParaView will no longer cache the remaining timesteps. ⚙

Screenshot Options

- When saving screenshots (or animations) with multiple views, these settings allow you to control the width of the border between multiple views, as well as the color to use for the border. `Multi View Image Border Color` sets the color for the border, while `Multi View Image Border Width` sets the width for the border in pixels. ⚙

- `Transparent Background`: When set, all screenshots will be saved with the background color replaced with a transparent background. Currently, this only works for `Render View` and similar views. ⚙

17.2 Camera settings

This tab allows you to control how you can interact in `Render View` and similar views. Basically, you are setting up a mapping between each of the mouse buttons and keyboard modifiers, and the available interaction types including

---

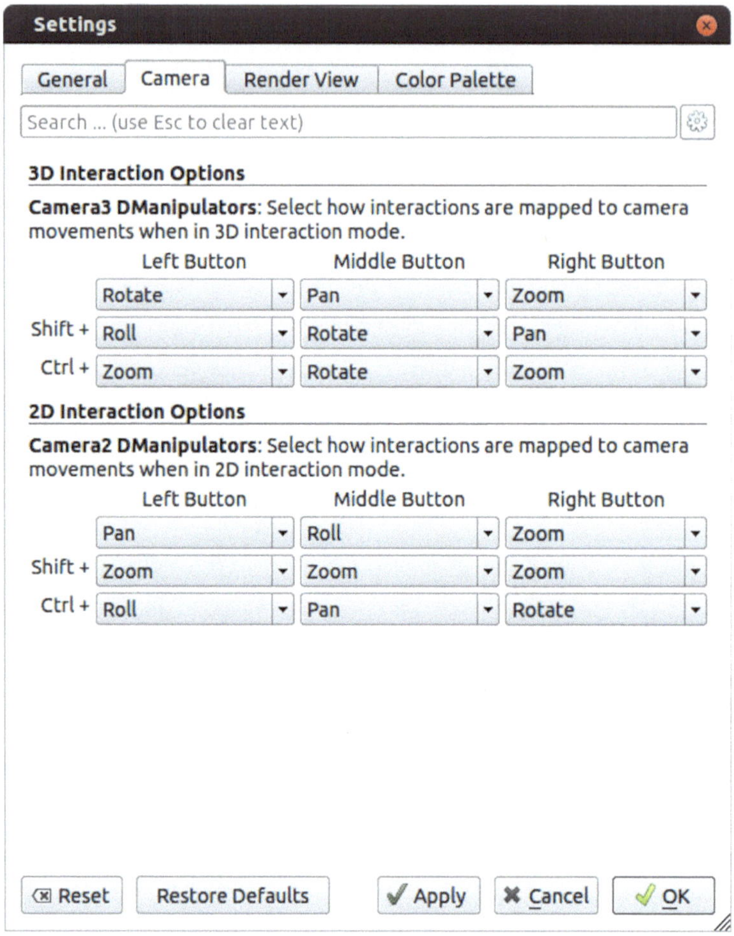

Figure 17.2: `Settings` dialog in *paraview* showing the `Camera` settings tab.

`Rotate`, `Pan`, `Zoom`, etc. The dialog allows you to set the interaction mapping separately for 3D and 2D interaction modes (see Section 4.4.2).

17.3 `Render View` **settings**

Refer to Sections 15.9.1 and 15.9.4 for various options available on the `Render View` tab.

17.4 `Color Palette`

The `Color Palette` tab (Figure 17.4) allows you to change the colors in the active color palette. The tab lists the available color categories viz. `Surface`, `Foreground`, `Edges`, `Background`, `Text`, and `Selection`. You can manually set colors to use for each of these categories or load one of the predefined palettes using the `Load Palette` option. To understand color palettes, let's look at an example.

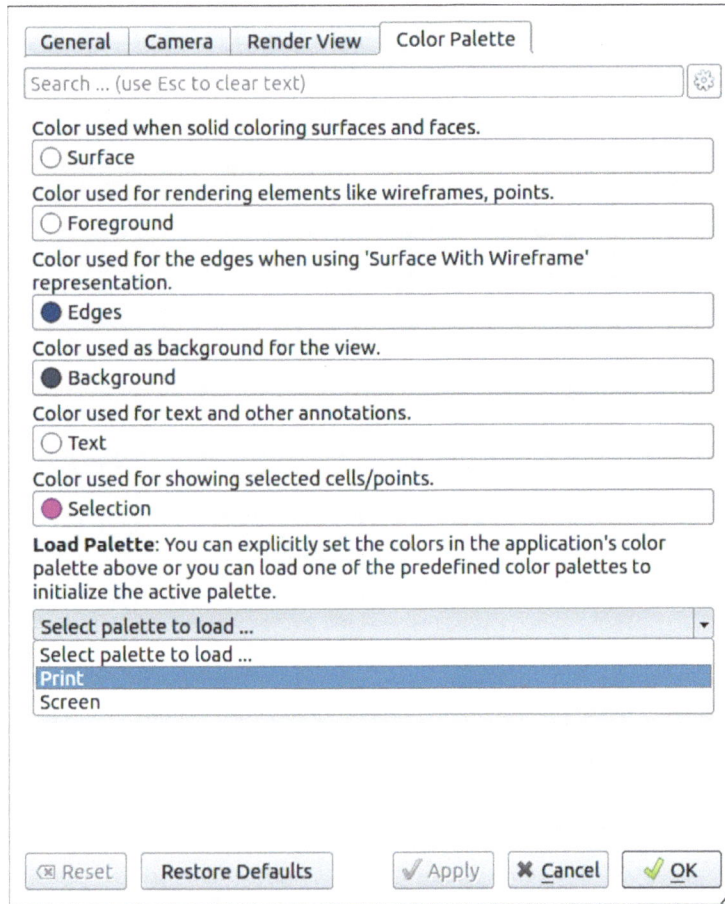

Figure 17.3: Settings dialog in *paraview* showing the Color Palette settings tab.

Let's start *paraview* and split the active view to create two Render View instances side by side. You may want to start *paraview* with the -dr command line argument to stop any of your current settings from interfering with this demo. Next, show Sphere as Wireframe in the view on the left, and show Cone as Surface in the view on the right. Also, turn on Cube Axis for Cone. You will see something like Figure 17.4 (left).

Now let's say you want to generate a image for printing. Typically, for printing, you'd want the background color to be white, while the wireframes and annotations to be colored black. To do that, one way is to go change each of the colors for each each of the views, displays and cube-axes. You can imagine how tedious that will get especially with larger pipelines. Alternatively, using the Settings dialog, change the active color palette to Print as shown in Figure 17.4 and then hit OK or Apply. The visualization will immediately change to something like Figure 17.4 (right).

Essentially, ParaView allows you to *link* any color property to one of the color categories. When the color palette is changed, any color property linked to a palette category will also be automatically updated to match the category color. Figure 17.4 shows how to link a color property to a color palette category in the Properties panel. Use the tiny drop-down menu marker to make the menu pop up that shows the color palette categories. Select any one of them to link that property with the category. The link is automatically severed if you manually change the color by simply clicking on the button.

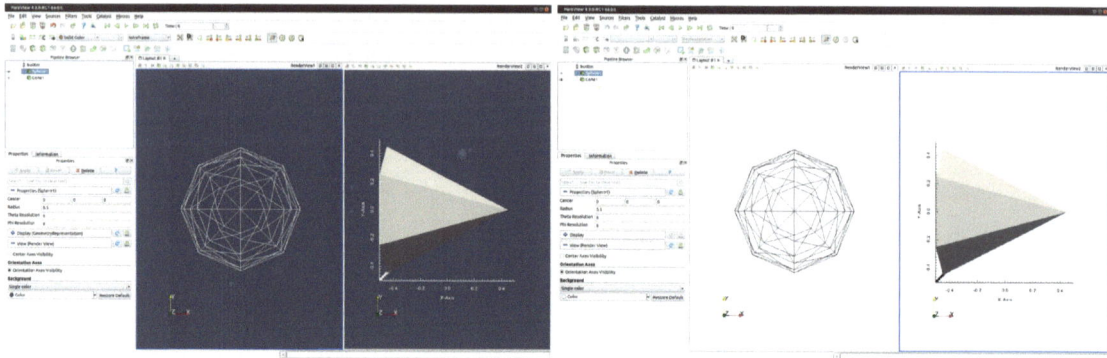

Figure 17.4: The effect of loading the `Print` color palette as the active palette. The left is the original visualization and the right shows the result after loading the `Print` palette.

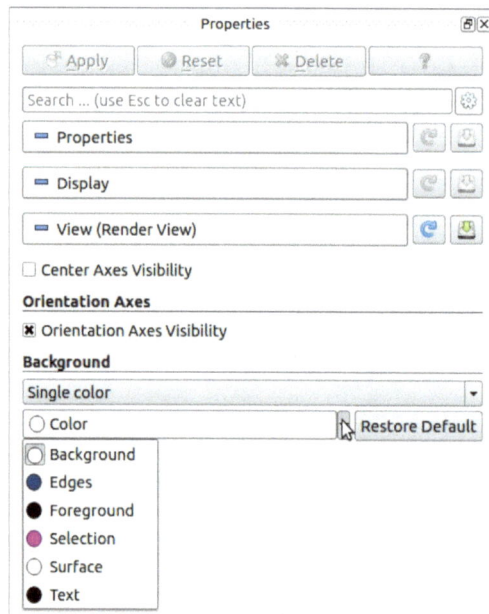

Figure 17.5: Popup menu allows you to link a color property to a color palette category in the `Properties` panel.

Part III

Extras

CFD POST-PROCESSING

This chapter will walk you through some examples of quantitative post-processing of computational fluid dynamics (CFD) results. The first two examples are from a dynamic simulation of a dam breaking. The first example analyzes the forces that the resulting fluid flow exerts on a barrier, while the second example computes the flow over the barrier. The third, and final, example is of a steady state compressible flow past a blunt fin. In this example, we compute the force acting on the fin due to the fluid flow.

18.1   Analysis of a breaking dam with OpenFoam

The first CFD example walks you through analyzing time-dependent results of an OpenFOAM simulation of a breaking dam problem. OpenFOAM[1] is an open-source CFD software package available through OpenCFD, Ltd. The simulation is of an incompressible flow problem, imitating a dam breaking and the water flowing over a small barrier downstream from the flow. The computed quanties are velocity (U), pressure (p), pressure minus hydrostatic pressure (p_{rgh}), and relative volume fraction (α_1). Instructions for running the problem with OpenFoam are available at.[18] For those not interested in running the simulation in order to try the example, a sample result is available at
http://www.paraview.org/files/data/OpenFOAM_UsersGuide_Example.tgz for a small mesh with 2,268 cells.

Results for three time steps are shown in Figure 18.1. Note that, normally, in the results, the first time step has field variables named with a .org extension to indicate that they are initial conditions for the simulation but that they are not in subsequent time steps. This is specific to the OpenFOAM data format. For the example we provided, we have removed this time step.

Once the results are obtained, the main file to load into ParaView will have a .foam extension. The sample results are in the file named damBreakParallel.foam. Once the file is loaded into ParaView, the following options should be set for the OpenFOAM reader:

- Choose Decomposed Case for the Case Type

- Check Create cell-to-point filtered data

- Check Add dimensional units to array names

To view an animation of the simulation results, select appropriate pipeline and viewing parameters. Then hit the VCR play button at the top of the ParaView window. This will run through all time steps of the simulation, which is 20 for the sample results.

With a description of the simulation, we proceed to computing the total horizontal pressure exerted on the barrier as the simulation proceeds. As is the case with many CFD simulations, the computational domain is significantly larger than the desired analysis regions, which, in this case, are the vertical walls of the barrier. Since we already have the needed field

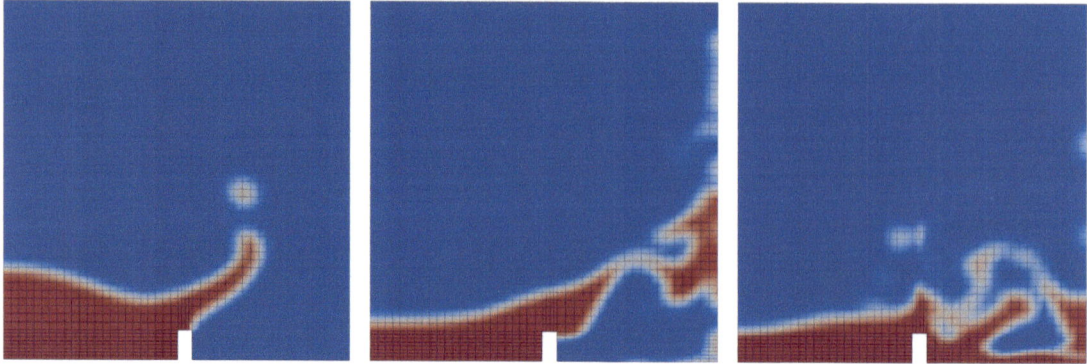

Figure 18.1: Three time steps of the OpenFOAM dam breaking problem. The pseudo-color is of the α_1 variable representing the volume fraction of water.

information (p) in the proper form, we only need to extract the portion of the computational domain in which we are interested.

Note that, depending on the information available in the data sets, there may be a variety of ways to perform this calculation. Here, we will present two separate ways to do this. First, start with a reduced data set by loading only the part of the domain that corresponds to the bottom; this option might not be available for all readers and/or data sets, but can be useful for analyzing large simulations efficiently, as ParaView never needs to load in the full data set into memory. To proceed with this example, change the parameters of the OpenFOAM reader to only read in the bottom boundary of the mesh by unchecking all of the mesh regions except for the lower wall (i.e., lowerWall). This results in 62 quadrilateral cells as opposed to the 2,268 hexahedral cells of the computation grid. To save even more on computation, you can whittle down the analysis domain to just the vertical walls of the cell by selecting these cells and then using the `Extract Selection` filter to create a new data set with only these cells in them. This is shown in Figure 18.2.

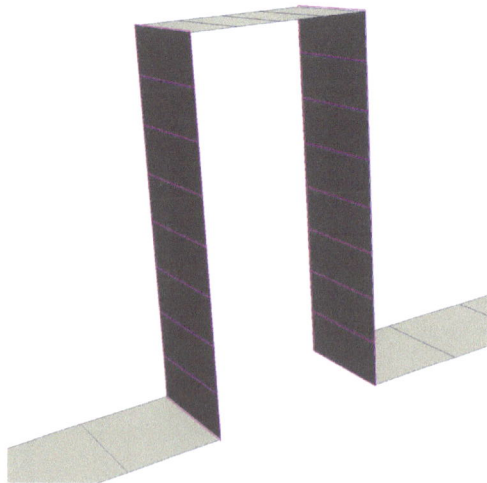

Figure 18.2: Selection of vertically-aligned cells for the dam break problem.

Note that the result of computing the horizontal force exerted by the water pressure would be the same regardless of whether or not the Extract Selection filter was used to reduce the data set further, since the normals of the non-extracted cells are in the y direction and would not contribute.

At this point, we have the field to which to integrate with respect, and the domain/cells over which we want to integrate. What is missing is the normals needed to make sure that the integrations sum up properly. While there are cell normals available in the drop-down menu for fields by which to color, they are not available in the data set itself. (They are made available and used for rendering.) By looking at the data arrays available in the output of the filter (under the Data Arrays section in the Information Tab of the Object Inspector, while the desired filter is highlighted in the Pipeline Browser), we see that there are no normals available there. So, the next step in the example is obtaining the normals at those points.

The problem now is that, while the Generate Surface Normals filter will compute this information, it only operates on polydata, and we currently have a multiblock data set with an unstructured grid coming out of our Extract Selection filter. To reduce our data into a single, unstructured data set, use the Merge Blocks filter. Next, convert the unstructured grid to a polydata using the Extract Surface filter. Now, with a single polydata coming out of our last filter, use the Generate Surface Normals filter to create the normals needed. As a safety precaution, make sure that the normals are pointing in the proper direction, which is outward from the computational domain. We could color the cells by the x-component of the normal. But, a more visually appealing way is to use the Glyph filter and select Normals as our Vector or Normals Glyph to show the normals' directions. If the normals are in the opposite direction, check the Flip Normals box in the Generate Surface Normals filter. Figure 18.3 shows our current data set with the proper direction for the normals.

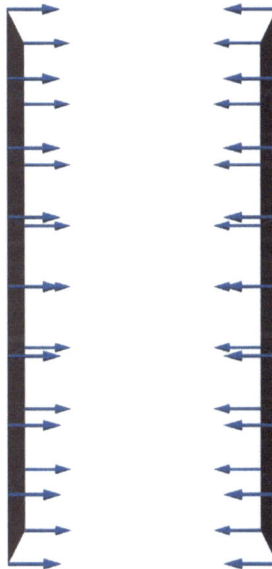

Figure 18.3: Cells discretizing the vertical wall boundary with the normals pointing outward.

We now have the two separate point data fields needed in order to compute the force on the wall: p_{rgh} and Normals. But, we need a force per unit area, i.e., a multiplication of the two. To perform the multiplication, use the Calculator filter. The calculator is aware of scalar and vector fields, and it knows how to operate on them. The parameters for the Calculator filter that we will use are:

- Set Attribute Mode to Point Data

- Set Result Array Name to Force per unit area

- In the text input "p [Pa]*Normals"

Finally, integrate this value over the desired cells through the `Integrate Variables` filter. The output will be a single point and a single cell with all of the integrated values included. The easiest way to see the results is by switching to the spreadsheet view. Since the integrated quantity of interest was a point field, select the Point Data attribute, and look for the "Force per unit area" array. The result should be $[-0.0466283, 0, 0]$ for the last time step (time step 20), if it was only integrated over the vertically-aligned cells. The result should be $[-0.0466283, -6.63415, 0]$, if it was integrated over the entire bottom boundary. The above method works when the boundary is already extracted. For many simulation results, however, only the computational cells and corresponding field data are written out to save computation and disk space. In this situation, you would set the following parameters for the reader:

- Set Case Type to Decomposed Case

- Check Create cell-to-point filtered data

- Check Add dimensional units to array names

- Make sure `internalMesh` is the only checked mesh region

The steps after that would be to use the `Merge Blocks` filter, followed by the `Extract Surface` filter. Then follow the steps of the previous example from the selection onward. While this provides the force on the wall at the last time step, you may be more interested in the maximum force magnitude acting on the barrier. The best way to analyze this is to use the `Temporal Statistics` filter, which computes the minimum, maximum, average, and standard deviation of values at a point or cell over all of the time steps. In this calculation, we are interested in the maximum magnitude, so uncheck all values except for Minimum and Maximum. After running the filter, you should see that the maximum force acting on the wall is 2.39608. While this filter gives us the maximum value, it is still unknown when this occurred. By selecting the point in the Spreadsheet view and using the `Plot Selection Over Time` filter to show how the force varies over time, it can be determined when the maximum occurred. This is shown in Figure 18.4.

The figure shows that the maximum force occurs at a time of 1.5. For this plot, we hid other variables of interest to focus attention on the force, but you can easily modify the plot variables and settings to show other interesting phenomena. Additionally, we set the left, bottom, and chart titles to better convey the results.

18.2 Calculating flow past the barrier

Another quantity of interest to calculate for this dam break problem is the amount of flow past the barrier. Again, there are multiple ways of doing this inside of ParaView. The most direct way is to use the `Surface Flow` filter. To start, load the results file into ParaView with the OpenFOAM reader. Follow the steps above for the second example, where we start out with the internalMesh block of the data set. The next step is to use the `Slice` filter to create a slice through the domain where we want to track the fluid flow. This is shown in Figure 18.5. While the flow of interest for this problem is in the x-direction, you can manipulate the slice plane widget to get compute flows through arbitrary planes.

The final filter needed is the `Surface Flow` filter, which takes care of multiplying the normals of the surface by the chosen vector (U in this case) to obtain the result. For the final time step, the result is 0.00118799. We could go through a similar process like the first example above, where we merge the blocks, generate a surface (this time with the `Slice` filter instead of through selection of the outer surface), create the surface normals, multiply the velocity by the surface normals, and, finally, integrate the results.

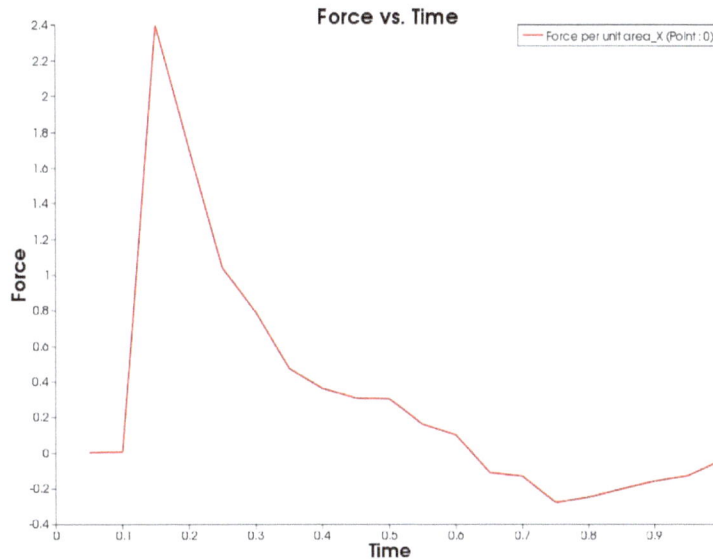

Figure 18.4: Selection Over Time plot.

18.2.1 Integrating the stress over a surface

This example is for computing the stress along a curved surface. The sample data set comes from the ParaViewData repository (http://paraview.org/files/v3.10/ParaViewData-3.10.1.zip). The file is bluntfin. vts, which is in the Data subdirectory. This data set is a vtkStructuredGrid data set containing compressible flow results of momentum, density, and stagnation energy. To begin, load the file. For the reader, you can choose to ignore the stagnation energy since it is not needed for the analysis we wish to perform. As this is a structured grid, storing the point and/or cell data can be quite costly compared to the memory of storing the grid geometry and topology. Also, since we plan to use the Gradient filter, there is also a cost for computing the gradient of stagnation energy.

The first step is to reduce the size of the data set with which we are working. We need to leave enough of the data set to compute an accurate gradient of velocity, but we certainly do not want or wish to compute the gradient over the entire original data set. In the previous examples with the unstructured grids, the easiest way to reduce the data set to the domain of interest was through selection and surface extraction. Now, however, you can take advantage of the regular topological structure of the grid by using the Extract Subset filter to easily extract the cells near the surface of interest. The volume of interest (VOI) to set is 0, 39, 0, 1, 0, 31. Leave 1 for the Sample Rate for each logical direction. This leaves a layer of single cells near the boundary of interest.

The next step is to compute velocity from momentum and density using the Calculator. The expression to use with the Calculator filter is *Momentum/Density*. To avoid confusion later, name the resulting array *Velocity* by inputting that into the Result Array Name field. Now that we have a velocity field, take its gradient to get the strain rate field by using the Gradient of Unstructured DataSet filter. Make sure to set Velocity as the array to process. Again, set the computed quantity to something significant; we choose "StrainRate" as the Result Array Name.

The next step is to reduce the data set to the surface of interest. The quickest way to do this is by using another Extract Subset filter, this time with a VOI of 0, 39, 0, 0, 0, 31. We use the surface normals again in order to integrate the forces properly over the boundary. As before, use the Extract Surface filter and then the Generate Surface Normals filter. For this example, check again that the normals are pointing outward. For this configuration, they are not, so check Flip Normals in the Generate Surface Normals filter. Now, compute the quantity to be integrated over the boundary surface. For a compressible fluid, the equation for normal stresses in the x-direction is $\sigma_{xx} = -p - \frac{2}{3}\mu\nabla \cdot \vec{v} + 2\mu\frac{\partial v_x}{\partial x}$.

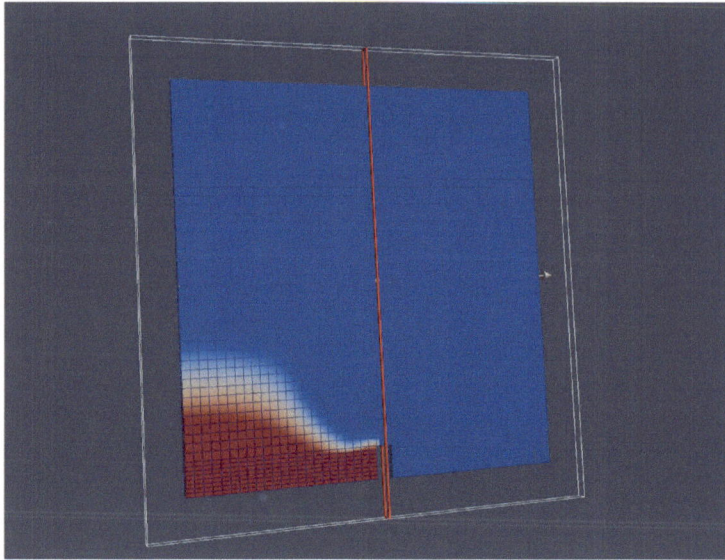

Figure 18.5: Using the `Slice` filter to create a slice.

The equation for shear stress is $\tau_{xy} = \mu(\frac{\partial v_y}{\partial x} + \frac{\partial v_x}{\partial y})$. To simplify, ignore the pressure and use $2 \cdot 10^5$ (kg/m s) as the dynamic viscosity, μ. Another simplification is to compute the divergence of the velocity field with the `Python Calculator` filter. The Expression input is "trace(StrainRate)", and we will use "Divergence" as the Array Name. Note that, as expected, the result of the trace of a matrix/second order tensor is a scalar value. Now we can use another `Python Calculator` filter to compute the actual quantity to integrate. The Expression to be used is:

make_vector(Normals[:,0]*.00002*(-2*Divergence/3 + 2*StrainRate[:,0,0] + StrainRate[:,0,1] + StrainRate[:,1,0] + StrainRate[:,0,2] + StrainRate[:,2,0]), Normals[:,1]*.00002*(-2*Divergence/3 + 2*StrainRate[:,1,1] + StrainRate[:,0,1] + StrainRate[:,1,0] + StrainRate[:,1,2] + StrainRate[:,2,1]), Normals[:,2]*.00002*(-2*Divergence/3 + 2*StrainRate[:,2,2] + StrainRate[:,1,2] + StrainRate[:,2,1] + StrainRate[:,0,2] + StrainRate[:,2,0]))

Inside the Python Calculator, the arrays are treated as numpy arrays, as long as ParaView was built to use numpy. Since we are creating a new point data array, the calculator has access to existing point data arrays. For arrays, you can specify which point-wise component to access. The first index is for the point index, and the numpy wildcard ":" is used to indicate that the operation is to be done for each point index. The single component arrays can be referred to by name alone or by name and [:] appended. The Normals array will have a shape of (number of points, 3), and the StrainRate array will have a shape of (number of points, 3, 3). The make_vector method is used to create a field with three components in it. For the `Python Calculator` filter, set the Array Name to "SurfaceStress". The result of ploting surface stress is shown in Figure 18.6.

Finally, use the `Integrate Variables` filter to get the desired force acting on our fin, which is (-0.0257839, -1.28476, -2.1637e-05).

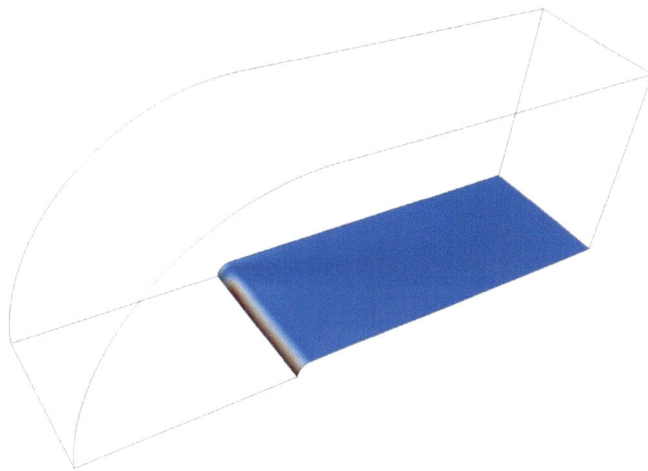

Figure 18.6: Plot of the surface stress.

CASE STUDIES

19.1   Enabling ParaView interaction with ITK and Slicer: collaboration on computational anatomy with Johns Hopkins Center for Imaging Science

A joint project by Johns Hopkins University 's Center for Imaging Science (JHU CIS) , under Michael Miller, and Kitware, under Will Schroeder, is leading to new functionality in ParaView to facilitate its use by JHU in order to empower its Computational Anatomy research.

JHU CIS research emphasizes probabilistic anatomical atlases, including many structures of the brain, which encode population shape statistics for both surfaces and image sub-volumes representing anatomical structures. ParaView, which is already the platform of choice at JHU CIS for visualization, will also be relied upon by this group to manage its sophisticated image analysis, which characterizes shape variation in the population on the basis of Large Deformation Diffeomorphic Metric Mapping (LDDMM) . By LDDMM , you can establish correspondences between equivalent points in anatomically defined coordinates and statistical measurements determined from them for a set of surfaces or segmented volumes of comparable structures.

In addition to being able to trigger ITK processing via VTK plugins that run on ParaView, an important component of this project is the management of a scene based on the notion of a scene graph, as well as on the MRML standard, as developed under Slicer. The implication of treating anatomy as a scene graph is that this approach allows independent computations on, and effective visualization of, many anatomically distinct structures that comprise an atlas.

19.1.1   Empowering ITK-based image analysis on ParaView via VTK plugins

ITK-based image analysis on ParaView is one of the main objectives of this collaboration between Kitware and JHU CIS . A first step toward this objective was realized with an ITK-based VTK plugin that was developed by Andinet Enquobahrie and Julien Finet. This plugin imbeds processing using the class `itk::RecursiveGaussianImageFilter`. The interface features a user-selectable scale factor. This ITK class was chosen because it produces immediate and visible results, irrespective of the scale factor selected. This infinite impulse response (IIR) filter is based on the work of Rachid Deriche in the 1980's and 1990's.

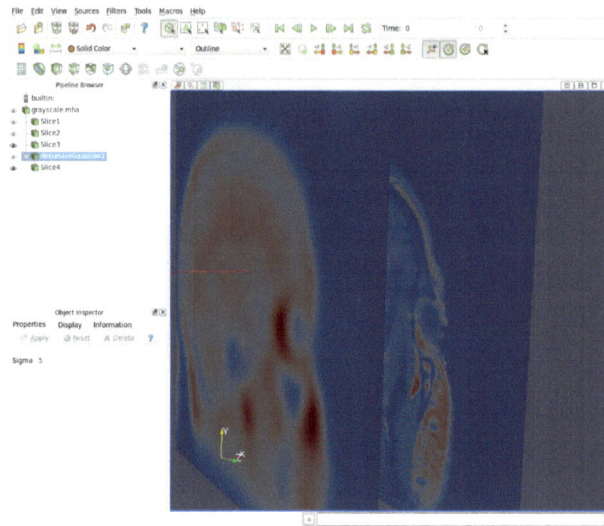

A second example was developed to demonstrate surface algorithms based on a `vtkPolyData` input that is converted to an `itk::QuadEdgeMesh` and processed by an `itk::QuadEdgeMeshSmoothing` class. the output of the processing is converted back to a `vtkPolyData`. The output `vtkPolyData` is viewed on the screen, superimposed with the wireframe of the original. The smoother effectively updates the position of each point with a weighted sum of its previous position and a neighborhood average, which, for a convex surface, tends to pull each point inwards. The number of such iterations is a parameter that you can set via this VTK plugin running on ParaView.

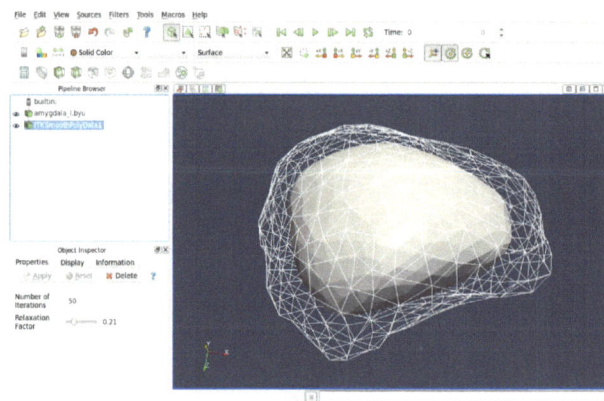

19.1.2 Slicer-compatible MRML-based scene management via KWScene

Preliminary results illustrate the compatibility of MRML-based scene management, via the new KWScene toolkit, between ParaView and Slicer. One litmus test for this scene graph is to 1) view an atlas composed of anatomical surfaces under Slicer, 2) save this atlas as a MRML scene, 3) input this scene to ParaView, 4) populate a representation of this scene internally, and then 5) output this new scene in MRML format. The results must also be viewable under Slicer.

Shown here is a visualization of components of the original JHU brain atlas scene under Slicer. The various anatomical components have been modified by hand in the MRML file to produce a different color for each structure, as well as to make them semi-transparent. This MRML is still visible under Slicer, and each atlas component appears distinct from the others.

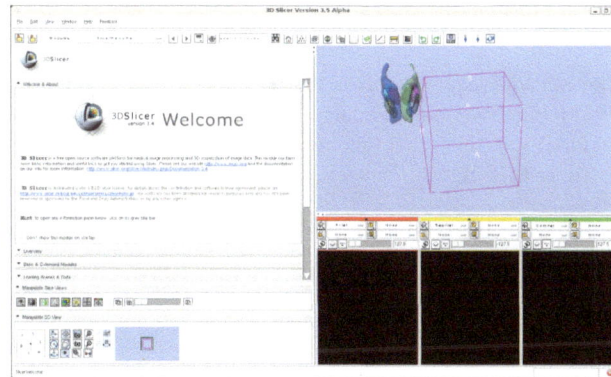

The same atlas-containing MRML scene can be read by and populated in ParaView, by way of a plugin based on a KWScene shared library, as shown below. All properties of these MRML ModelNodes (in this case, .byu-type triangulated surfaces), including color and opacity, are preserved.

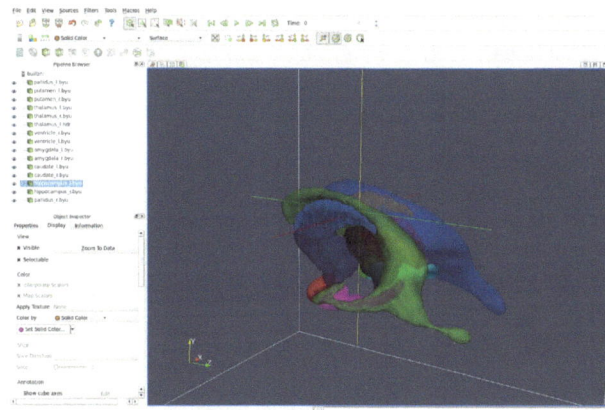

The scene instantiated in ParaView can be saved as a new MRML file. This new MRML file is also viewable under Slicer, as seen below, and all MRML entries of these ModelNodes, such as color and opacity, are once again preserved. Differences in viewing parameters are apparent, as, currently, KWScene emphasizes support for data-related nodes such as Model and Volume.

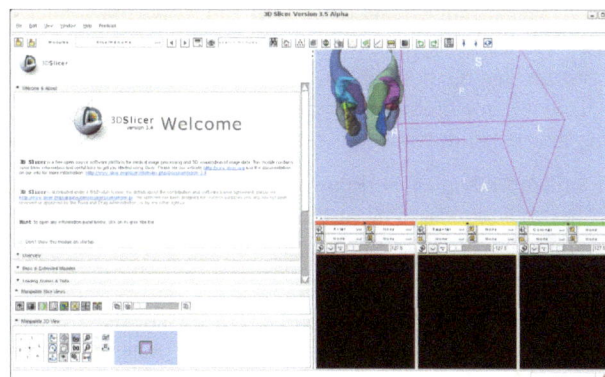

MRML entries of image volumes (VolumeNode-type), including triplanar viewing parameters (Slice and SliceComposite nodes), are also preserved.

19.1.3   Intuitive interactivity of ParaView, broad functionality of ITK, descriptiveness of Slicer-MRML

This project benefits from the sophisticated requirements of the JHU CIS group's Computational Anatomy research, which, in turn, has elicited a new combination of open-source software platforms that build on their strengths, namely, the intuitive interactivity afforded by ParaView, the broad functionality of image analysis classes available under ITK, and the descriptiveness and flexibility of Slicer-MRML.

19.2   Exploratory climate data visualization and analysis using VTK and ParaView in UV-CDAT

In recent years, substantial progress in understanding Earth's climate system has driven an explosion, both in scale and complexity, of climate-related data. Current climate models are capable of generating petabytes of data from a single run. The complexity of these datasets is also intensifying as models encompass an increasingly wide range of earth systems, adding many new variables to the datasets and requiring integration of an increasingly wide range of observational data sources. The knowledge discovery process in climate science requires effective tools to discover, access, manipulate, and visualize the datasets of interest. Recent developments are driving the need for a new generation of climate knowledge discovery tools, as the scientist's traditional toolkit is becoming overwhelmed and rendered obsolete by the "data tsunami". Key technical challenges include the seamless integration of advanced exploratory visualization tools, workflow and provenance support, and high performance computing.

To address these technical challenges, researchers at NASA , LANL , and Kitware have been developing sophisticated climate data visualization and analysis capabilities as part of the UV-CDAT framework. In the next few sections, we will describe various visual data exploration and computational features provided by VCS[16] and ParaView as part of the UV-CDAT framework.

19.2.1   The VCS package

The PCMDI Visualization Control System (VCS) is expressly designed to meet the needs of climate scientists. Because of the breadth of its capabilities, VCS can be a useful tool for other scientific applications as well. VCS allows wide-ranging changes to be made to the data display, provides for hardcopy output, and includes a means for recovery of a previous display.

VCS provides the high-level interfaces, tools, and application integrations required to make the analysis and visualization power of VTK readily accessible without exposing details such as actors, cameras, renderers, and transfer functions. VCS provides support for 1D, 2D, and 3D visualizations, and it can be run as a desktop application or distributed over a set of nodes for hyperwall or distributed visualization applications. VCS 2D plots are the most commonly used by the climate scientists for understanding information and relationship contained in the data. VCS 2D plots are also typically used for the publlication purposes. VCS 3D views into high-dimensional datasets offer a widened perspective and a more comprehensive gestalt, facilitating the recognition of significant features and the discovery of important patterns.

VCS is part of UV-CDAT, which supports complex workflows using VisTrails,[4] integrating numerous analysis and visualization processes (Figures 1 & 2)) with many intermediate and final data products. Workflow systems have been shown to be an effective tool for addressing the challenge of combining disparate computational modules while transparently automating provenance collection.[5, 15]

While VCS 2D plots are important and commonly used, we will cover 3D plots here in more detail, as they provide new analysis capabilities that are not present in other analysis and visualization tools.

19.2.2 VCS 3D plot types

The VCS 3D offers scientists a set of coordinated, interactive 3D views (i.e., plots) into their datasets. Each plot type offers a unique perspective by highlighting particular features of the data. Multiple plots can be combined synergistically (within a single cell or across multiple cells) to facilitate understanding of the natural processes underlying the data.

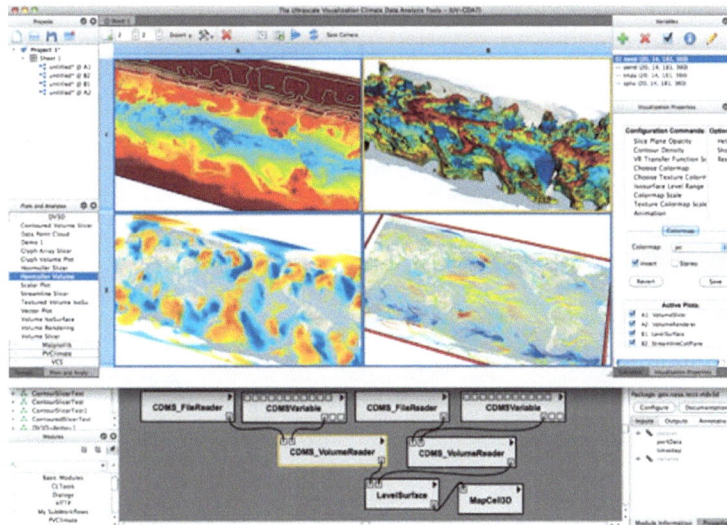

Figure 19.1: VCS 3D within the UV-CDAT GUI.

The Slicer plot provides a set of slice planes that can be interactively dragged over the dataset. A slice through the data volume at the plane's location is displayed as a pseudocolor image on the plane. A slice through a second data volume can also be overlaid as a contour map over the first. This tool allows scientists to very quickly and easily browse the 3D structure of the dataset, compare variables in 3D, and probe data values.

The Volume Render plot maps variable values within a data volume to opacity and color. It enables scientists to create an overview of the topology of the data, revealing complex 3D structures at a glance. Due to the complexity of creating useful transfer functions, the art of generating volume renderings has, in the past, been relegated to visualization professionals. VCS 3D offers interfaces that greatly simplify this process, enabling interactive volume rendering to play an important role in scientists' data exploration processes.

The Isosurface plot displays an isosurface derived from one variable's data volume and colored by the spatially-correspondent values from a second variable's data volume. It can produce views similar to a volume rendering while facilitating the comparison of two variables.

The Hovmoller plots are similar to the 3D slicer and volume render plots described above, except that they operate on a data volume structured with time (instead of height or pressure level) as the vertical dimension. This plot allows scientists to quickly and easily browse the 3D structure of spatial time series.

The Vector Slicer plot provides a set of slice planes that can be interactively dragged over a vector field dataset. A slice through the field at the plane's location is displayed as a vector glyph or as a streamline plot on the plane. This plot allows scientists to browse the structure of variables (such as wind velocity) that have both magnitude and direction.

19.2.3 VCS plot features

The plots offer the following features:

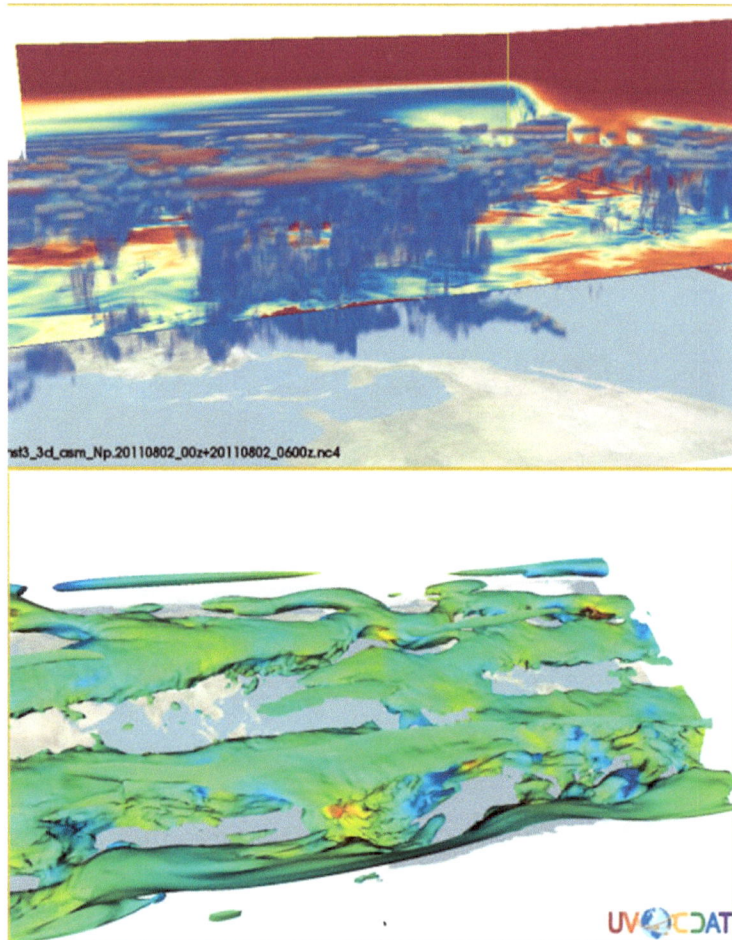

Figure 19.2: An isosurface plot (bottom) and a combination volume render and slicer plot (top).

- The ability to animate over one of the data dimensions (typically time).
- The ability to develop custom visualization and analysis pipelines through the VisTrails workflow interface.
- A rich selection of interactive query, browse, navigation, and configuration options, facilitating exploratory visualization.
- Integration with the VisTrails spreadsheet, which provides multiple, synchronized plots for desktop or hyperwall.
- Integration with the VisTrails provenance architecture to provide transparent collection and comprehensive management of workflow and data provenance.
- Active and passive 3D stereo visualization support for VCS 3D provided by the underlying VTK architecture.
- Seamless integration with CDAT's climate data management system (CDMS)[11] and other climate data analysis tools to provide extensive climate data processing and analysis functionality.

19.2.4   The VCS GUI interface

The VCS package within UV-CDAT is composed of a set of VisTrails modules. Each VCS module offers a distinctive GUI interface (accessible from the VisTrails workflow builder), enabling the configuration of workflow parameters. These modules can be selected from a palette and linked to create custom workflows using the VisTrails workflow builder. The VCS spreadsheet cells also offer a wide range of interactive key-press and mouse-drag operations, facilitating the configuration of colormaps, transfer functions, and other display and execution options. For example, pressing a button in a configuration panel, and then clicking and dragging in a spreadsheet cell displaying a VCS 3D volume render plot, initiates a leveling operation that controls the shape of the plot's opacity or color transfer function. The volume render plot changes interactively as you drag the mouse around the cell.

All configuration operations are saved as VisTrails provenance. The provenance trail contains a record of all workflow construction and configuration operations that contributed to the current visualization, making it easy to revert to an earlier configuration of the workflow at any stage of development.

19.2.5   VCS workflows

A VCS workflow begins with a set of modules encapsulating CDMS operations for accessing and processing climate data from the local file system or from the Earth System Grid Federation (ESGF). The CDAT toolkit provides a wide range of climate data analysis operations, including simple arithmetic operations, regridding, conditioned comparisons, weighted averages, various statistical operations, etc. A VCS 3D translation module converts the processed CDMS data volumes into VTK image data instances to initialize the visualization branch of a VCS 3D workflow. VCS visualization modules encapsulate complex VTK pipelines with numerous supporting objects such as actors, cameras, renderers, interaction observers, data mappers, and transfer functions. Each visualization pipeline implements a unique interactive 1D, 2D, or 3D plot. Each branch of a VCS workflow terminates in a VCS cell module, which represents a custom cell in the UVCDAT spreadsheet.

19.2.6   ParaView plots and UV-CDAT spatio-temporal parallel pipeline

The integration of ParaView into the UV-CDAT framework has brought a wealth of analysis and visualization capabilities to the framework. The serial abilities of ParaView have been tightly integrated into UV-CDAT, which brings with it several benefits. The parallel capabilities of ParaView can also be accessed using a set workflow. A new addition to ParaView is the calculation of the Meridional Overturning Circulation (MOC) and the Meridional Heat Transport (MHT) . Also, in response to the demands and use cases of the UV-CDAT program, a new parallel pipeline has been developed to take advantage of temporal parallelism, called the UV-CDAT spatio-temporal pipeline.

Several new climate-specific readers and filters have been implemented in ParaView for the UV-CDAT framework. These include an Unstructured POP reader, an MOC and MHT reader, and a Project Sphere filter. The Unstructured POP reader loads POP Ocean data as an unstructured grid. Better analysis and visualizations can be obtained from this more accurate representation of the data. The Project Sphere filter takes data defined on a spherical grid, like climate data, and projects it onto a flat plane.

19.2.7   Meridional Overturning Circulation and Meridional Heat Transport

The MOC and the MHT are two quantities considered important to the analysis of Earth's ocean currents. Changing the temperature of ocean currents will affect its density, causing it to increase or decrease in depth. In general, ocean currents will heat up and rise near the equator, and they will cool down and sink near the poles. The amount of overturning of the ocean currents is referred to as the MOC . The MHT is the transport of heat through ocean currents from the low latitudes near the equator to the high latitudes towards the poles.

Serial programs were first used to compute these two quantities. As the size of the generated data became ever larger, the time required to compute them became too prohibitive, and they were dropped as part of the standard diagnostics. To remedy this, two parallel filters were created in ParaView and integrated in UV-CDAT, which calculate the MOC and the

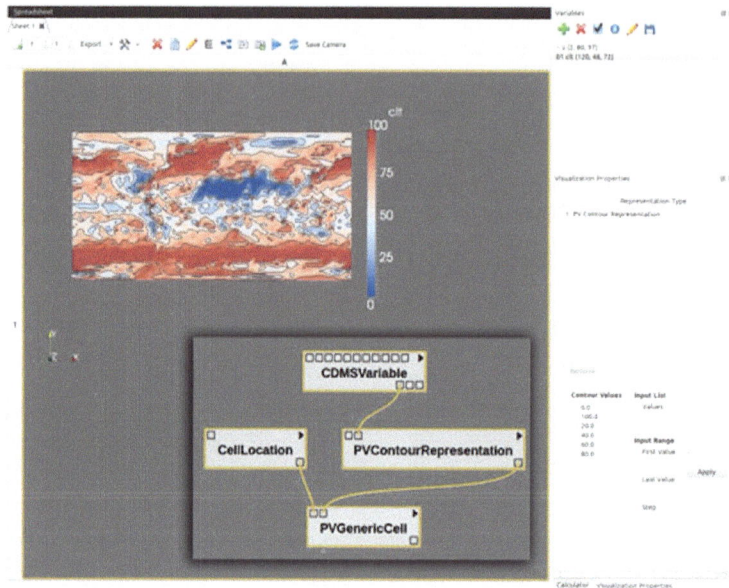

Figure 19.3: ParaView plot and corresponding VisTrails pipeline workflow.

MHT in parallel. The performance gains from parallelizing these computations were substantial, with run times being reduced from a couple of hours to a few minutes.

19.2.8 UV-CDAT spatio-temporal parallel pipeline

Many climate datasets have, in addition to a high spatial resolution, a high temporal resolution. In many instances, simulations output daily or monthly averages, with datasets possibly covering a total timespan of decades. Due to this high temporal resolution, there is a critical need to have a fast, scalable method for processing a large number of timesteps. In response, the UV-CDAT spatio-temporal pipeline was devised to solve UV-CDAT Use Case 1 and Use Case 2.

19.2.9 Use case 1

Use Case 1 involves a dataset with high spatial and temporal resolution. The task is to produce an image sequence of the dataset by producing one image per timestep. One key aspect here is that there are no dependencies between timesteps. In addition, each timestep can be processed independently.

In a fully data-parallel model, all available processors would take part in reading the first timestep, perform any required analysis, and then take part in producing the final image output. Then, all processors would load the second timestep, and the cycle would repeat until all timesteps have been processed. In this case, timesteps are accessed sequentially, and only spatial parallelism is utilized.

In the UV-CDAT spatio-temporal pipeline, parallelism is extended both spatially and temporally. This means that multiple timesteps can be processed simultaneously. This is permissible since each timestep can be processed independent of each other. In order to achieve temporal parallelism, the available processors are divided into groups, called time compartments. The number of total time compartments is dependent on the number of processes and the size of a time compartment, which is constant over all time compartments. Each time compartment can now load and process a timestep independently, resulting in multiple timesteps being worked on simultaneously. The figure below illustrates how

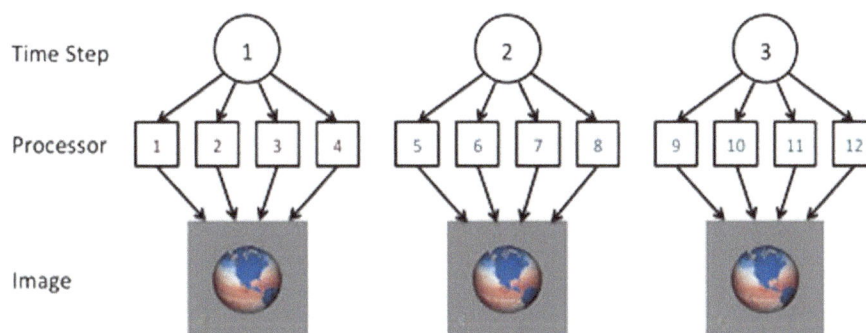

Figure 19.4: Use Case 1 - High spatial resolution, high temporal resolution, image sequence production.

processors are broken up into time compartments and how work is distributed among them. When there are more timesteps than time compartments, the files are assigned in round-robin fashion to time compartments, so it is possible for a time compartment to process multiple timesteps. Within a time compartment, its assigned timesteps are processed one at a time.

The amount of temporal parallelism versus spatial parallelism is controlled by the size of one time compartment, which is a user configurable parameter. When the time compartment size is large, there are fewer total time compartments, which results in less temporal parallelism and more spatial parallelism. On the other hand, if the time compartment size is small, there are more time compartments. Therefore, the amount of temporal parallelism is higher, and the amount of spatial parallelism is lower.

19.2.10   Use case 2

Similar to Use Case 1, Use Case 2 also involves analyzing climate data, which has both high spatial and temporal resolution. The difference with Use Case 1 is that, instead of having each timestep be processed independently, some type of reduction operation among several timesteps must be performed, with the output being various statistics. One example would be calculating yearly averages from monthly data. In this case, every 12 timesteps comprising one year must be averaged together. Supported reduction operations include average, min, max, and standard deviation. The UV-CDAT spatio-temporal pipeline can also be used to support Use Case 2, as is illustrated below. Each time compartment loads one-or-more timesteps like before, but with an additional reduction step, which combines the results of several time compartments into a single data product.

19.2.11   UV-CDAT spatio-temporal pipeline performance

Initial results from the UV-CDAT spatio-temporal pipeline's performance show vast performance gains. In Use Case 1, there was an improvement from hours to minutes when switching to the spatio-temporal pipeline. Use Case 2 also showed an order of magnitude improvement when using the spatio-temporal pipeline. Similar results have been shown over multiple supercomputers and multiple file systems.

19.2.12   Conclusions

The inundation of data generated by ever-increasing resolution in both global models and remote sensors is presenting both a challenge and an opportunity for earth science analytics. New tools and methods are needed to reap the benefits of

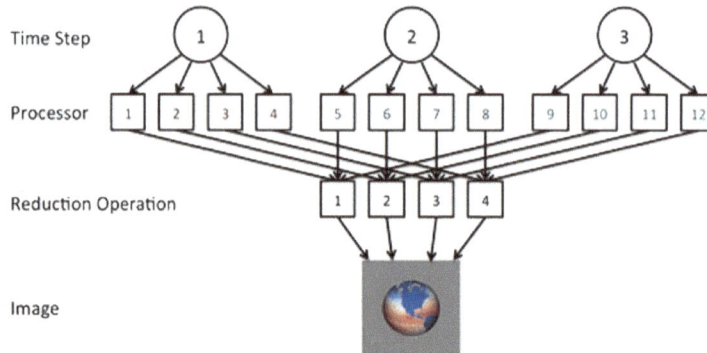

Figure 19.5: Use Case 2 - High spatial resolution, high temporal resolution, time average.

this overabundance of information. Key technical challenges include the seamless integration of advanced visualization tools, workflow and provenance support, and high performance computing.

The complexity of the climate knowledge discovery process is increasing due to the increasing complexity of climate datasets. Graphical representations (which are very effective at addressing data complexity) can be enhanced by an increase in the number of "degrees of freedom" in the visualization process. Three-dimensional views into complex high dimensions datasets can offer a widened perspective and a more comprehensive gestalt, facilitating the recognition of significant features and the discovery of important patterns.

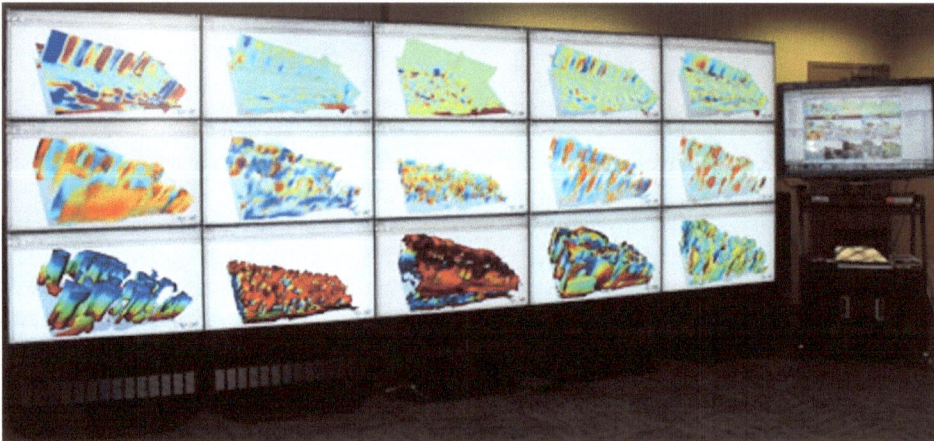

Figure 19.6: The VCS 3D distributed visualization framework deployed on the NASA NCCS hyperwall.

Resources supporting this work were provided by the NASA High-End Computing (HEC) Program through the Center for Climate Simulation (NCCS) at Goddard Space Flight Center. We would like to thank Dean N. Williams, Berk Geveci, Gerald Potter, and the entire UV-CDAT team for this work.

19.3 ParaView in immersive environments

The ubiquity of immersive systems is increasing. The availability of low-cost Virtual Reality (VR) systems,[13] coupled with a growing population of researchers accustomed to newer interface styles, makes this an opportune time to help domain science researchers cross the bridge to utilizing immersive interfaces. The next logical step is for scientists, engineers, doctors, etc., to incorporate immersive visualization into their exploration and analysis workflows; however, from past experience, we know that having access to equipment is not sufficient. There are also several software hurdles to overcome. The first hurdle is simply the lack of available usable software. Two other hurdles more specific to immersive visualization are: subdued immersion (e.g., the software might only provide a stereoscopic view or might provide stereo with simple head tracking but no wand) and lack of integration with existing desktop workflows (e.g., a desktop CFD workflow may require data conversions to operate with an immersive tool).

ParaView has gained immense popularity in the scientific community as a universal visualization system. Early on, we decided to integrate support for immersive environments directly into ParaView, rather than linking to an external library. We felt that there were sufficient components in ParaView's design that could be extended to support immersive rendering and interactions and that limiting dependencies would make our efforts more impactful and sustainable for the long term.

19.3.1 Architecture

ParaView provides a user friendly environment via its graphical user interface, which grants researchers with immediate opportunities for performing visualization tasks. At a very high level, the overall ParaView architecture is represented in the figure below.

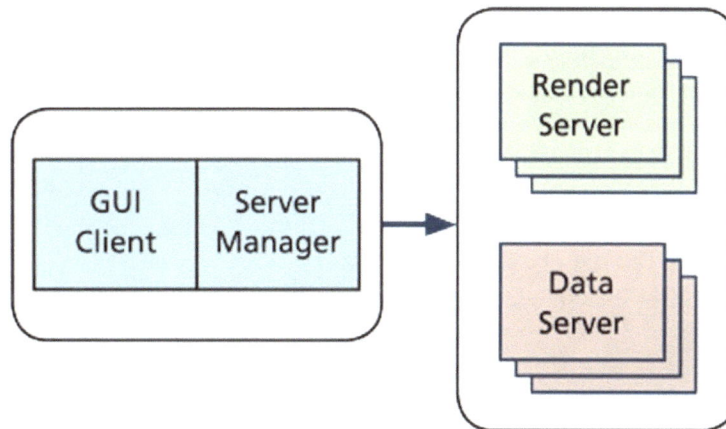

Figure 19.7: High-level overview of the ParaView architecture.

The Server Manager is the layer responsible for exchanging data and information between the client and the servers. As the name suggests, the Data Server is responsible for reading raw data, filtering data, and writing out data, which then can be rendered by the Render Server. It should be noted that the Data Server and the Render Server modules can exist either across a network or together with the GUI client on a single machine. We determined the Render Server to be the apt place to drive Immersive displays. The typical use of the Render Server is for parallel rendering and image compositing. More broadly, however, it is simply a framework where multiple views of the same data can be rendered synchronously.

The Client reads a configuration file and sets the appropriate display parameters on the Render Server. The parameters passed include coordinates of each display with reference to the base coordinate of the tracking system. A similar technique is used to pass device data to each of the participating nodes. The client reads the device data from a locally- or remotely-connected device and sends it across to the rendering nodes. Either the Virtual Reality Peripheral Network (VRPN)[2] or the Virtual Reality User Interface (VRUI) Device Daemon[3] protocols can be used to collect the input data. The figure below demonstrates the client receiving head tracking data via VRPN from a remote tracking device and routing it to cameras on every Render Server.

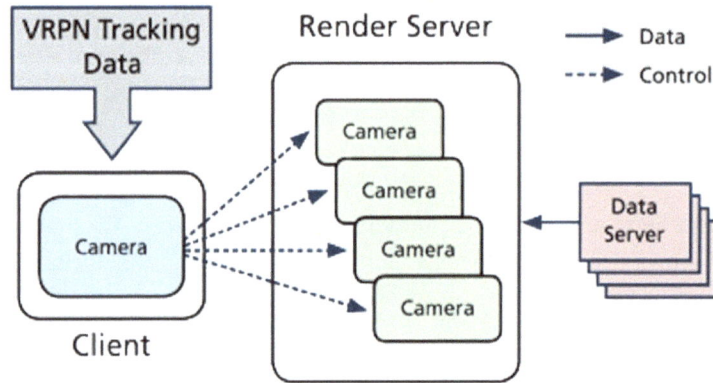

Figure 19.8: Client distributing head tracking data to render server cameras.

19.3.2 Implementation: off axis rendering

Like many computer graphics systems designed for desktop interaction, the VTK library calculates the perspective viewing matrix with the assumption that the viewer looks along an axis from the center of the image. This assumption is generally acceptable for desktop interfaces, but breaks down when applied to immersive interfaces where the view is affected by the location and movement of the head.

We added a new rendering option that allows a VTK-camera to be set to "OffAxisProjection" mode, opening up new parameters that can be used to precisely set the projection matrix. The key parameter required for this is the relationship between the eye and the screen. This could be done in relative terms. However, with the goal of having this work in large immersive displays, it is more natural to specify screen and eye positions relative to a specific origin. Therefore, the following new methods have been added to the VTK camera class:

- `SetUseOffAxisProjection <bool>`

- `SetScreenBottomLeft <x> <y> <z>`

- `SetScreenBottomRight <x> <y> <z>`

- `SetScreenTopRight <x> <y> <z>`

- `SetEyePosition <x> <y> <z>`

These are sufficient for monoscopic rendering, but most immersive displays operate stereoscopically, so we need to provide an eye separation and the direction of the head to properly adjust the location of each eye:

- `SetEyeSeparation <distance>`

- `SetEyeTransformMatrix <homogeneous matrix>`

With off-axis projection in place within VTK, adding immersive rendering to ParaView became a matter of configuring the screens and collecting and routing head tracking information to continuously set the proper rendering parameters. Additionally, we wanted to provide an immersive user interface, so hand (or wand) tracking data is also typically collected. We can map that data through the ParaView proxy system to affect visualization tools.

Figure 19.9: Stereo rendering with head tracking using VTK in a four-sided VR environment.

19.3.3 Interactor styles

In addition to providing "OffAxisProjection", we added support for new interactor styles via ParaView's newly-added VR Plugin.

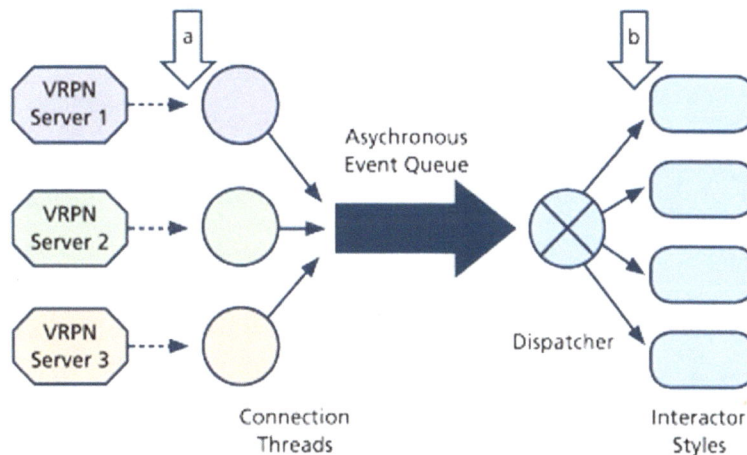

Figure 19.10: ParaView VR Device Plugin: (a) VRPN Server or VRUI DD Connections are specified here. (b) Device Events and corresponding Interaction-Styles are specified here.

19.3.4 Results and conclusion

Adding immersion to ParaView uses existing VR tracking protocols (VRPN and VRUI) in conjunction with ParaView's current capabilities for multi-screen rendering to enable immersive viewing and interaction. As with open-source packages released by Kitware, Immersive ParaView also relies on CMake for compilation of the application. We tested our additions to ParaView using several different immersive environments including a portable IQ-station[13] (a low-cost display based on commercial off-the-shelf parts) and a four-sided CAVE. The four-sided CAVE was tested using a single render server with two NVidia QuadroPlex's.

Immersive ParaView makes strides towards a fully-featured, open-source visualization system that can leverage immersive technologies to serve broad scientific communities. It offers a low barrier to entry, drawing users to immersive displays through familiar software and migrating visualization sessions. As it attracts a user base and forms a community, we expect Immersive ParaView to become sustainable, to gain support, and to raise awareness and utilization of immersive displays. We ultimately aim to improve scientific workflows as low-cost VR systems and to have Immersive ParaView and other immersive visualization tools become integral components in scientists' labs. We would like to thank Idaho National Lab (INL) for its support of this effort.

19.4   Immersive ParaView experiences at Idaho National Laboratory

The Center for Advanced Modeling and Simulation (CAMS) at INL offers an advanced visualization facility that includes a four-sided CAVE-style immersive display system, a large 3x3 tiled display, and a low-cost immersive system, dubbed the IQ-station[13] (see the figure below). Given these immersive environments, the CAMS team has a vested interest in making it very easy for scientists to bring their data into their facilities and to enable them to quickly explore and interact with the data. Highly customized tools requiring specific data formats work very well in the CAVE, but these tools do not meet the needs of the new or occasional user who does not have the means to develop custom code. The common user use-model drives the need for a general purpose visualization tool that is compatible with immersive environments.

Figure 19.11: ParaView running on a portable VR system.

ParaView was recognized as a great fit for scientists to use in an immersive environment, as it has all the necessary features to bring desktop analysis and visualization to the advanced visualization systems. In 2010, the CAMS team began a collaboration with Kitware, Indiana University, and the University of Wyoming to add features necessary for immersion (i.e., VR interfaces) to ParaView, including some new features to the underlying VTK library.[14]

The result of this collaboration is a collection of code changes labeled as "Immersive ParaView". These extensions to the code base enable ParaView to display and interact with objects in an immersive environment. This work followed a development cycle that included: analysis and exploration of similar efforts from earlier releases of ParaView and other tools; a first-pass implementation modifying VTK for basic operation and gaining understanding of the various connections required for immersive applications; and a second-pass implementation that re-engineered and overhauled the

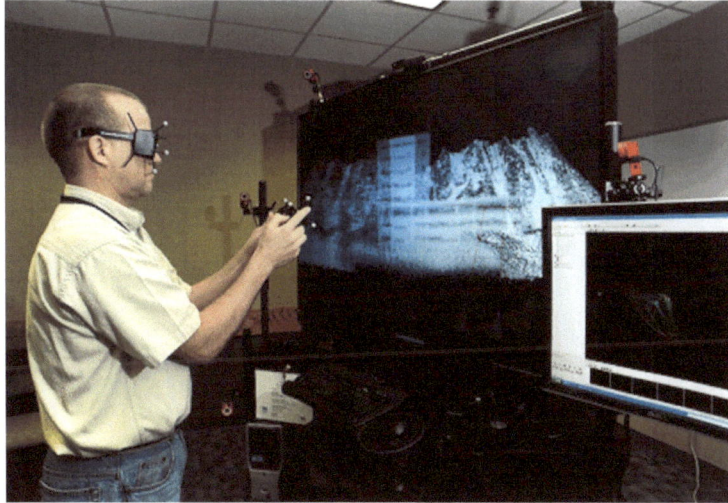

Figure 19.12: ParaView application running on IQ station.

code to improve correctness and maintainability.

19.4.1   Testing the prototype implementation

The new immersive functionality makes use of ParaView's client/server operational mode. One-or-more server processes are configured to render all the views needed to fill the displays of the immersive system. The client then resides on a separate screen and remains the primary means by which the visualization pipeline is built and configured.

Once the client/server connection is established, the plugin manager is used to load the "VR Plugin" into both the client and server processes. Doing so reveals a new widget panel (a new addition based on our evaluation, see below) that allows you to initiate a VR session.

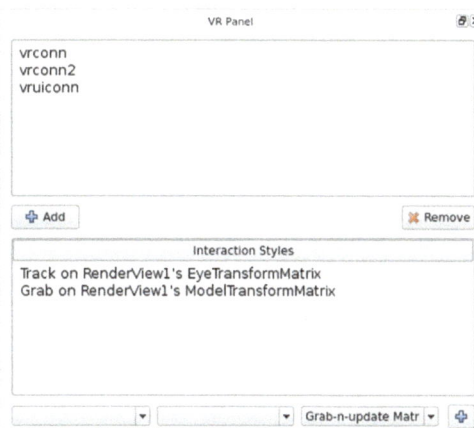

Figure 19.13: VR Plugin widget panel: Create a new connection manager by utilizing controls from the top half of the widget and, later, configuring various interactor styles using the bottom half of the widget.

Our tests at the INL CAMS facility included the use of the crushed can sample dataset, as well as the use of some computational data provided by INL researchers. With the recent off-axis stereo feature in VTK, we were able to get correct immersive rendering both in the four-sided CAVE and on the smaller-scale IQ-station. The tracking feature is part of the "VR Plugin" and can use either the VRPN[17] or the VRUI Device Daemon protocol.[8] With tracking enabled, immersive rendering responds properly to head movement. Additionally, the world can be grabbed and moved with a hand-held wand.

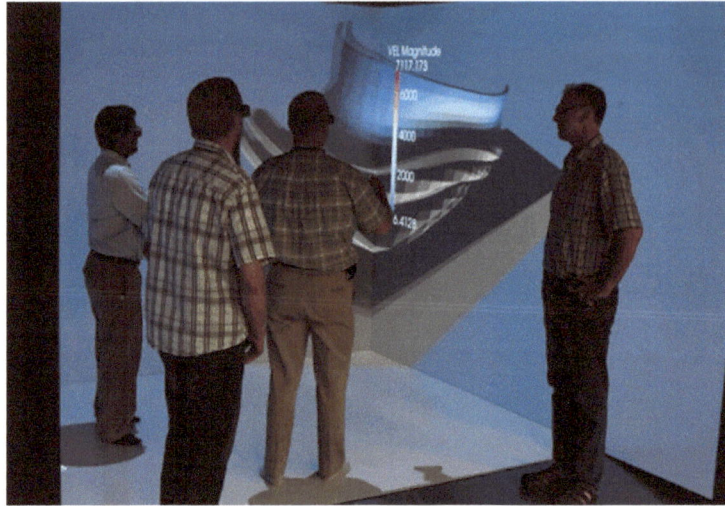

Figure 19.14: Testing the prototype implementation in the INL four-sided immersive environment.

Testing the prototype demonstrated the practicality of adding immersion through the VR plugin system. Given the functional baseline code, it was decided to address the identified shortcomings that were encountered. These were primarily in the process of configuring the immersive features. As part of preparations for a wider user base, we focused on creating a new VR widget panel and on adding Python scripting access to the new VR plugin features.

This work has been supported by INL and is publicly released as open-source software in the ParaView repository.

VISUALIZATION AND ANALYSIS OF ASTROPHYSICAL AMR DATASETS

20.1   Introduction

Recent advances in high-performance computing, combined with numerical techniques such as AMR , have greatly benefited astrophysicists in modeling complex phenomena describing the origins of cosmic structures. By discretizing the computational domain with multiple, overlapping, uniform grids of varying resolution, high-fidelity accuracy can be attained in a region of interest (ROI) , while lower-resolution is used elsewhere to minimize memory and storage requirements. In this approach, multi-resolution simulations exhibiting large length- and time-scales are realized; however, typical data sizes produced from such simulations are prohibitive. Naturally, infrastructure for carrying out analysis and visualization of astrophysical datasets at such large scales is required. In this chapter, we present recent and on-going developments in ParaView, specifically targeting large-scale astrophysical AMR datasets.

At the core of this new technology is a demand-driven approach that promotes exploratory visualization and enables astrophysicists to easily and efficiently mine their data. Techniques for visualizing and inspecting astrophysical datasets are presented, including detection and analysis of halos. Throughout the chapter, figures from sample astrophysical datasets, generated using the Enzo[6] flow-solver, are used to illustrate the various steps in the underlying analysis. For halo detection, the HOP algorithm is employed, provided by yt[20] (a Python-based astrophysics toolkit that is integrated with ParaView).

20.2   Mechanisms for interacting with astrophysical data

The basic idea of demand-driven visualization is the ability to selectively load the portion of the data required to address the given query provided by users. For example, users may request to visualize the data at a specific level of resolution or to visualize just a slice of the data. Or, they may be interested in a subset of the field variables.

The premise of this approach is rooted in the observation that most insights are derived only within a small sub-set of the dataset and constitutes as one of the leading design considerations of this work. This section details the mechanisms available for loading and inspecting both particle- and grid-based (fluid) astrophysical datasets. Specifically, the demand-driven operations of the AMR and particle readers are presented. Note, although examples are presented using an Enzo sample dataset, the present implementation also has native support for FLASH. Further, sub-setting operators, such as the axis-aligned AMR slice and multiresolution ROI extraction, are illustrated in combination with quantitative analysis enabled via ParaView's plotting capabilities. Last, use of yt's HOP algorithm through the ParaView interface is illustrated along with more advanced visualizations, such as streamlines and contouring that yield additional insights into underlying phenomena.

20.2.1 Demand-driven AMR and particle readers

Most astrophysics codes combine the fluid quantities (e.g., density, velocity, etc.) defined on the AMR grid hierarchy with particle quantities (e.g., mass, velocity, etc.) in a single set of coupled governing equations. Hence, capability for dealing with both types of data is required. In ParaView, there are two different types of readers: (1) AMR readers for the fluid quantities and AMR grid hierarchy, and (2) particle readers for particles and associated data.

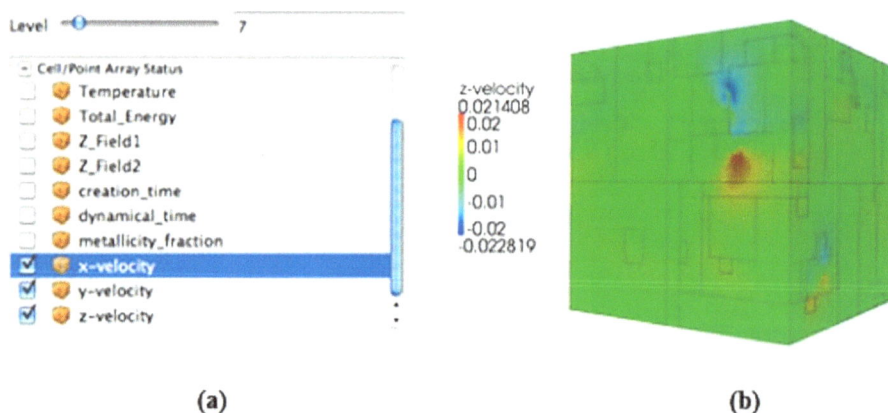

Figure 20.1: AMR Reader: (a) The reader panel that provides functionality for selectively loading cell/point data, as well as controlling the maximum desired level of resolution. (b) Surface mesh of the Enzo AMR Red-Shift dataset with the outline of each block overlaid.

Typical operations the AMR reader provides for the analysis of fluid data are the ability to specify the maximum level of resolution and to select which attributes to load. This functionality is extremely useful when loading large-scale datasets, since loading the entire dataset in memory is not feasible most of the time. By loading just a couple of low resolution levels, users gain insight as to where potential regions of interest are and extract those regions for further analysis. Figure 20.2.1 (a) depicts the reader panel, accessible from ParaView, that illustrates the user controls currently enabled. Notably, the ability to select a maximum level of resolution and which field variables to load is depicted. By default, ParaView only loads data at the lowest resolution and without field variables selected. Further, only the blocks on the surface are being processed for rendering. Figure 20.2.1 (b) shows the resulting surface mesh when prescribing a maximum resolution of seven colored by the z-component of the velocity. Subsequently, the data in the volume can be inspected using slices, which is described in more detail in the next section.

Similar functionality is also enabled for the particles reader. Figure 20.2.1 (a) depicts the particles reader panel controls and (b) shows the resulting particles dataset. As with the AMR reader, the ability to select which particle attributes to load is enabled. Further, using a frequency parameter, particles can be sub-sampled. In this case (Figure 20.2.1 (a)), the reader will load every fifth particle. Sub-sampling is commonly employed when analyzing particle simulations to reduce cluttering since there are typically billions of particles for a given simulation. Additionally, particles can be filtered out based on location or by particle type, e.g., in the case of Enzo datasets, Dark Matter, Star, or Tracer particles can be easily hidden or shown. This feature is particularly useful when downstream modules require specific particle input. For example, if a halo-finder is connected downstream, only dark matter particles are applicable as an input data type. In addition, the particles reader provides filtering of particles based on location; this is commonly employed to over-plot the particle distribution in the volume within a thin slice. For example, in the case depicted in Figure 20.2.1 (b), only particles in the range $[0.2, 0.4]$ along the x-axis and desired particle data are loaded. The corresponding parameter configuration is depicted in the particles reader panel in Figure 20.2.2 (a).

A salient feature of ParaView for rendering particle datasets is the use of the PointSprite plug-in. The plug-in provides an additional representation that allows visualization of particles as spheres using the GPU texture. This approach is both

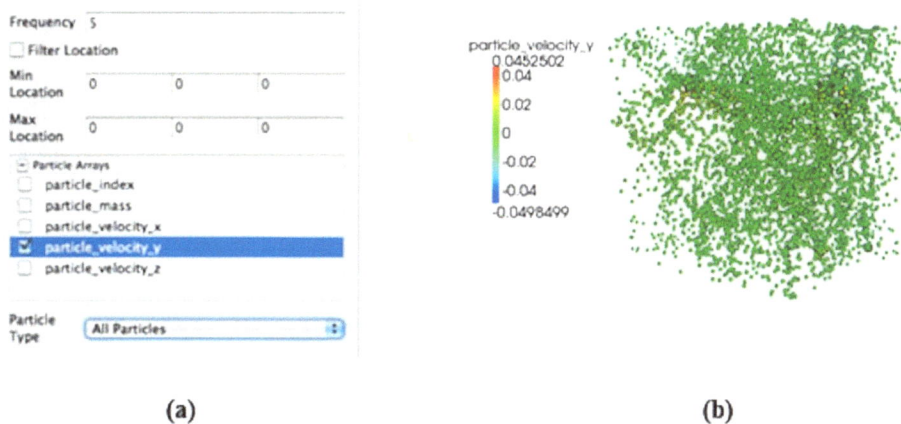

(a)   **(b)**

Figure 20.2: Particles Reader: (a) Reader panel that provides functionality for sub-sampling. In this case, every fifth particle is loaded through selective loading of particle arrays while filtering particles within a bounding box defined by its min and max coordinates, as well as filtering particles by type. (b) Corresponding particle dataset represented using point-sprites where each particle radius is proportional to the y-velocity.

more efficient and visually more appealing. Figure 20.2.1 illustrates the difference between the two representations. Additionally, the radius of the spheres can be scaled so that it is proportional to some particle quantity, (e.g., particle mass, density), which can lead to further insight. A common use-case is to scale the radius of the sphere according to the magnitude of the velocity. In this example, since the particle velocity components are stored as different field variables, they are first combined to a vector field (named "Velocity" in this case) using the Calculator filter. The resulting visualization is shown in Figure 20.2.1. Notably, this yields further insight, since it is easy to pin-point the regions of interest where particles are moving faster in a single glance.

20.2.2 Axis-aligned AMR slice

One of the most fundamental, simplest, yet very effective approaches of analyzing 3D AMR datasets is extraction of axis-aligned AMR slices through the dataset. There are several benefits to this approach, including the efficient and simple calculation of which blocks to load and the ability to exploit the multi-resolution hierarchical data-structure within the slice. For large datasets in particular, scientists initially load the data at a low-resolution, create a slice, and sweep within the volume until a region of interest is encountered. Once a region of interest is identified, scientists can increase the resolution to gain further insights into the physical phenomena and, subsequently, use other filters or perform other quantitative analysis, create plots, etc., within the slice.

Figure 20.2.2 (a) shows the AMR slice control panel. The user prescribes the level of resolution, the offset from the origin, and a plane normal. The resulting visualization is shown in (b). The effect of increasing the resolution on a slice is illustrated in Figure 20.2.2 (a) and (b), respectively.

Often times, visualizing the contours of a particular slice or in the volume is desirable in qualitative analysis of the scalar fields. If the data is node-based, traditional contouring algorithms can be readily applied; however, most AMR codes are cell-centered. Without proper handling of AMR data, the use of commonly employed algorithms, such as the Marching Cubes algorithm, is complicated by discontinuities at the inter-level interfaces. A dual mesh-based approach is employed in ParaView for proper handling of contours of cell-centered AMR datasets. This is a two-stage approach where the dual mesh is first constructed, and then the contouring algorithm is applied to the dual mesh. Resulting visualizations from the contouring are illustrated in Figure 20.2.2 (a), which depicts contours of the y-component of the velocity along an AMR

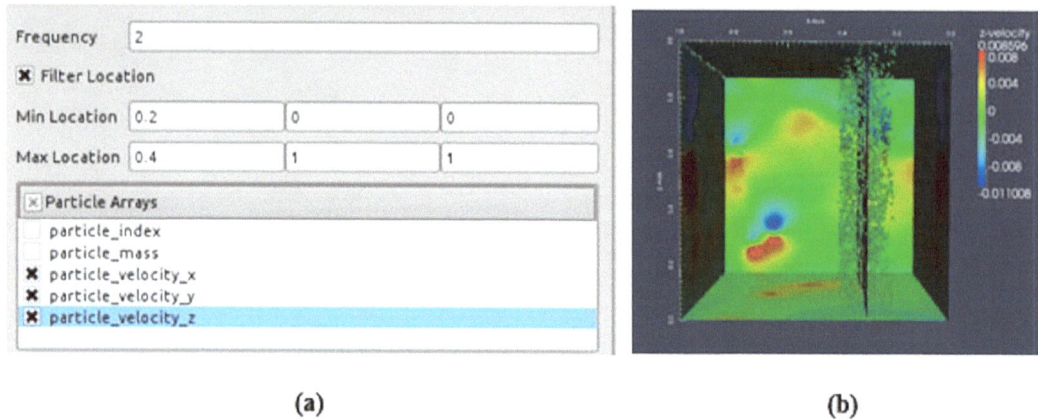

Figure 20.3: Filtering particles by location: (a) Particles reader panel configuration. (b) Resulting slice of particles overlaid on top of the AMR surface mesh, rendered using the Cull Frontface representation.

slice and (b) where contouring is applied in the volume.

Although visualizing datasets via slicing and generating contours is effective and insightful, quite often, generating plots depicting data distributions within the space of other variables is required. Take, for example, visualizing the data of a slice in a 2D plot as a function of density (x-axis) and velocity (y-axis). ParaView's intrinsic plotting capabilities combine qualitative and quantitative analysis in the same window. This particular use-case is depicted in Figure 20.2.2, where the corresponding 2D profile of the slice is generated.

20.2.3 Multi-resolution ROI extraction

Once a region of interest is identified, it is useful to be able to extract the region and corresponding data to a uniform grid with a prescribed resolution for further analysis. Among the most notable applications of this capability is data-reduction. For example, suppose a halo region is identified and further analysis needs to be conducted. Extracting the region to a fixed-resolution grid effectively reduces the amount of data and can potentially enable analysis to be continued on a typical workstation, as opposed to a supercomputer. ParaView provides this functionality with the AMR ROI Extraction filter. This use-case is illustrated in Figure 20.2.3, where the region is identified using a slice and extracted.

As illustrated in Figure 20.2.3 (a), the ROI extraction filter provides the mechanism to specify the following:

- the location at which the solution is interpolated (the nodes or cell centers of the receiving grid) and

- the level of resolution (the number of grid points in the receiving grid), while

- the ROI is defined as a bounding box enclosing the region of interest.

20.2.4 Halo detection and analysis

Halo detection and analysis is very typical in astrophysics. Using dark matter particles and fluid data, halo detection algorithms identify regions where new structures are forming, traditionally called halo regions or, just, halos. ParaView has two halo detection algorithms available. The first one is a Friend-of-Friends (FOF) algorithm developed by LANL . The second one is HOP and is available through the yt plug-in, a popular Python-based astrophysics toolkit. Users can

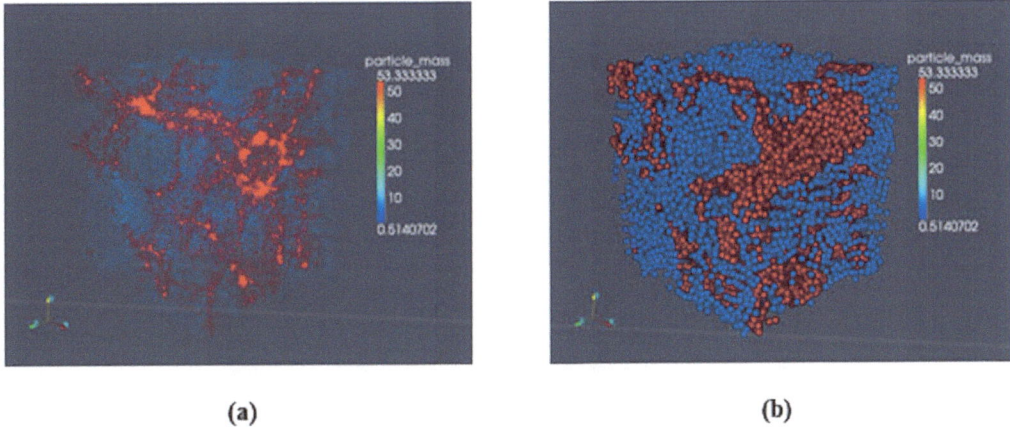

Figure 20.4: Rendering of sample particle dataset: (a) Particles rendered as points. (b) Particles rendered using the PointSprite representation.

invoke HOP from the ParaView GUI interface and perform halo-detection. The resulting output from the HOP algorithm is propagated in ParaView and visualized as a set of spheres forming around each halo.

As noted earlier, the HOP algorithm operates on both particles and fluid data. Hence, users must provide both inputs to the HOP halo-finder. Figure 20.2.4 (a) shows the output of the HOP algorithm as depicted in ParaView. The region encapsulated in the sphere (shown in white) corresponds to the halo region. Once the halo region is known, further analysis can be conducted. For example, by using the sphere center as a seed point, streamlines can be generated to visualize the flow surrounding the halo. Last, quantitative analysis can be conducted as illustrated earlier in Figure 20.2.4 (b).

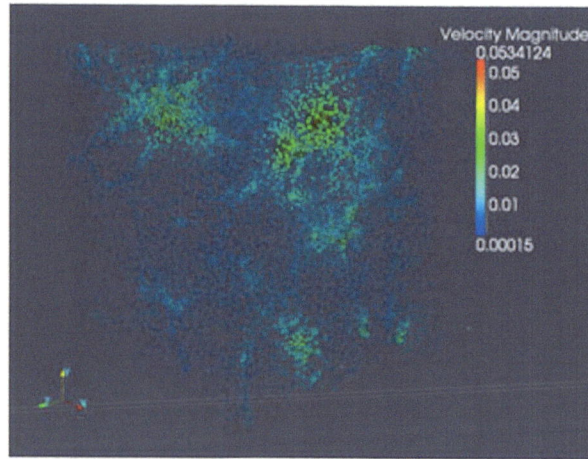

Figure 20.5: Rendering of sample particle dataset using the PointSprite representation where the radius of each sphere is scaled proportionally to the magnitude of the velocity.

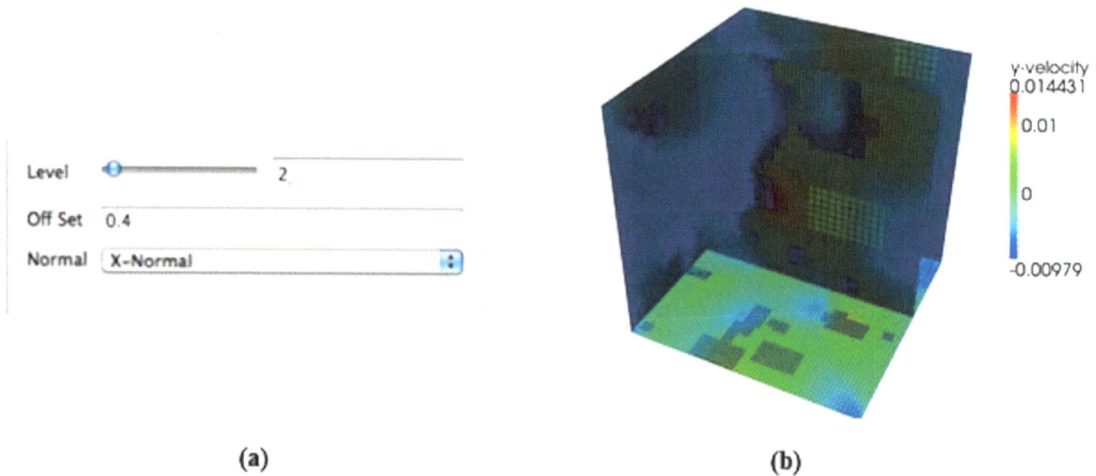

(a)   (b)

Figure 20.6: AMR Slice: (a) Slice filter panel controls that allow users to set the offset of the slice and normal, as well as request a higher resolution data to be loaded. (b) Resulting 2D AMR slice data with $dx = 0.4$ from the global dataset origin overlaid on the surface mesh of the computational domain.

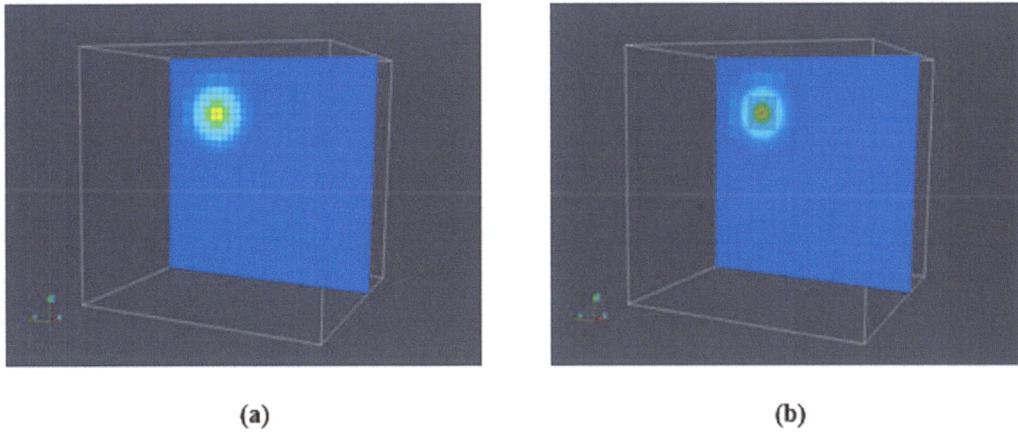

(a)   (b)

Figure 20.7: Varying Resolution on AMR Slice: (a) Slice with resolution set at level 1. (b) Slice after increasing the resolution to level 3.

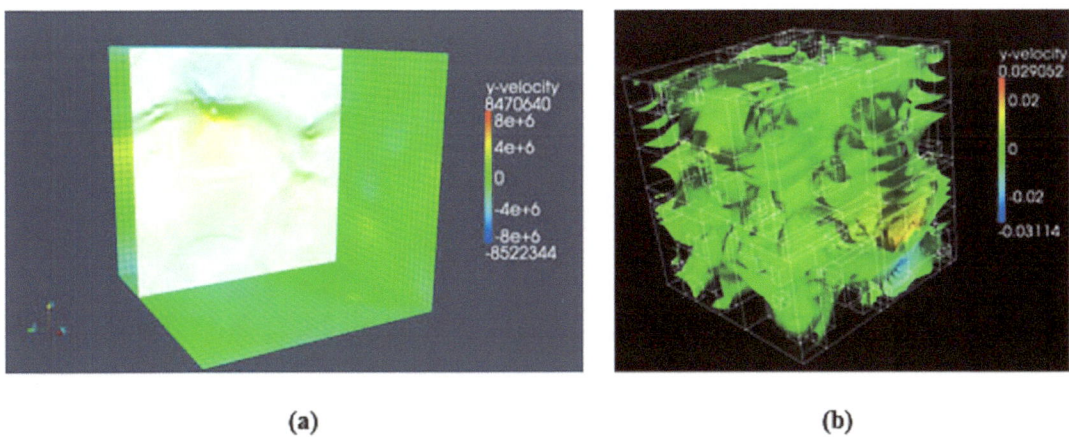

(a)   (b)

Figure 20.8: AMR Contouring using the sample Red-Shift dataset: (a) Overlaying contours on a slice. (b) 3D contours.

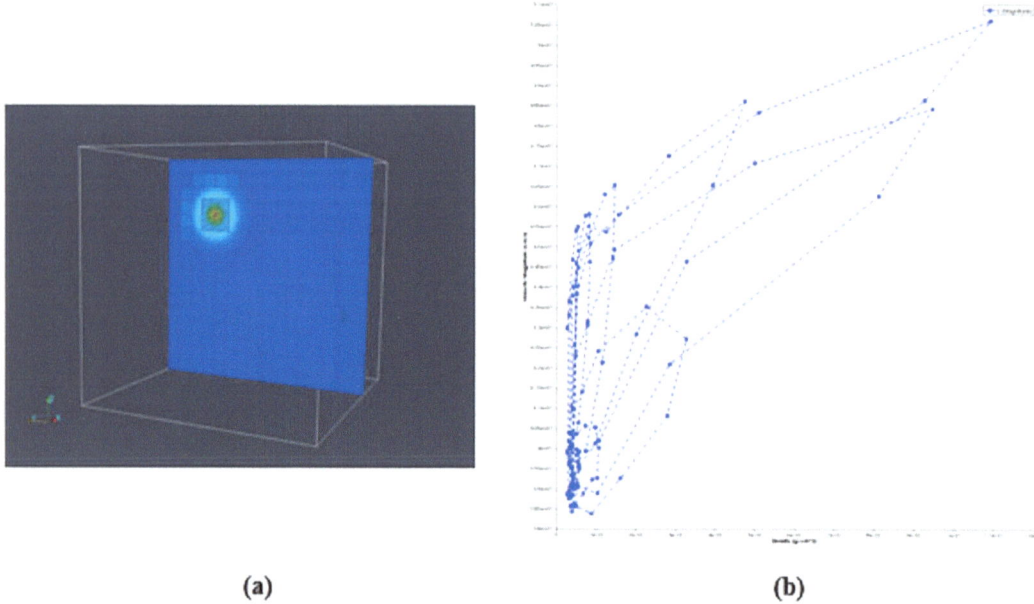

Figure 20.9: Quantitative analysis of a particular slice: (a) Slice containing halo region. (b) 2D profile of the data in the halo region plotted in the Density-Velocity plane.

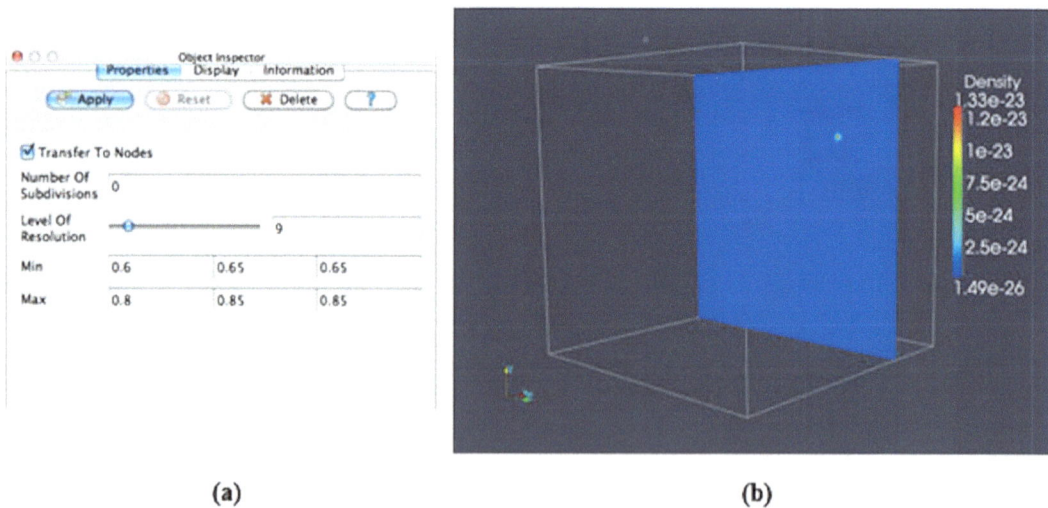

Figure 20.10: ROI Extraction: (a) AMR ROI Extraction filter panel showing the controls available to users. (b) Resulting visualization after ROI is extracted enclosing the highest density region.

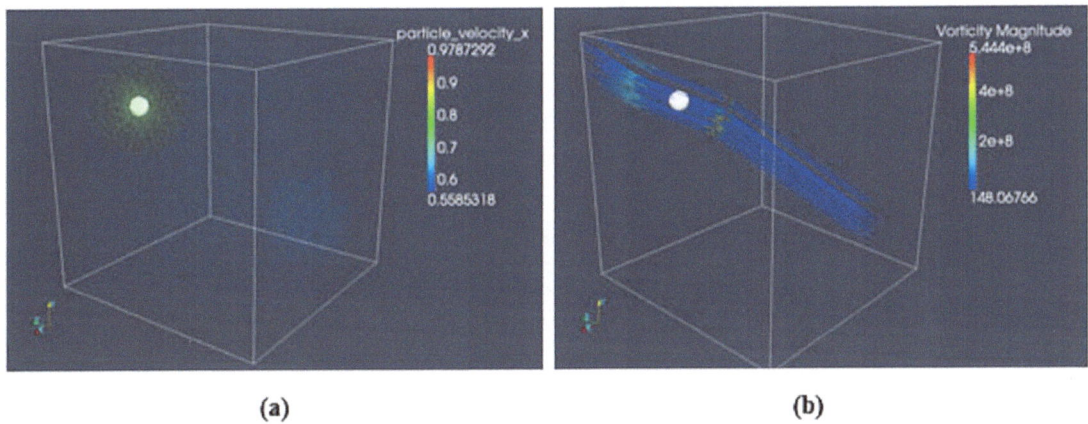

Figure 20.11: Halo Detection and Analysis: (a) Resulting output after running the HOP algorithm. The halo region is encapsulated in the sphere, shown in white, overlaid on top of the particle input dataset. (b) Streamlines seeded at the halo region, visualizing the flow around the halo.

Part IV

Appendix

BIBLIOGRAPHY

[1] OpenFOAM. http://www.openfoam.com/.

[2] Virtual Reality Peripheral Network. http://www.cs.unc.edu/Research/vrpn.

[3] VRUI. http://idav.ucdavis.edu/~okreylos/ResDev/Vrui.

[4] S. P. Callahan, J. Freire, E. Santos, C. E. Scheidegger, C. T. Silva, and H. T. Vo. Vistrails: Visualization meets data management. In *Proceedings of the 2006 ACM SIGMOD International Conference on Management of Data*, SIGMOD '06, pages 745–747, New York, NY, USA, 2006. ACM.

[5] S. B. Davidson and J. Freire. Provenance and scientific workflows: Challenges and opportunities. In *Proceedings of the 2008 ACM SIGMOD International Conference on Management of Data*, SIGMOD '08, pages 1345–1350, New York, NY, USA, 2008. ACM.

[6] Enzo Developers. Enzo. http://enzo-project.org/.

[7] Ken Moreland. The ParaView Tutorial. http://www.paraview.org/Wiki/The_ParaView_Tutorial.

[8] O. Kreylos. Environment-independent vr development. In G. Bebis, R. Boyle, B. Parvin, D. Koracin, P. Remagnino, F. Porikli, J. Peters, J. Klosowski, L. Arns, Y. Chun, T.-M. Rhyne, and L. Monroe, editors, *Advances in Visual Computing*, volume 5358 of *Lecture Notes in Computer Science*, pages 901–912. Springer Berlin Heidelberg, 2008.

[9] Numpy developers. NumPy. http://www.numpy.org/.

[10] Pat Marion. What is InterpolateScalarsBeforeMapping in VTK? http://www.kitware.com/blog/home/post/414.

[11] R. Drach, P. Dubois, and D. Williams. Climate Data Management System, version 5.0. http://www2-pcmdi.llnl.gov/cdat/manuals/cdms5.pdf, 2007.

[12] W. J. Schroeder, K. M. Martin, and W. E. Lorensen. The design and implementation of an object-oriented toolkit for 3d graphics and visualization. In *Proceedings of the 7th Conference on Visualization '96*, VIS '96, pages 93–ff., Los Alamitos, CA, USA, 1996. IEEE Computer Society Press.

[13] W. R. Sherman, P. O'Leary, E. T. Whiting, S. Grover, and E. A. Wernert. Iq-station: A low cost portable immersive environment. In G. Bebis, R. Boyle, B. Parvin, D. Koracin, R. Chung, R. Hammound, M. Hussain, T. Kar-Han, R. Crawfis, D. Thalmann, D. Kao, and L. Avila, editors, *Advances in Visual Computing*, volume 6454 of *Lecture Notes in Computer Science*, pages 361–372. Springer Berlin Heidelberg, 2010.

[14] N. Shetty, A. Chaudhary, D. Coming, W. R. Sherman, P. O'Leary, E. T. Whiting, and S. Su. Immersive paraview: A community-based, immersive, universal scientific visualization application. In *Proceedings of the 2011 IEEE Virtual Reality Conference*, VR '11, pages 239–240, Washington, DC, USA, 2011. IEEE Computer Society.

[15] T. Silva, J. Freire, and S. P. Callahan. Provenance for visualizations: Reproducibility and beyond. In *Computing in Science & Engineering*, 2007.

[16] T. Maxwell. DV3D. http://portal.nccs.nasa.gov/DV3D/.

[17] R. M. Taylor, II, T. C. Hudson, A. Seeger, H. Weber, J. Juliano, and A. T. Helser. Vrpn: A device-independent, network-transparent vr peripheral system. In *Proceedings of the ACM Symposium on Virtual Reality Software and Technology*, VRST '01, pages 55–61, New York, NY, USA, 2001. ACM.

[18] The OpenFOAM Foundation. OpenFOAM Users Guide.
http://www.openfoam.com/docs/user/damBreak.php#x7-620002.3.12.

[19] The ParaView Community. Setting up a ParaView server.
http://www.paraview.org/Wiki/Setting_up_a_ParaView_Server.

[20] yt Developers. yt. http://yt-project.org/about.html.

INDEXES

paraview UI Index

pvpython Index